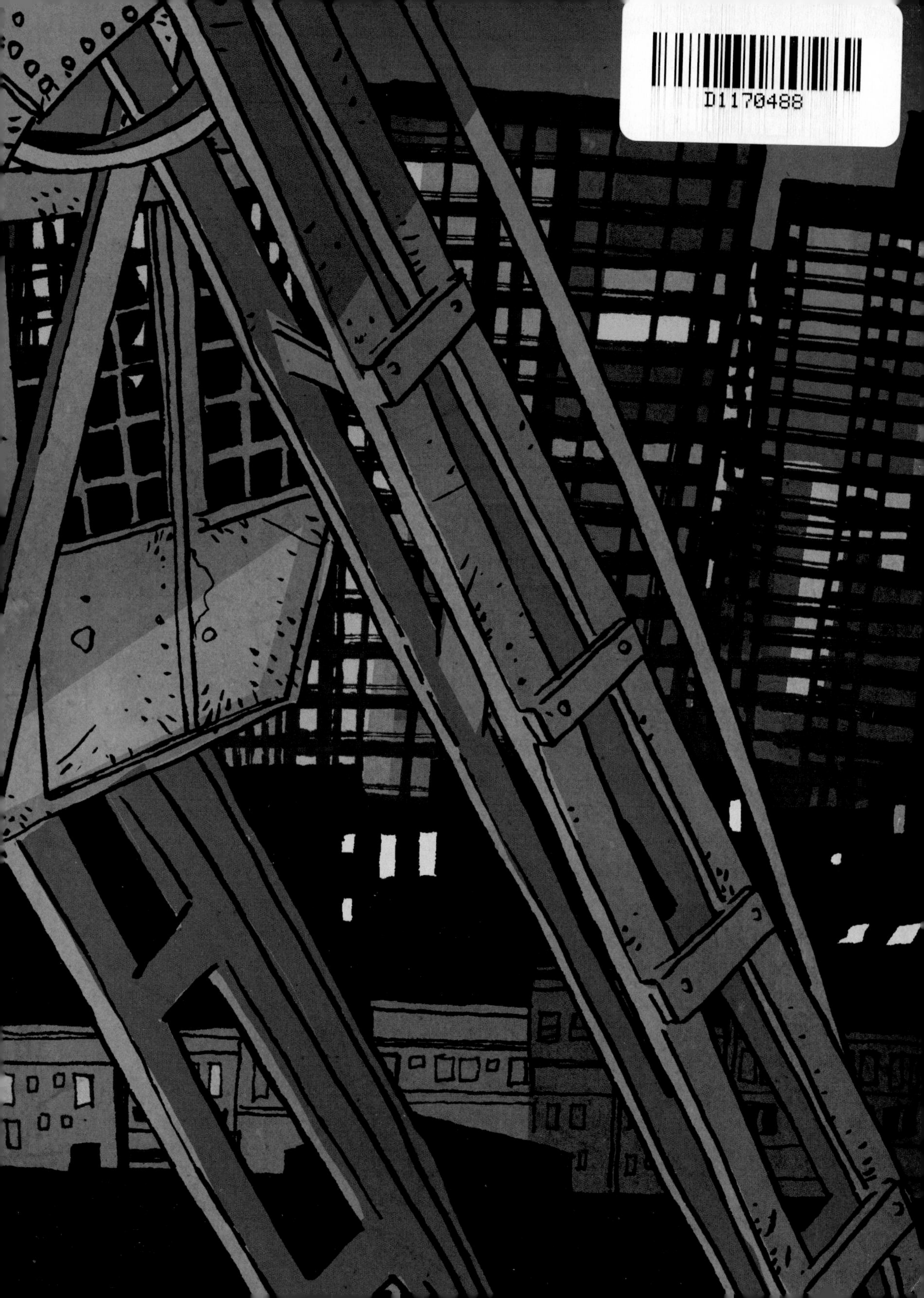

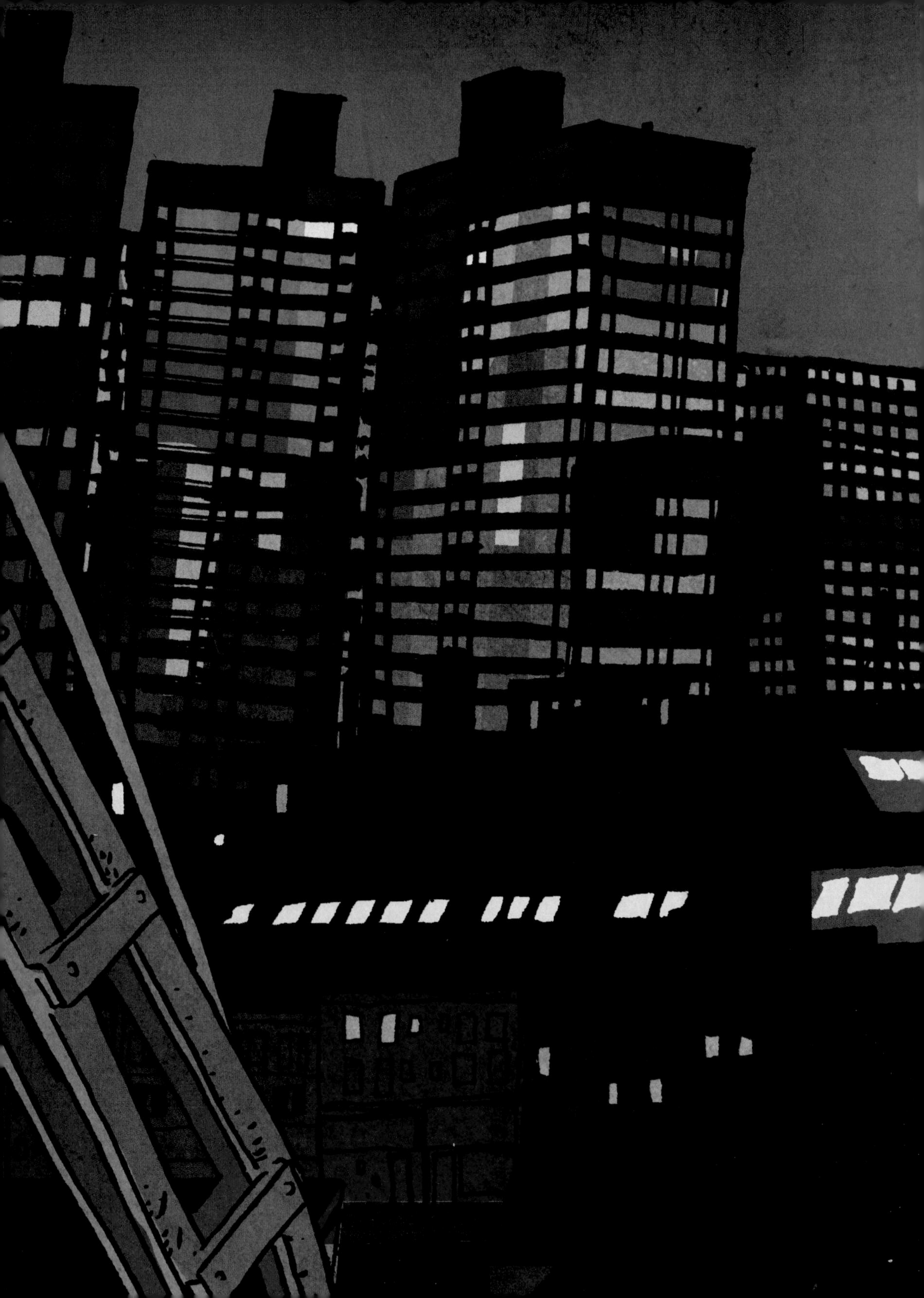

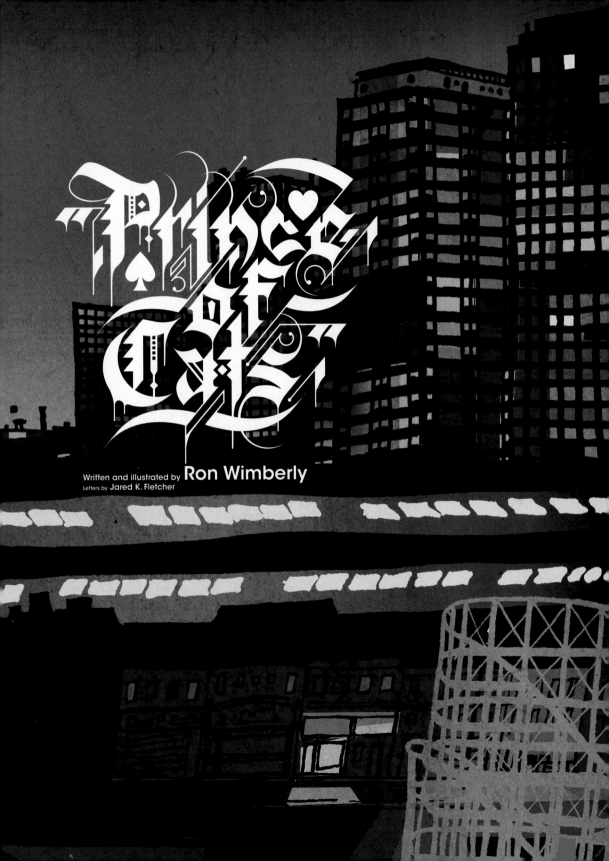

"Prince of Cats"

Written and illustrated by **Ron Wimberly**
Letters by **Jared K. Fletcher**

Jonathan Vankin and Will Dennis Editors Gregory Lockard Assistant Editor Robbin Brosterman Design Director – Books Louis Prandi Publication Design

Karen Berger Senior VP – Executive Editor, Vertigo Bob Harras VP – Editor-in-Chief

Diane Nelson President Dan DiDio and Jim Lee Co-Publishers Geoff Johns Chief Creative Officer John Rood Executive VP – Sales, Marketing and Business Development
Amy Genkins Senior VP – Business and Legal Affairs Nairi Gardiner Senior VP – Finance Jeff Boison VP – Publishing Operations Mark Chiarello VP – Art Direction and Design
John Cunningham VP – Marketing Terri Cunningham VP – Talent Relations and Services Alison Gill Senior VP – Manufacturing and Operations
Hank Kanalz Senior VP – Digital Jay Kogan VP – Business and Legal Affairs, Publishing Jack Mahan VP – Business Affairs, Talent
Nick Napolitano VP – Manufacturing Administration Sue Pohja VP – Book Sales Courtney Simmons Senior VP – Publicity Bob Wayne Senior VP – Sales

Thanks to Jorden Haley

Library of Congress Cataloging-in-Publication Data

Wimberly, Ronald.
  Prince of cats / Ronald Wimberly.
    p. cm.
  ISBN 978-1-4012-2068-6 (alk. paper)
  1. Graphic novels. I. Title.
PN6727.W563P75 2012
741.5'973–dc23
                                    2012025796

SUSTAINABLE
FORESTRY
INITIATIVE

Certified Chain of Custody
At Least 25% Certified Forest Content
www.sfiprogram.org
SFI-01042
APPLIES TO TEXT STOCK ONLY

R&J B-sides Mixtape

So I'm your DJ tonight. My name is Dπ
and boys and girls, have I got a treat
for you. I'll be cutting the B-side of
Romeo and Juliet from Shakespeare's
greatest hits with a hot little piece
of wax called "Gratuitous Ninja."
The outcome is Ninjaupera, post-modern
absurdity for the critically pretentious
or the laughably subversive.
Either way, enjoy.

WITHDRAWN

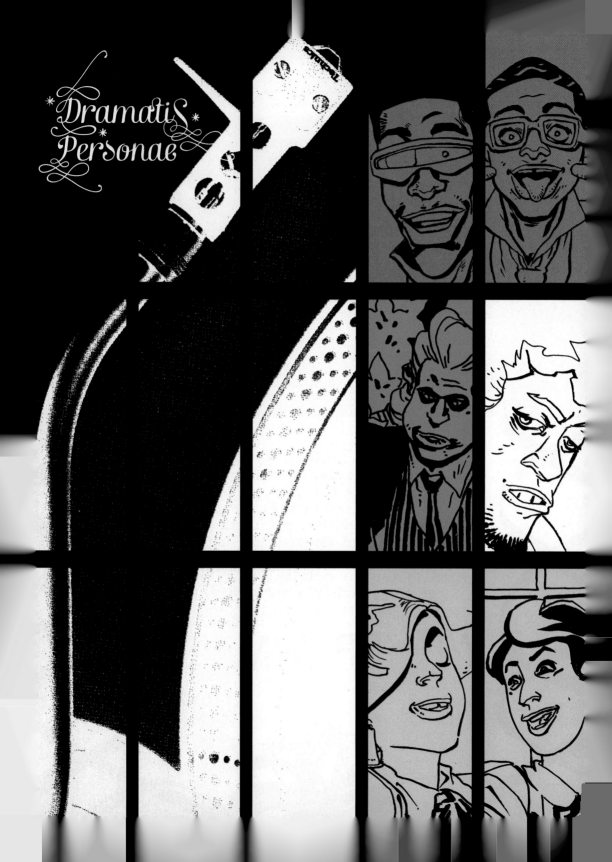

Dramatis Personae

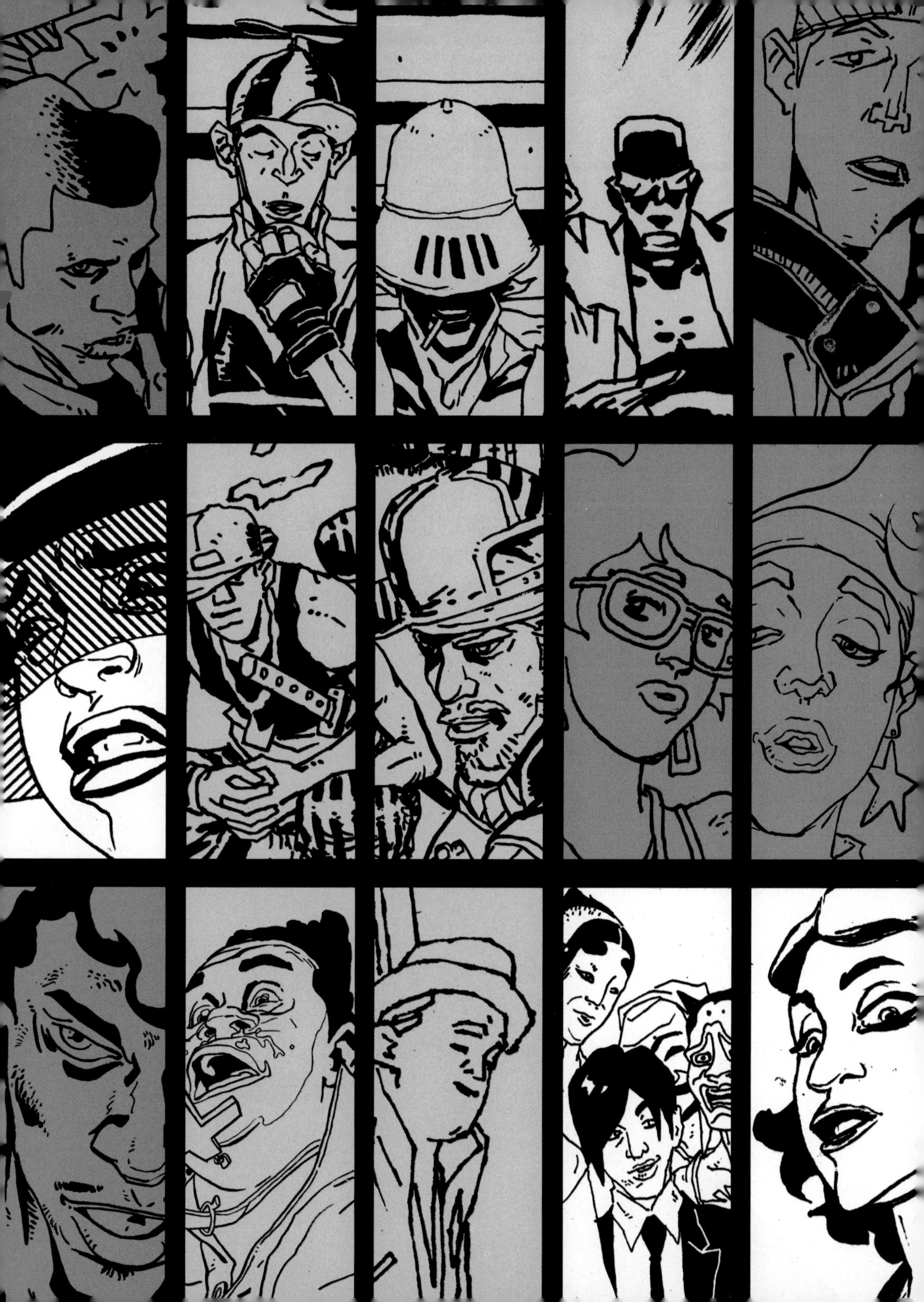

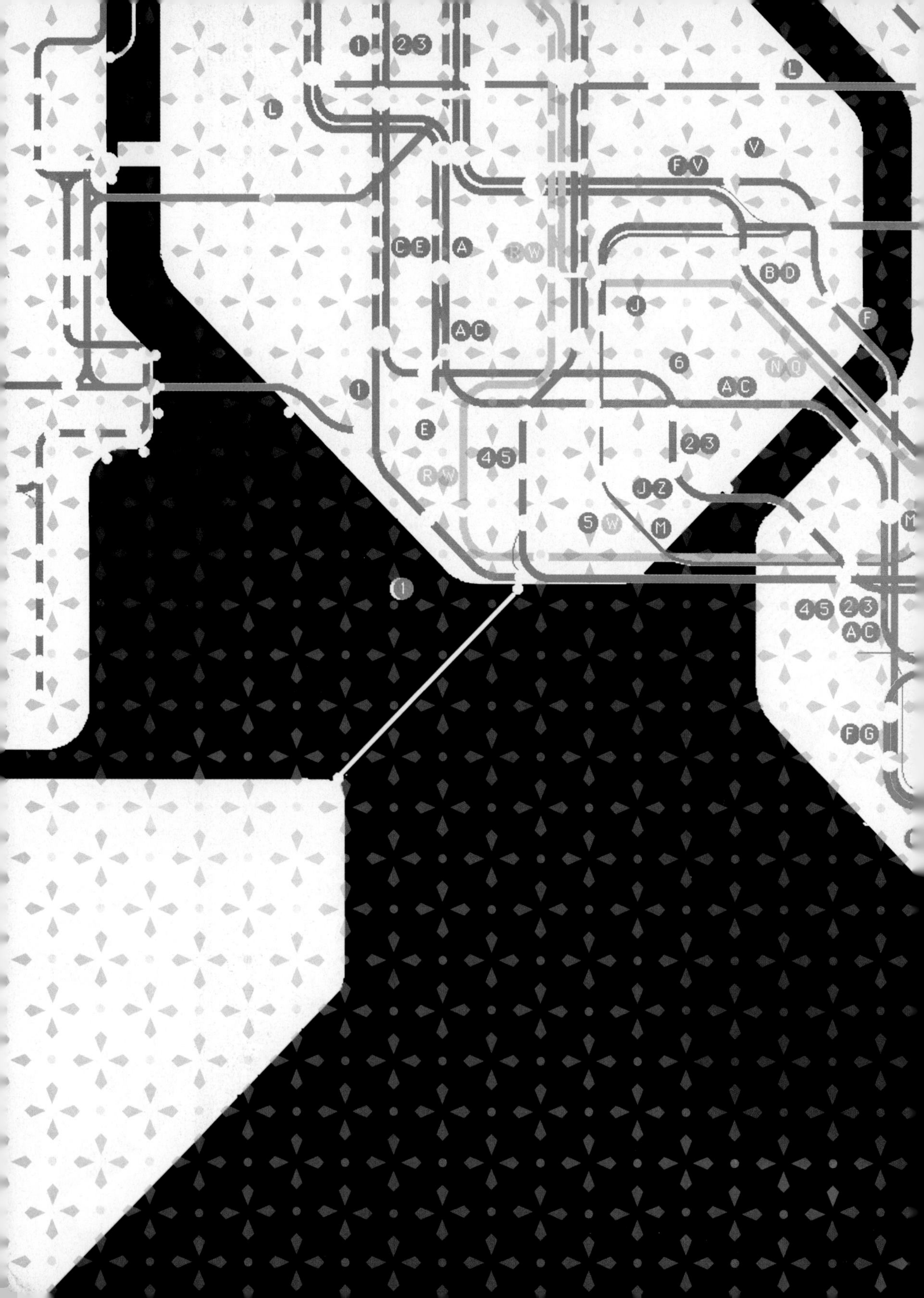

1
23
L
L
V
FV
CE
A
RW
BD
J
F
AC
6
NQ
1
AC
E
23
45
RW
JZ
5W
M
1
45
23
AC
FG

Remember back in the day,
Niggas wore waves,
Gazell-e Shades, corn braids, dueled aplenty
But never ended deadly, they wore dull blades
And kept it friendly, even though enemy.
Fast forward from nineteen hundred eighty-three
To whet steel corners, with new mutiny
In Brooklyn Babel, Where we lay our scene;
Here hood born Youth, adolescence Addled
Spill civil blood, make civil hands unclean;
Traded rattles for father's swords and battled,
Saddled with their parents' spiteful legacy
Love, its collateral casualty
A thin line is blurred, a child interred
To redeem American dreams deferred...

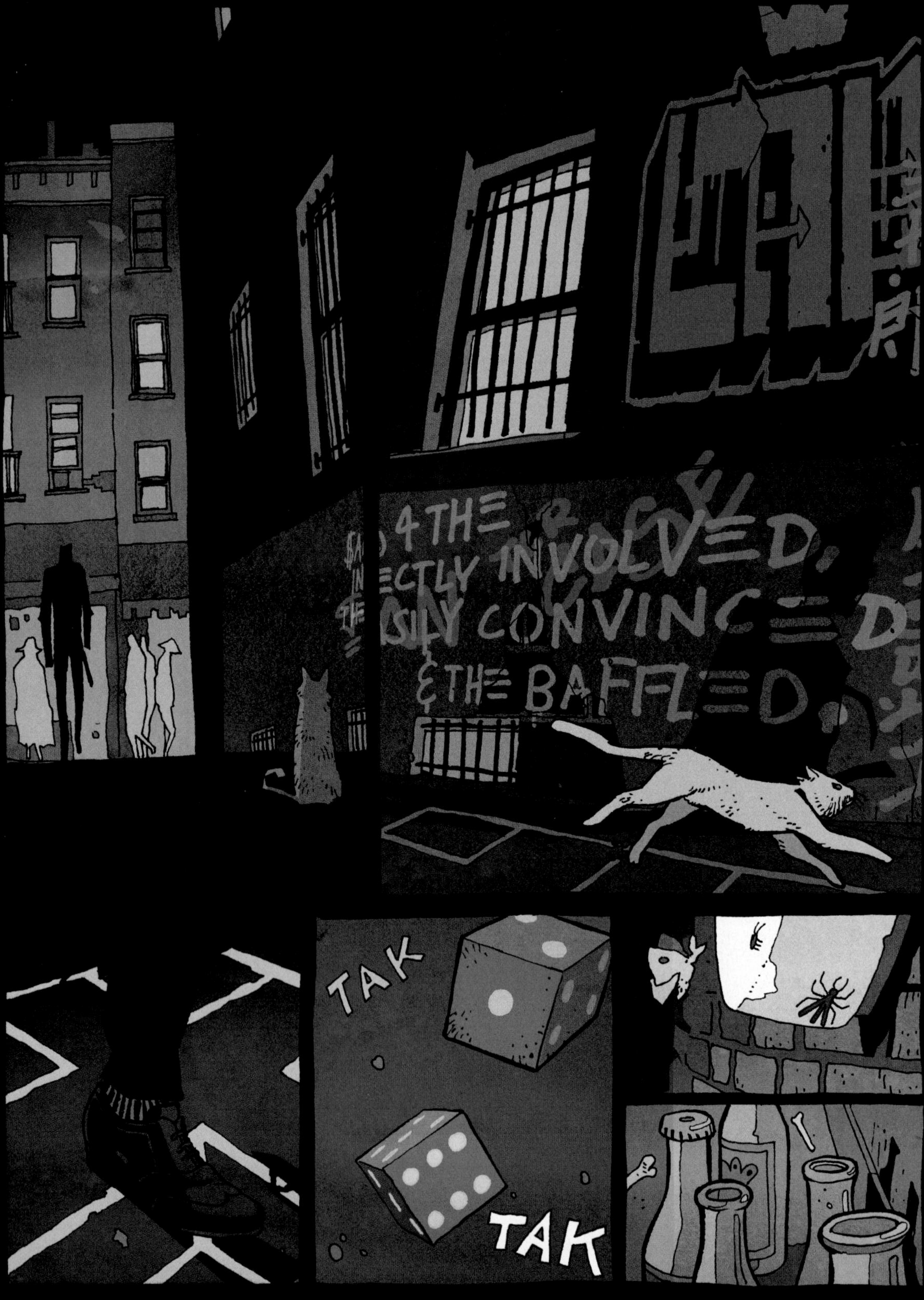
4 THE
INVOLVED,
CONVINCED
& THE BAFFLED.
TAK
TAK

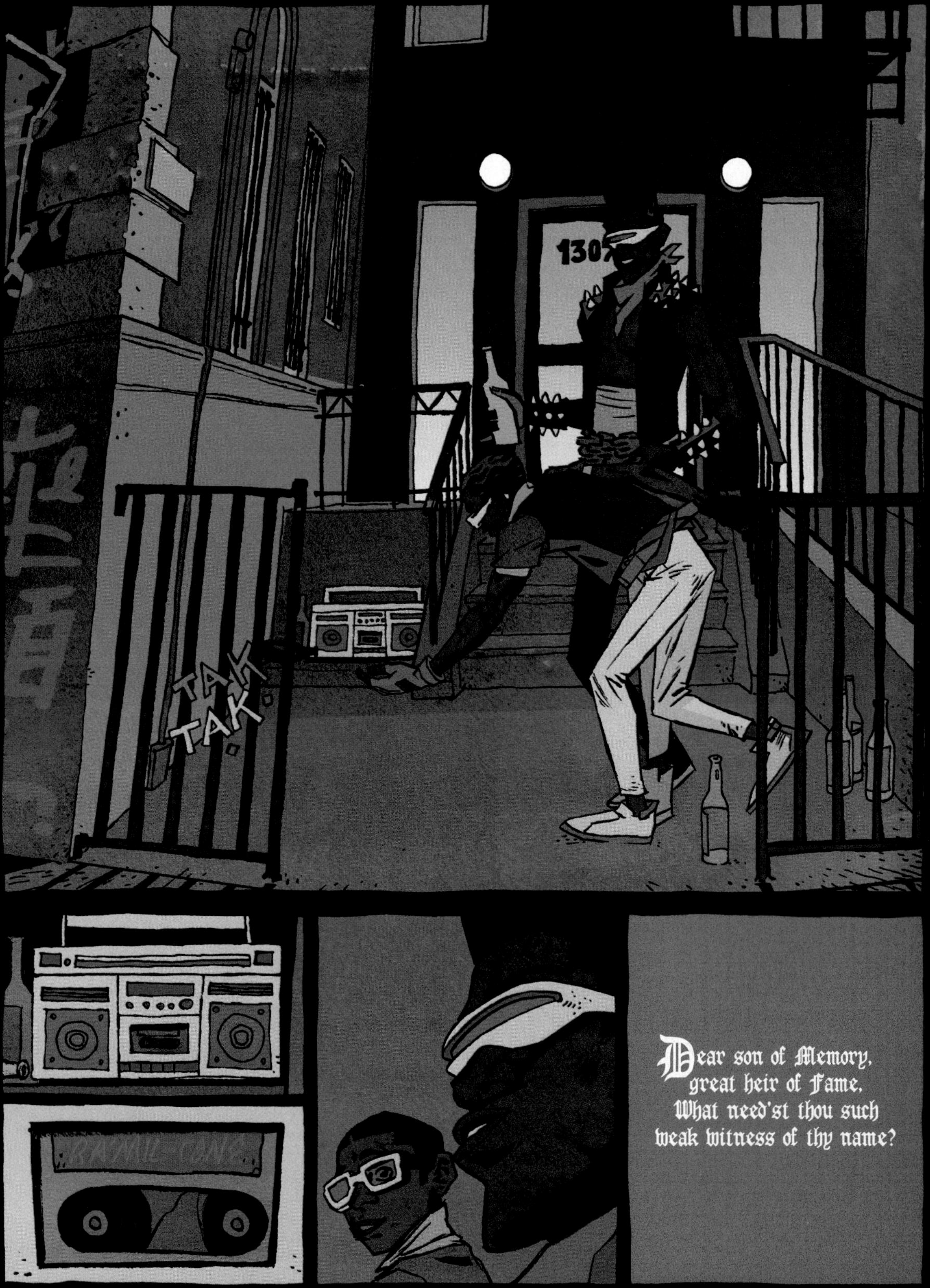
TAK TAK.
Dear son of Memory,
great heir of Fame,
What need'st thou such
weak witness of thy name?

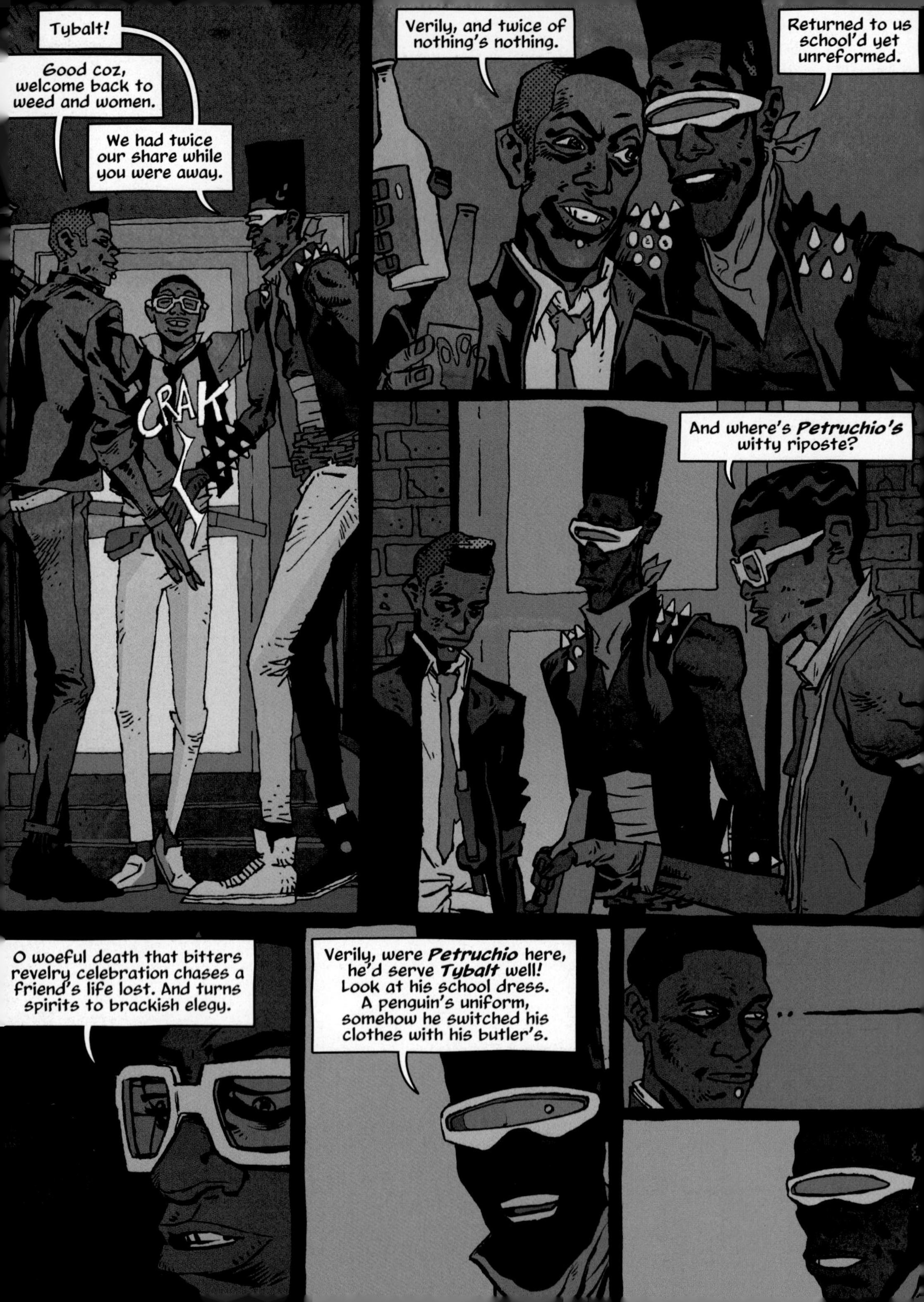

Tybalt!
Good coz, welcome back to weed and women.
We had twice our share while you were away.
CRAK
Verily, and twice of nothing's nothing.
Returned to us school'd yet unreformed.
And where's *Petruchio's* witty riposte?
O woeful death that bitters revelry celebration chases a friend's life lost. And turns spirits to brackish elegy.
Verily, were *Petruchio* here, he'd serve *Tybalt* well! Look at his school dress. A penguin's uniform, somehow he switched his clothes with his butler's.
...

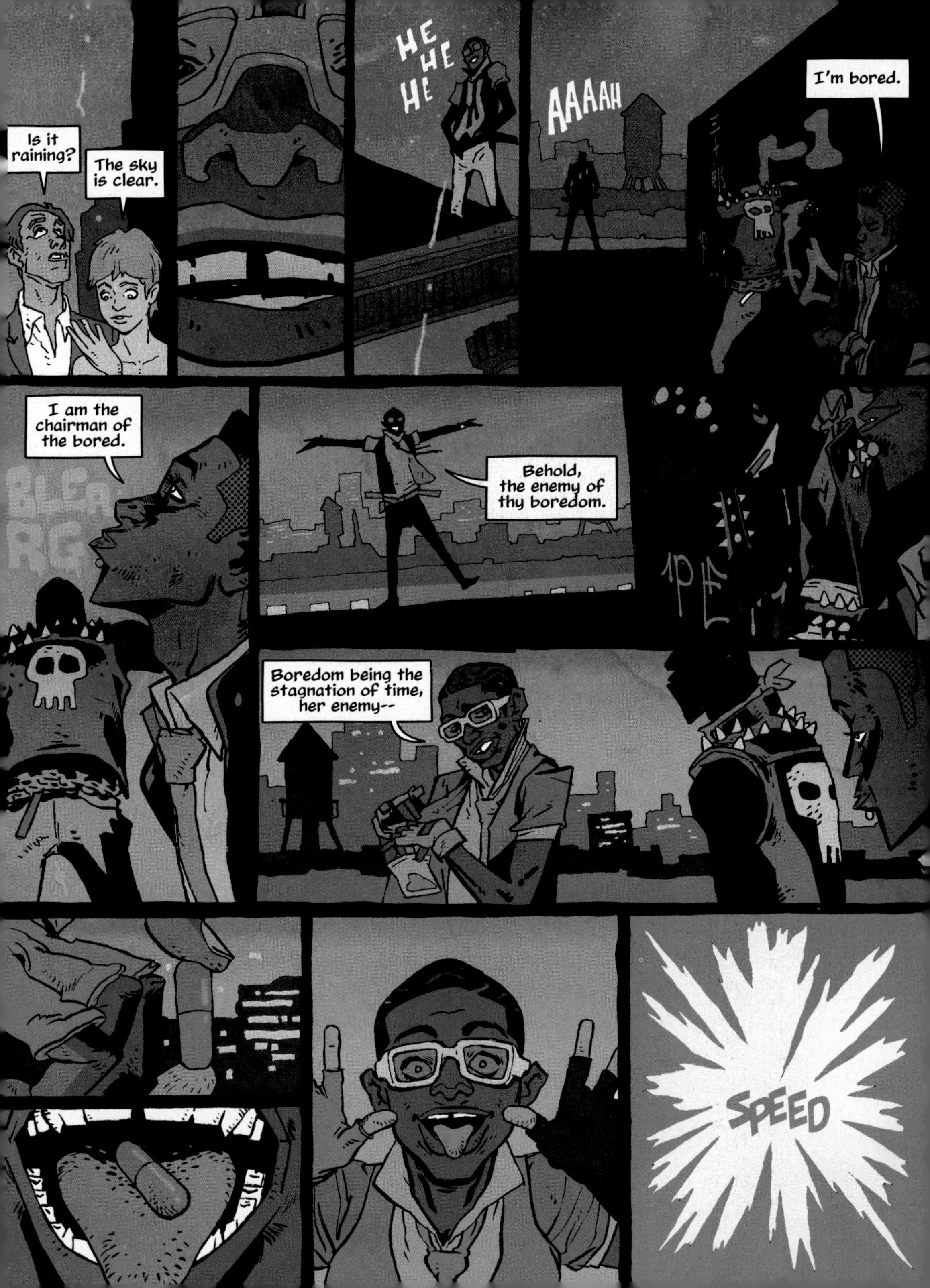

Is it raining?
The sky is clear.
HE HE HE
AAAAH
I'm bored.
I am the chairman of the bored.
BLEARG
Behold, the enemy of thy boredom.
Boredom being the stagnation of time, her enemy--
SPEED

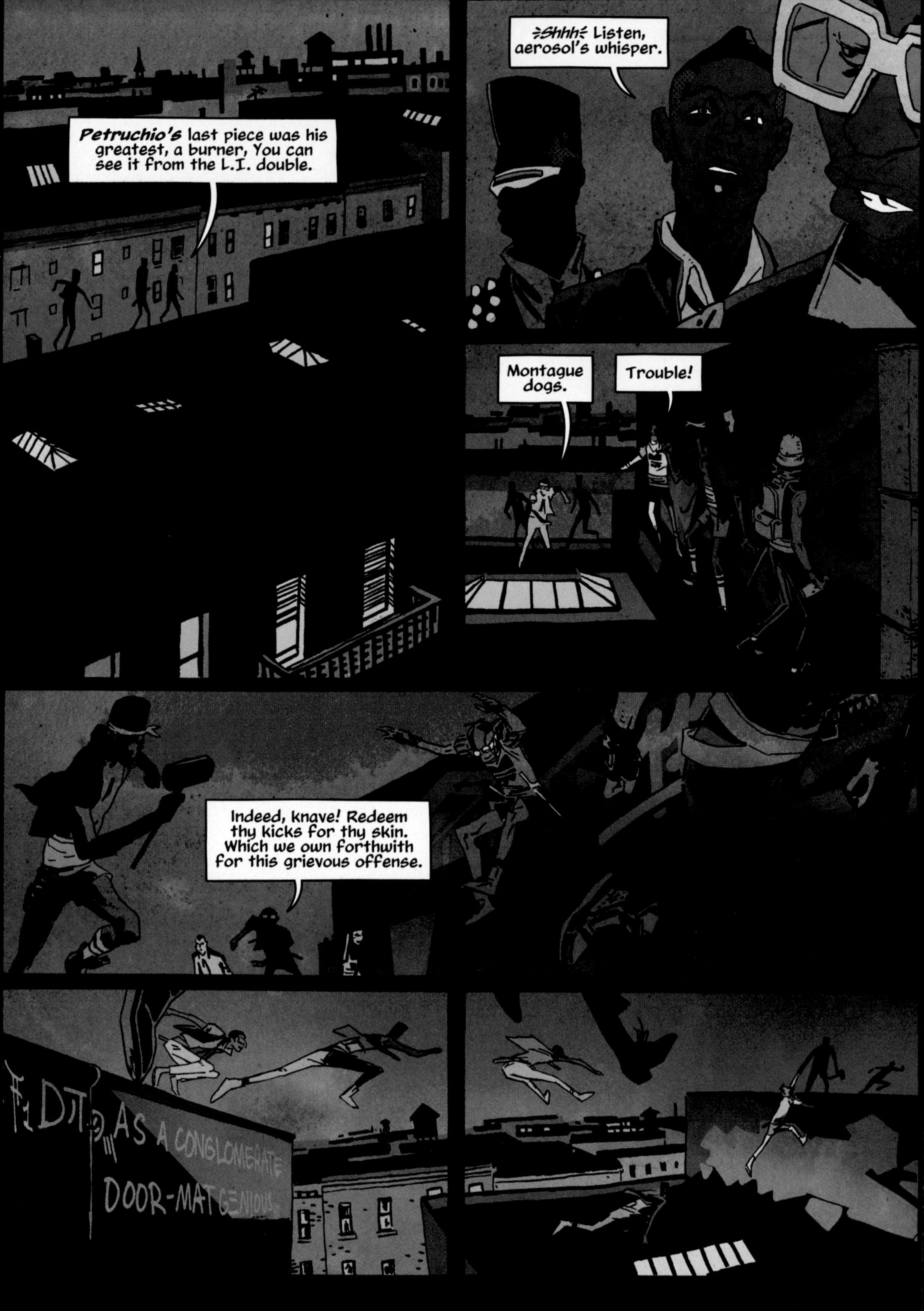
Petruchio's last piece was his greatest, a burner, You can see it from the L.I. double.
Shhh Listen, aerosol's whisper.
Montague dogs.
Trouble!
Indeed, knave! Redeem thy kicks for thy skin. Which we own forthwith for this grievous offense.
AS A CONGLOMERATE
DOOR-MAT GENIOUS

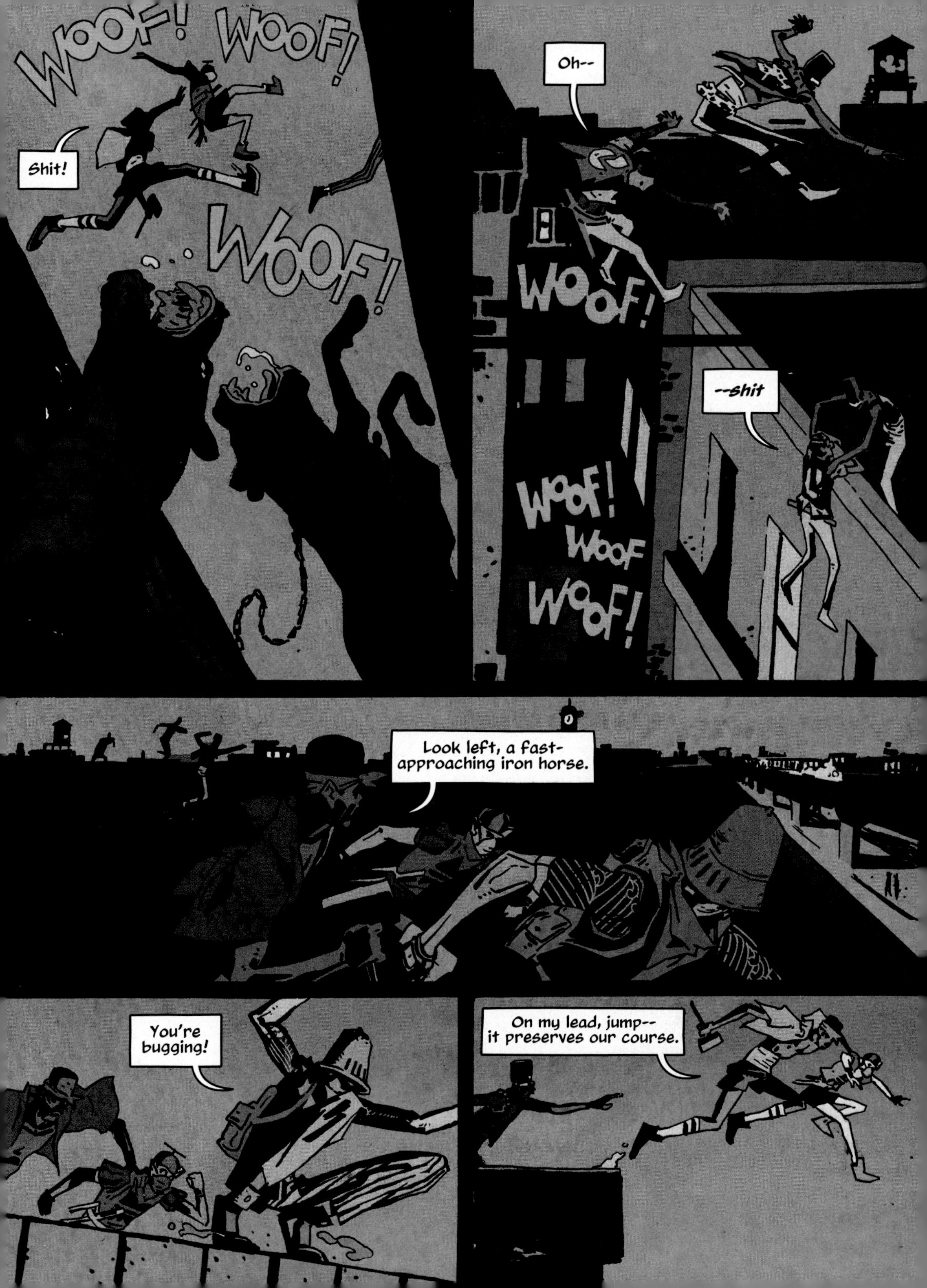
WOOF! WOOF!
Shit!
WOOF!
Oh--
WOOF!
--shit
WOOF!
WOOF
WOOF!
Look left, a fast-approaching iron horse.
You're bugging!
On my lead, jump--it preserves our course.

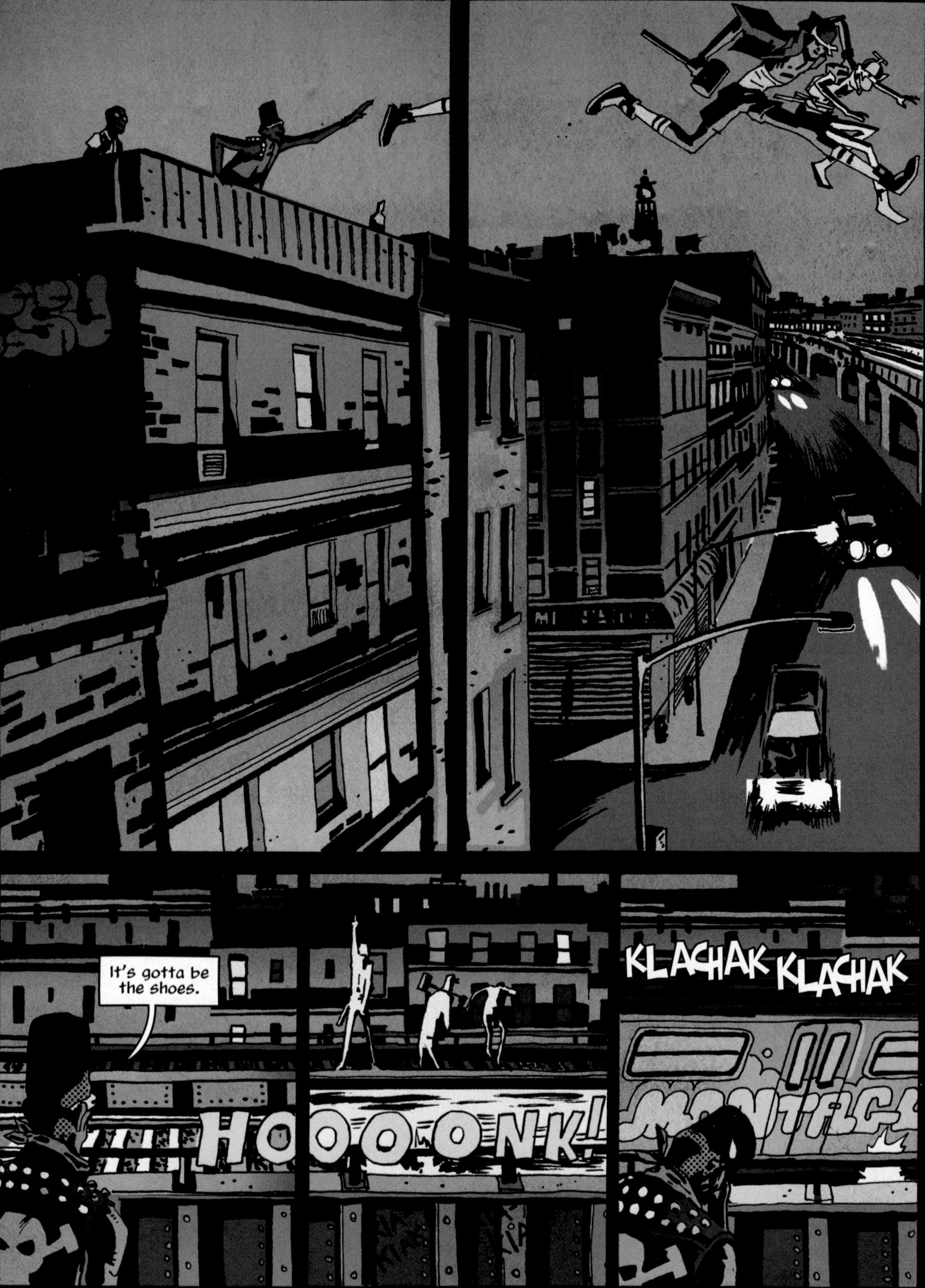
It's gotta be the shoes.
HOOOONK!
KLACHAK KLACHAK

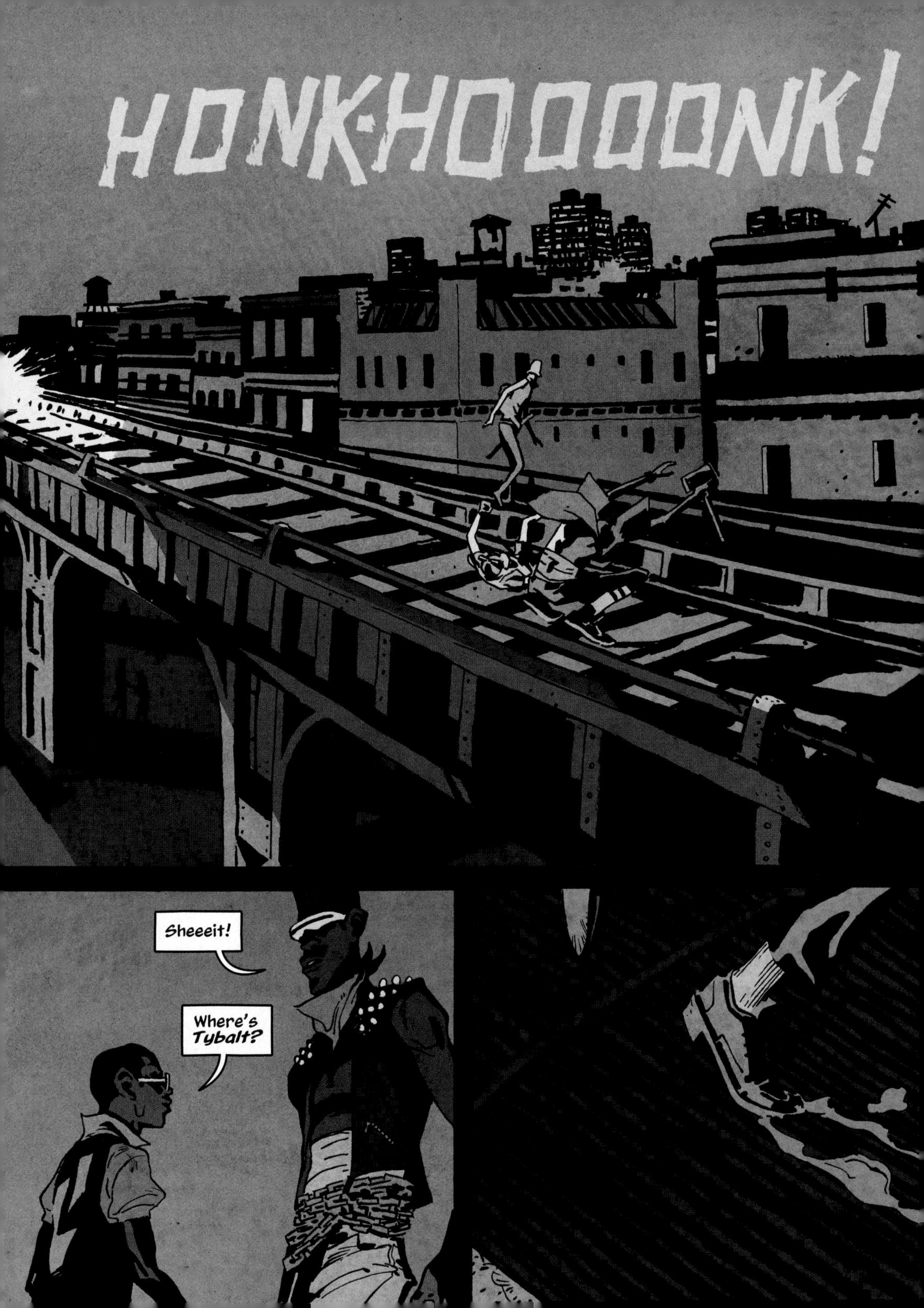
HONK-HOOOONK!
Sheeeit!
Where's *Tybalt?*

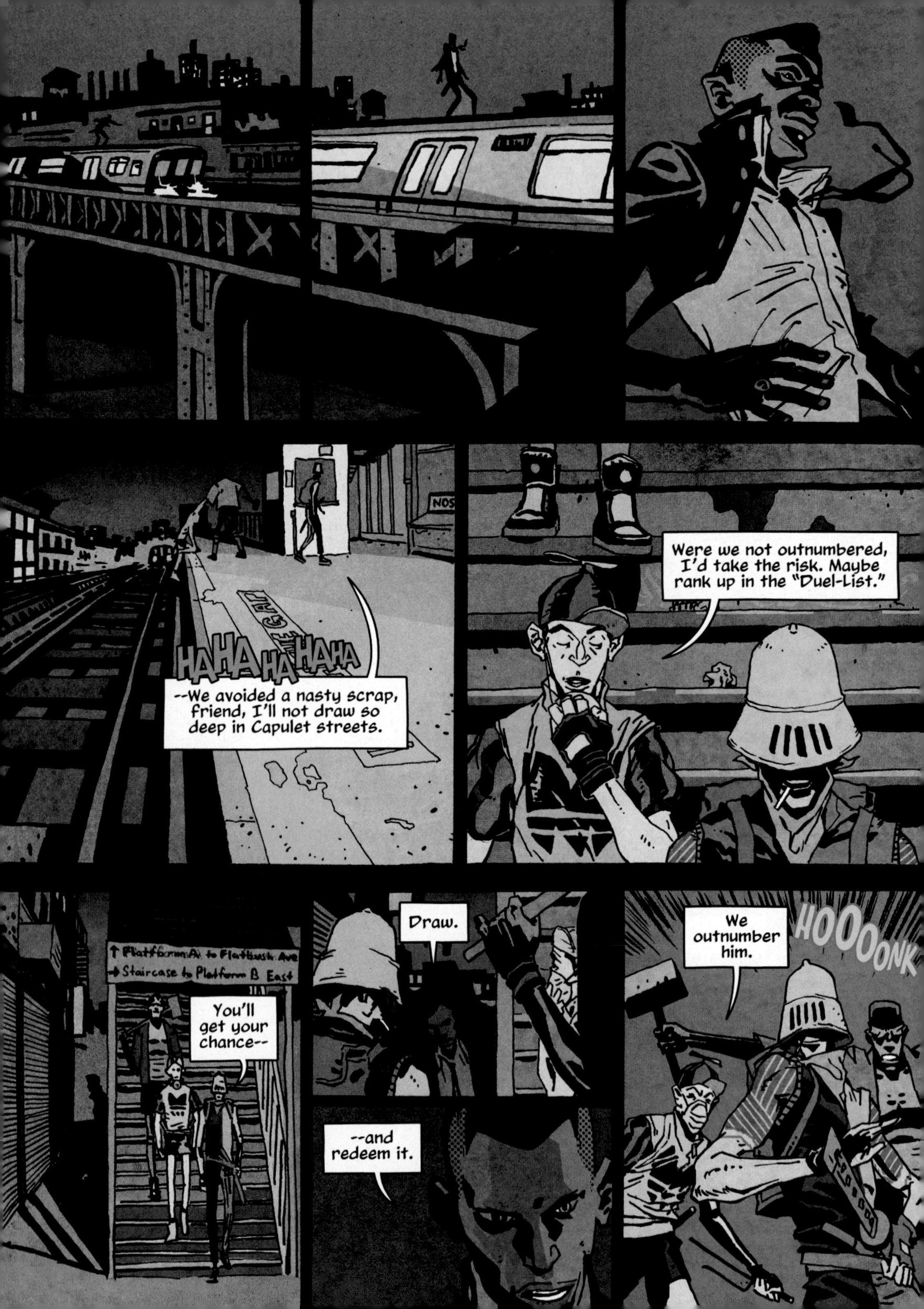
HAHAHAHAHA
--We avoided a nasty scrap, friend, I'll not draw so deep in Capulet streets.
Were we not outnumbered, I'd take the risk. Maybe rank up in the "Duel-List."
↑ Platform A: to Flatbush Ave
→ Staircase to Platform B East
You'll get your chance--
Draw.
--and redeem it.
We outnumber him.
HOOOONK

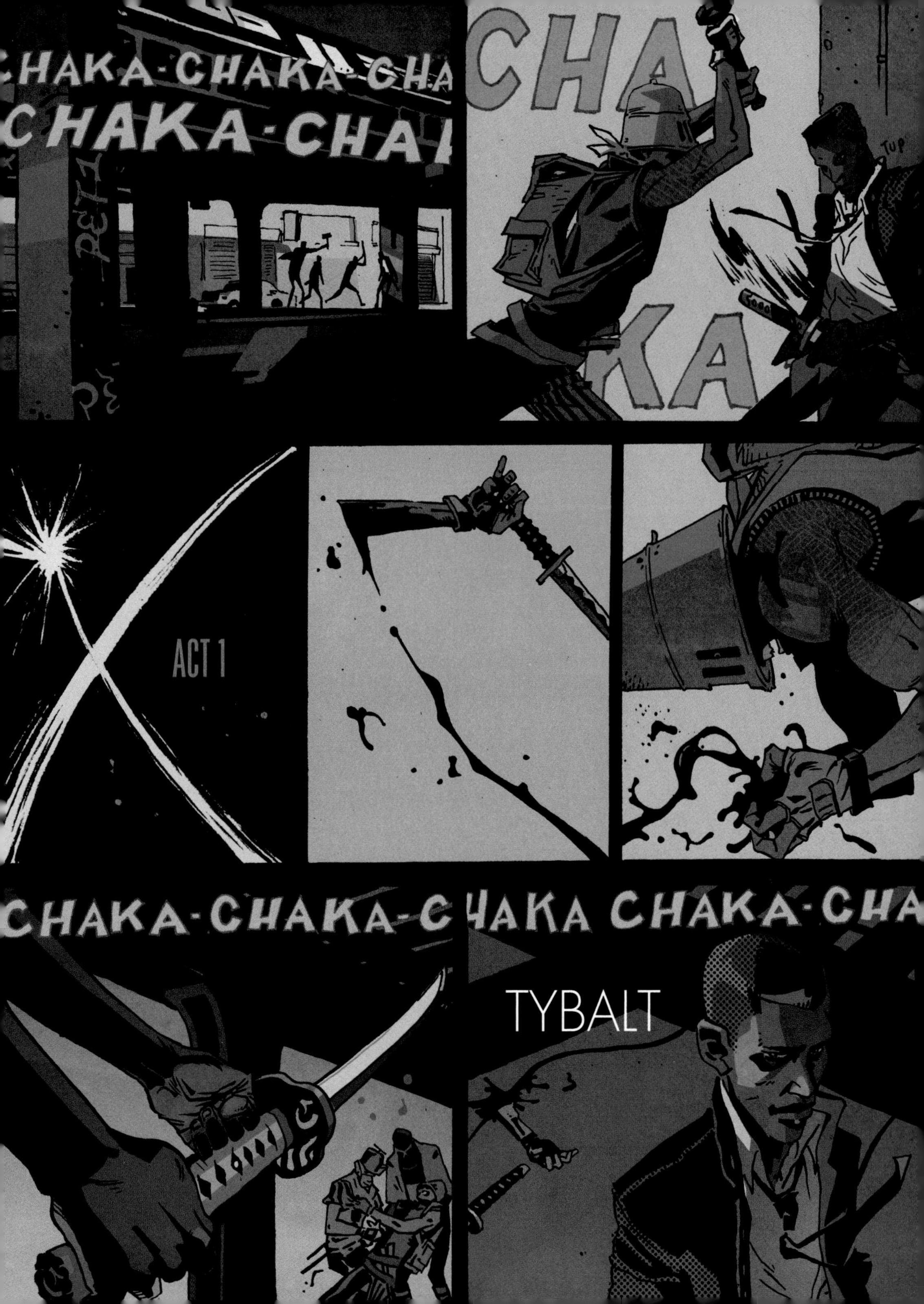
CHAKA-CHAKA-CHA
CHAKA-CHA
CHA
TUP
KA
ACT 1
CHAKA-CHAKA-CHAKA CHAKA-CHA
TYBALT

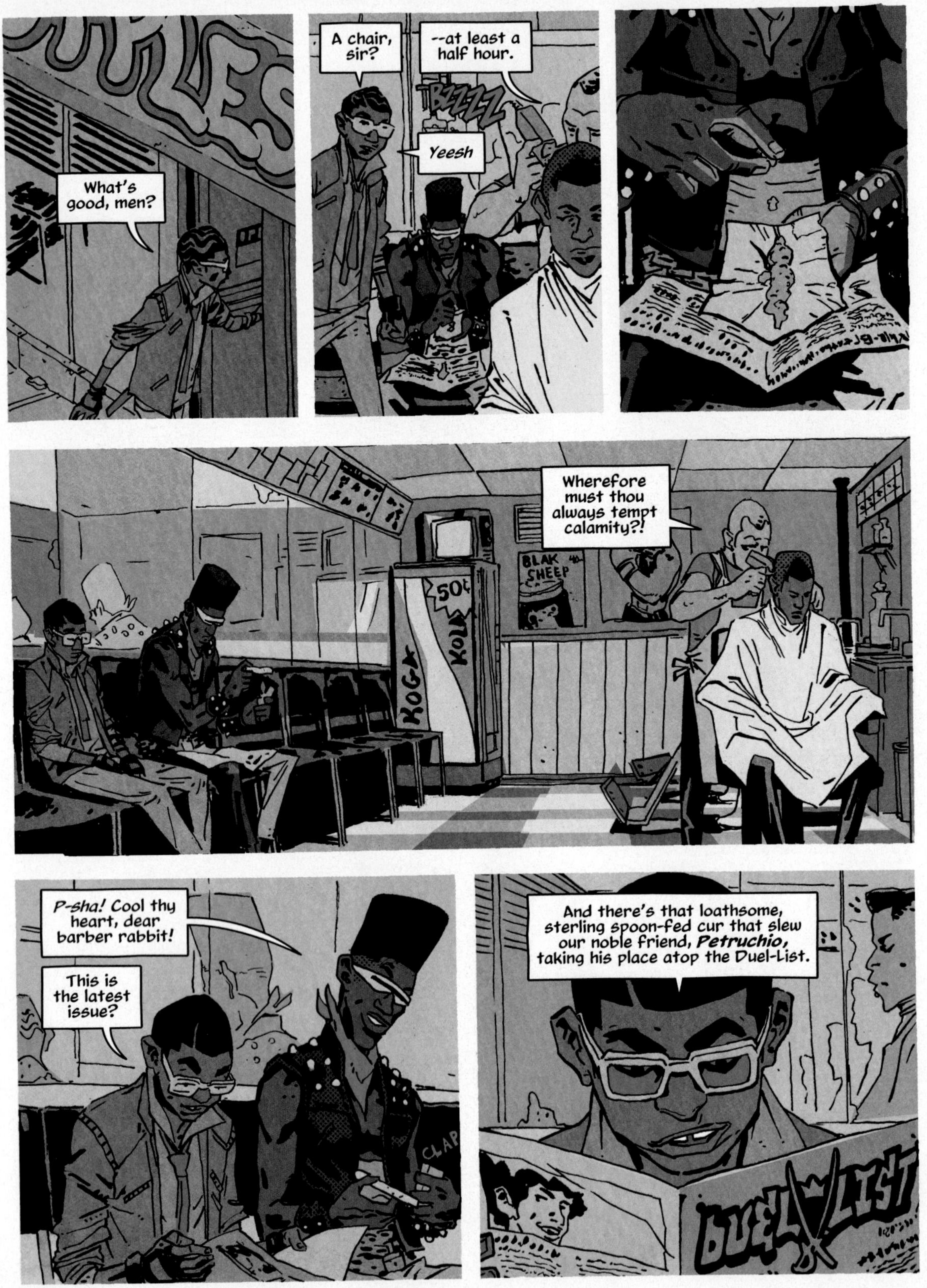
What's good, men?
A chair, sir?
--at least a half hour.
BZZZZ
Yeesh
Wherefore must thou always tempt calamity?!
BLAK SHEEP
50¢
KOLA
KOLA
P-sha! Cool thy heart, dear barber rabbit!
This is the latest issue?
CLAP
And there's that loathsome, sterling spoon-fed cur that slew our noble friend, Petruchio, taking his place atop the Duel-List.
DUEL LIST

Milk-Breathed Montague Makes Moves

Robert Greene

This issue, Newly crowning the duel-list
Is Montague progeny, Romeo,
Whose deft Tsubamae Gaeshi dismissed
The one armed defense of Petruchio.
Ye may have yet to hear young Romeo's name
No doubt ye heard his father's, Lord Montague
Who made it known through slum-glorious game,
the weight he moved, the foes he fought and slew.
Much has been made of Romeo's pedigree

Yet with this touché his reputation bought.
He's proven apples fall not far from trees,
He's of his brazen father's mettle wrought.
Though none made witness of the Title duel
Petruchio's ranking paper was retrieved.
As is the official duel-list rule
It's captor, Romeo, it's ranking received.
Petruchio did not survive the match.

-For memorial details see 'the dispatch'

Duel List

01. Romeo Montague
02. Benvolio Montague
03. Luciano Canolio
04. Donatello Canolio
05. "Notorious" Barabus
...
06. Tybalt Capulet
07. Jaquelyn
08. Malachi
09. Metatron
10. Moiritsuke

31 Fulton Street

chop shop

So what it read, coz?
Thy deeds went unreported, cousin. No doubt, the duelist you disarmed was unranked ....The top four is flush with clan Montague.
Ha! Think it you so easy to rank, coz? Thou'll not find the answer to the street's tests in thy professor's book of formulas. You get an F, you're toe-tagged in death--
--More children pierced over childish bullshit.
Not bullshit, Barber, but the beef of our lord.
Verily, cousin! For our lord, I'd cut beef.
Cousin, thy cuts are more rare than well done. Thou hast a beef tongue, yet unseasoned.
Hold! Stir no more in this chair, son, or thy cut will be the rare one --and spoiled.
Well, *Romeo's* technique was a prime cut, and with it, Petrucio's youth consumed.
YLES

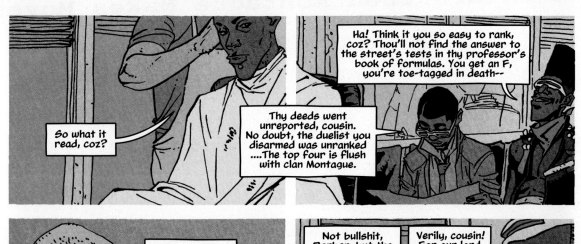

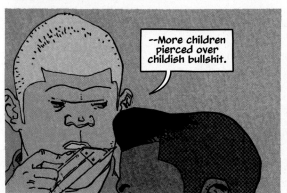

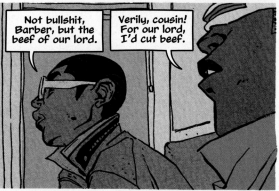

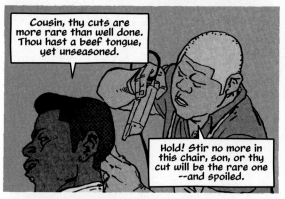

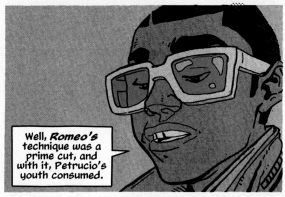

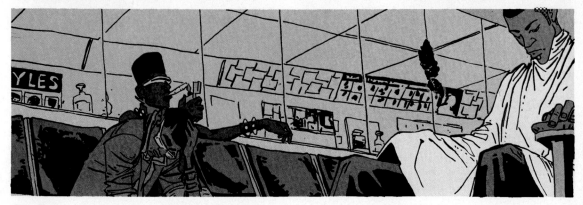

God rest his sword... But...I'd love to see the Tsubamae Gaeshi.

Hehe...Verily, and rap with Charon on the subject, whilst you ride with him across the Styx.

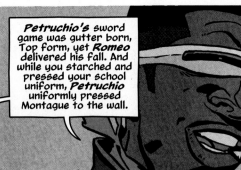

Petruchio's sword game was gutter born, Top form, yet **Romeo** delivered his fall. And while you starched and pressed your school uniform, **Petruchio** uniformly pressed Montague to the wall.

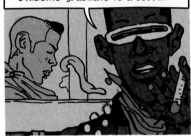

...And thy blade's edge ain't the only thing softened In private school. The lessons may not be cheap but street tuition is steep, and often students graduate to a coffin--

KSHT KSHT

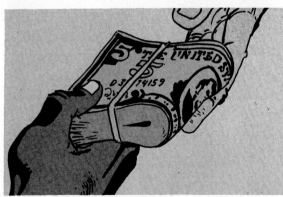

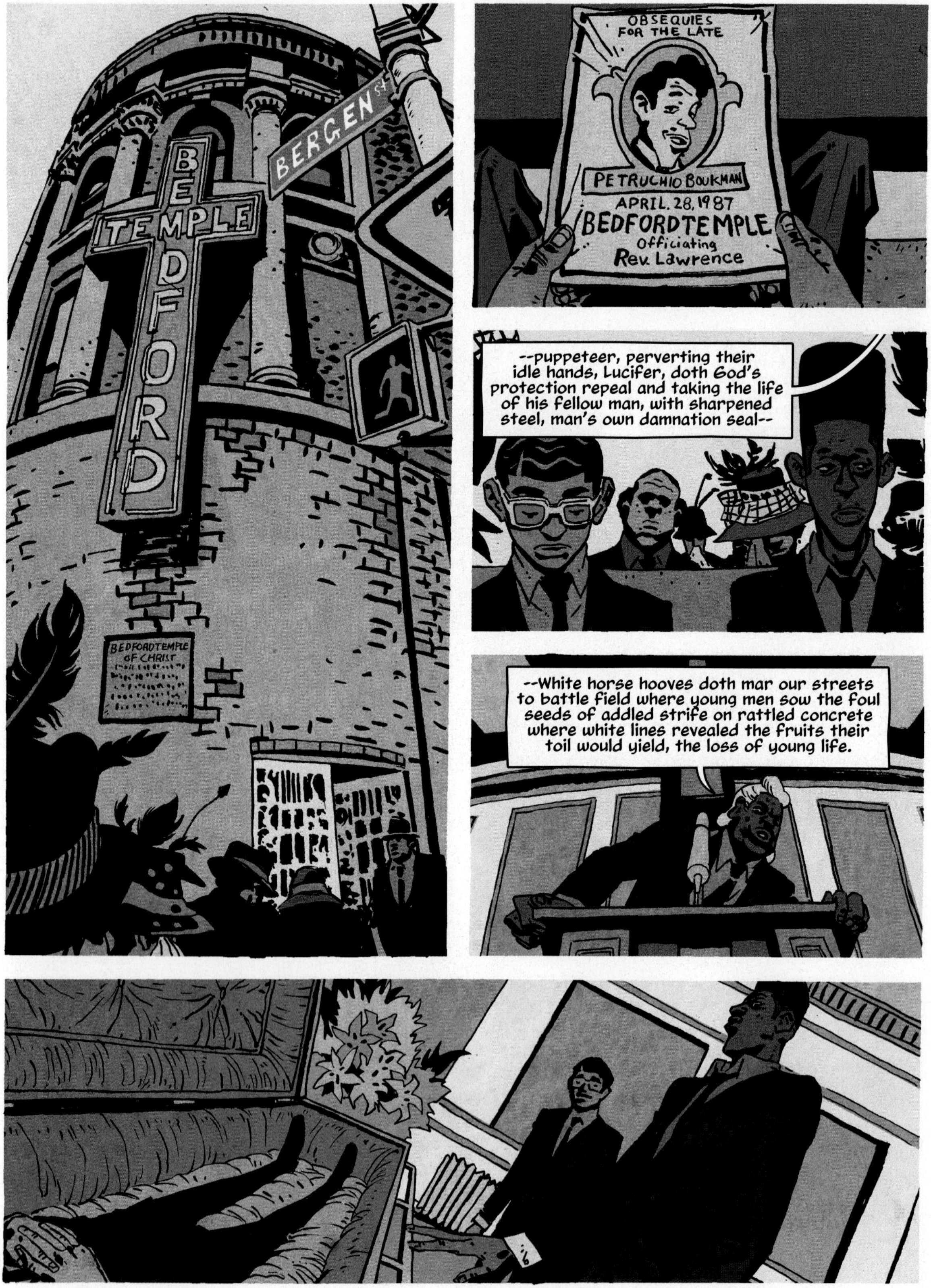

BERGEN St
TEMPLE
BEDFORD
BEDFORDTEMPLE OF CHRIST
OBSEQUIES FOR THE LATE
PETRUCHIO BOUKMAN
APRIL. 28, 1987
BEDFORDTEMPLE
Officiating
Rev. Lawrence
--puppeteer, perverting their idle hands, Lucifer, doth God's protection repeal and taking the life of his fellow man, with sharpened steel, man's own damnation seal--
--White horse hooves doth mar our streets to battle field where young men sow the foul seeds of addled strife on rattled concrete where white lines revealed the fruits their toil would yield, the loss of young life.

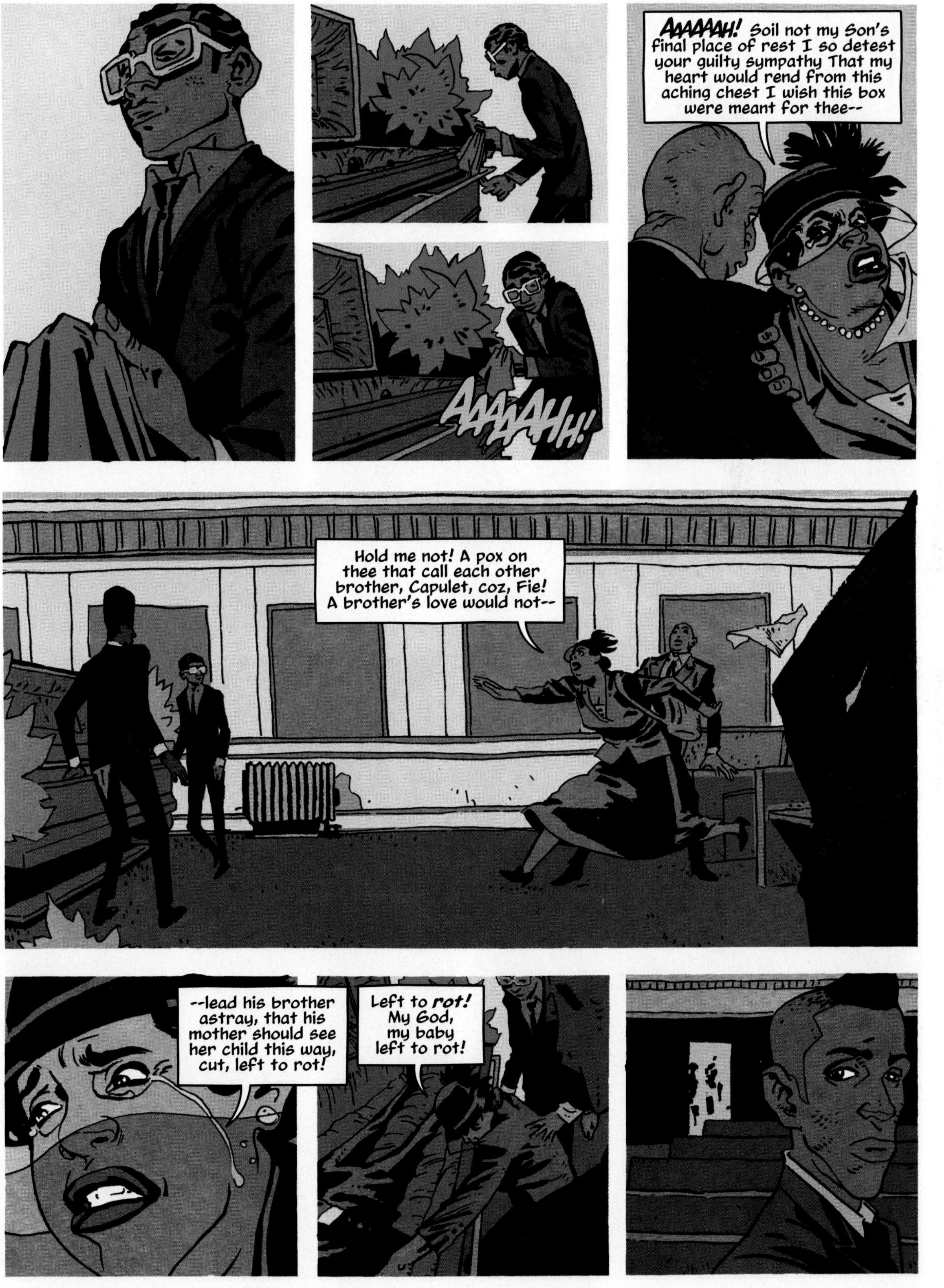
AAAAAHH!
AAAAAAH! Soil not my Son's final place of rest I so detest your guilty sympathy That my heart would rend from this aching chest I wish this box were meant for thee--
Hold me not! A pox on thee that call each other brother, Capulet, coz, Fie! A brother's love would not--
--lead his brother astray, that his mother should see her child this way, cut, left to rot!
Left to rot! My God, my baby left to rot!

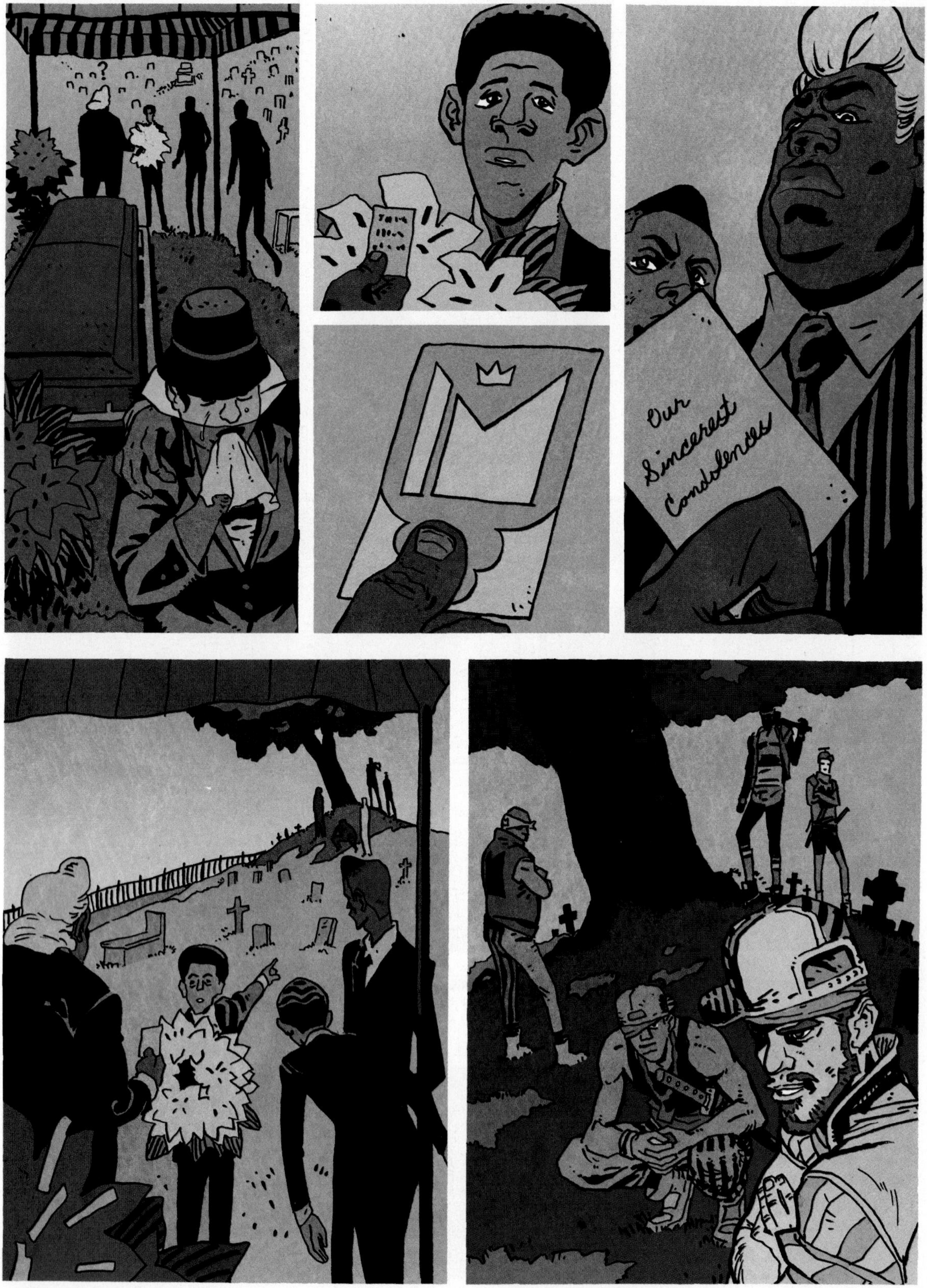
Our Sincerest Condolences

As the Lord revealed them to Matthew, twenty-six verse fifty one--

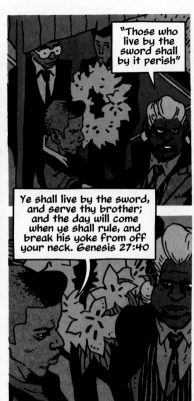

"Those who live by the sword shall by it perish"

Ye shall live by the sword, and serve thy brother; and the day will come when ye shall rule, and break his yoke from off your neck. Genesis 27:40

Impressive. Though ye may misunderstand the text, maybe ye would better serve thy brethren from the pulpit.

I'd rather serve my brother's vengeance to a Montague dog and usher him into thy care, Friar.

Business looks good.

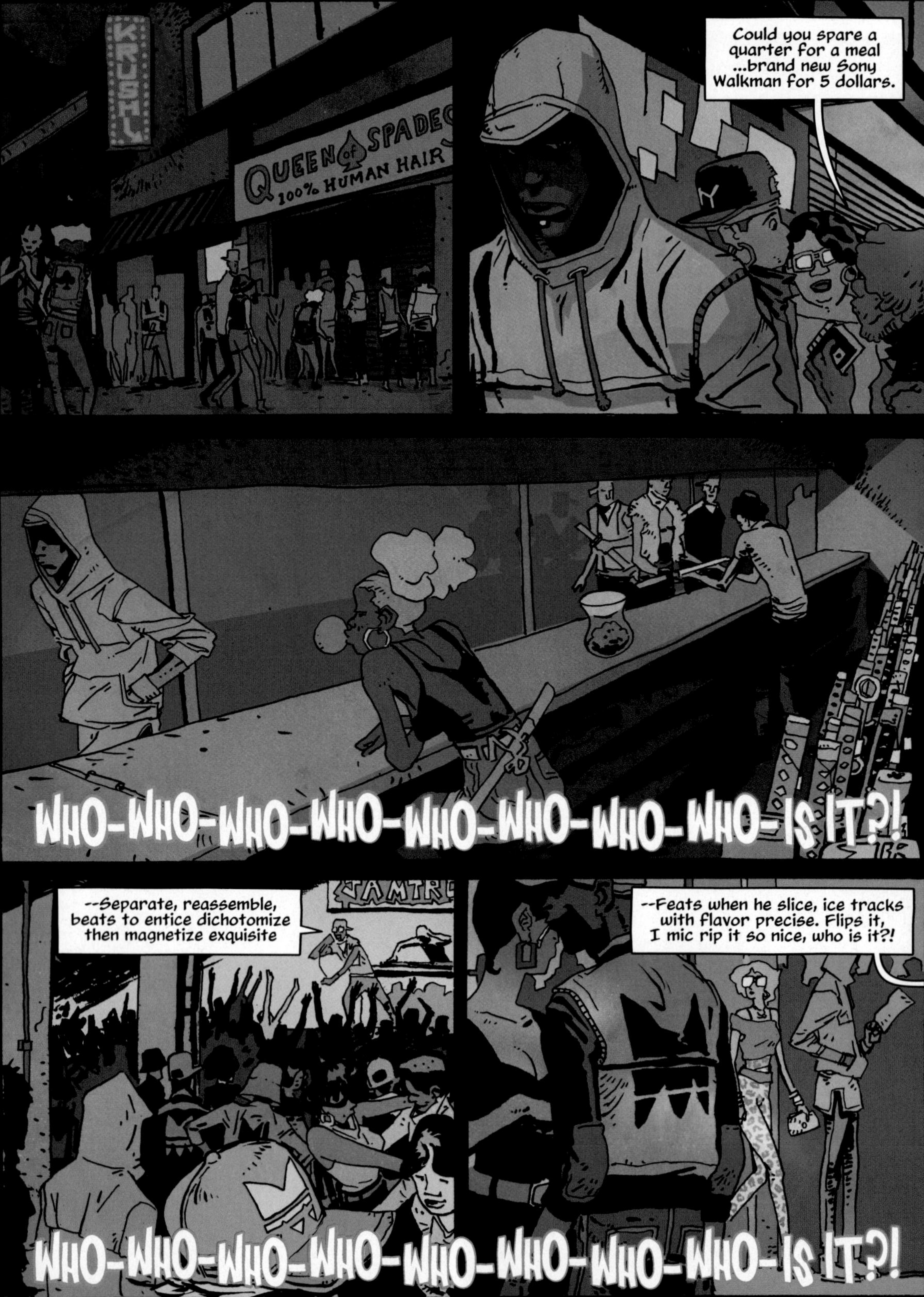

KRUSH
QUEEN of SPADES
100% HUMAN HAIR
Could you spare a quarter for a meal ...brand new Sony Walkman for 5 dollars.
WHO-WHO-WHO-WHO-WHO-WHO-WHO-WHO-IS IT?!
--Separate, reassemble, beats to entice dichotomize then magnetize exquisite
--Feats when he slice, ice tracks with flavor precise. Flips it, I mic rip it so nice, who is it?!
WHO-WHO-WHO-WHO-WHO-WHO-WHO-WHO-IS IT?!

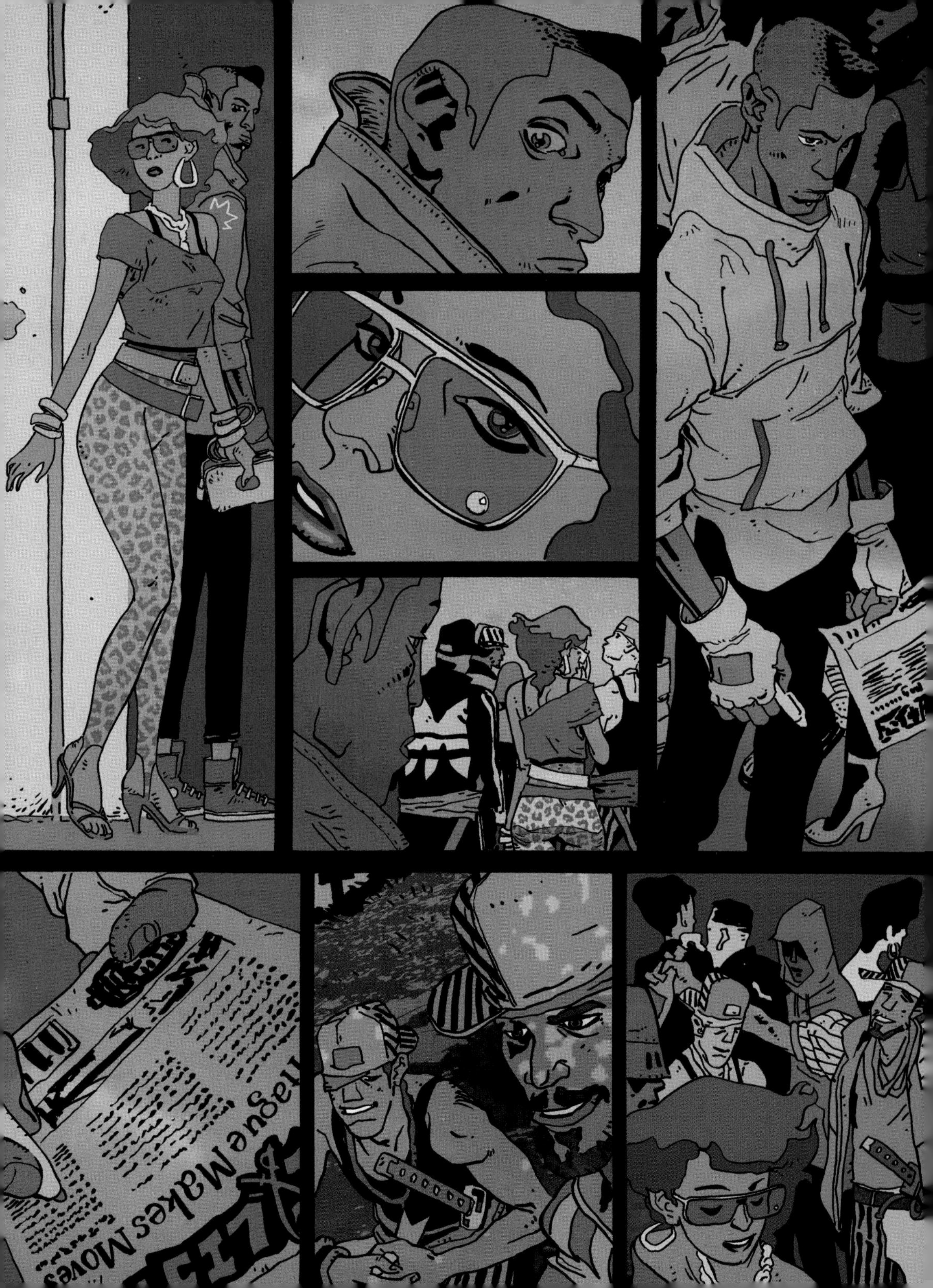

ague Makes Moves

Romeo Remains, Canolios are Slain

Robert Greene

Romeo remains, Canolios are slain.
A ruddy new blade debuts at rank four.
That merked the smartly dressed duo and did stain
With Montague blood the new rub dance floor

Tybalt, nephew of the Capulet Lord
Did swordless, enter the Montague den
Brandishing boxcutter, defied a horde
of Montague men and still did defend

His life against the Montague's attempts.
When he, on accident scuffed Lu's New Kicks
Lu drew quick yet caught Tybalt's Coup de temps
in open eye, and then Tybalt, through Trick

Did cleverly disarm the one brother,
And after hewing through three Montague men,
dispatched efficiently the other,
Young Donatello, quickly after his Kin.
In all, five Montague did lose their lives.
See memorial details on page five.

chop shop

Duel List

01.   Romeo Montague
02.   Benvolio Montague
03.   "Notorious" Barabus
04.   Tybalt Capulet
05.   Jacquelyn

. . .

06.   Malachi
07.   Murder Maeve
08.   Moiritsuke
09.   Little Julius
10.   Dipi Ittosai

--Verilly, he's cute, *Juliet*, admit.

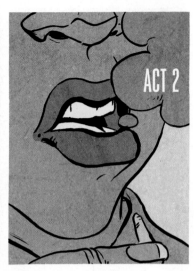

ACT 2

Yuck! He's my cousin, *Roxie!*

Juliet

...And a Capulet, unfortunately.

Hey!

--but look at this picture.

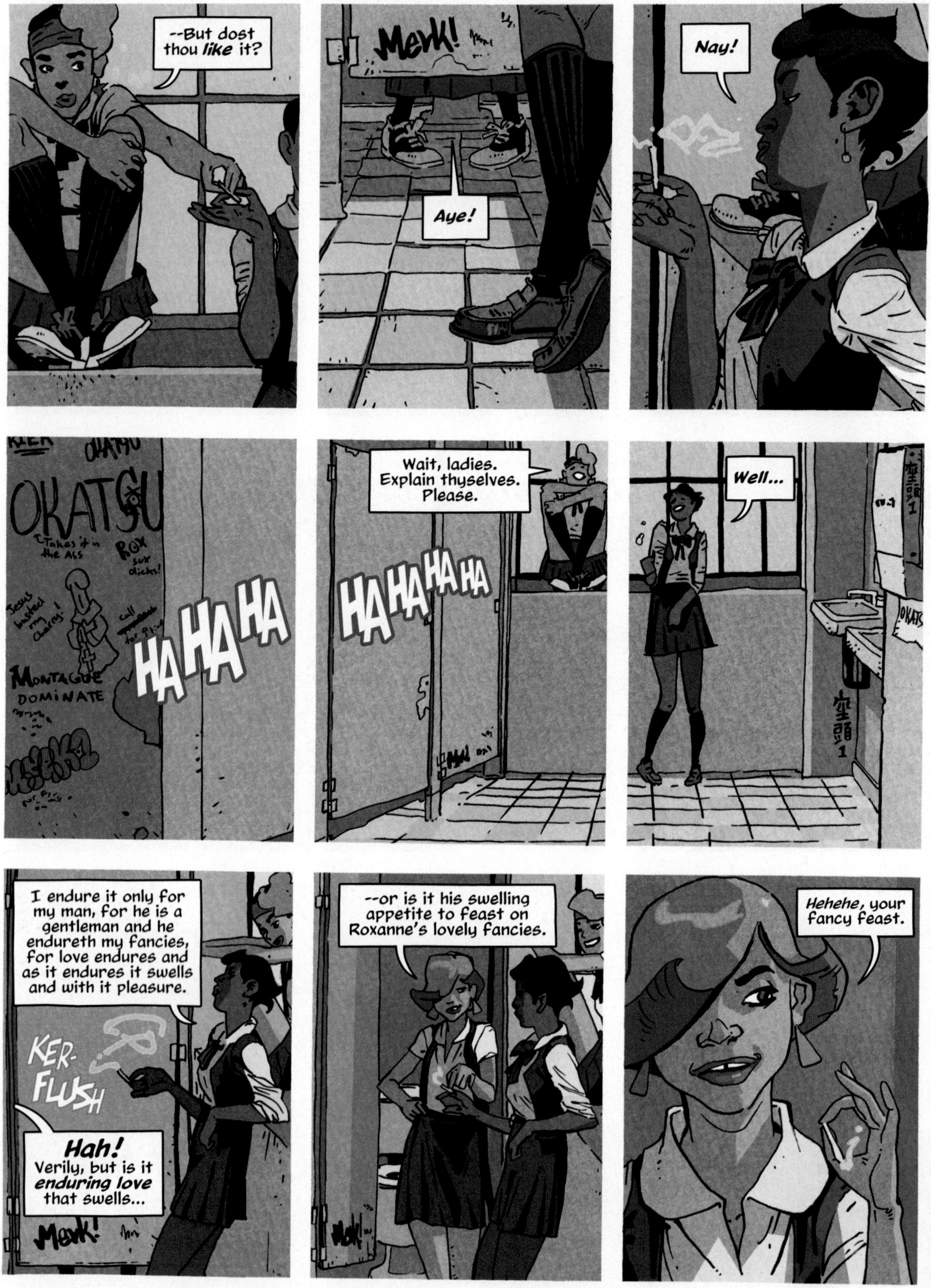
--But dost thou *like* it?
Merk!
Aye!
Nay!
OKATSU
Takes it in the Ass
ROX sux dicks!
Jesus busted my cherry!
MONTAGUE DOMINATE
HAHAHA
HAHAHAHA
Wait, ladies. Explain thyselves. Please.
Well...
I endure it only for my man, for he is a gentleman and he endureth my fancies, for love endures and as it endures it swells and with it pleasure.
KER-FLUSH
Hah! Verily, but is it ***enduring love*** that swells...
Merk!
--or is it his swelling appetite to feast on Roxanne's lovely fancies.
Hehehe, your fancy feast.

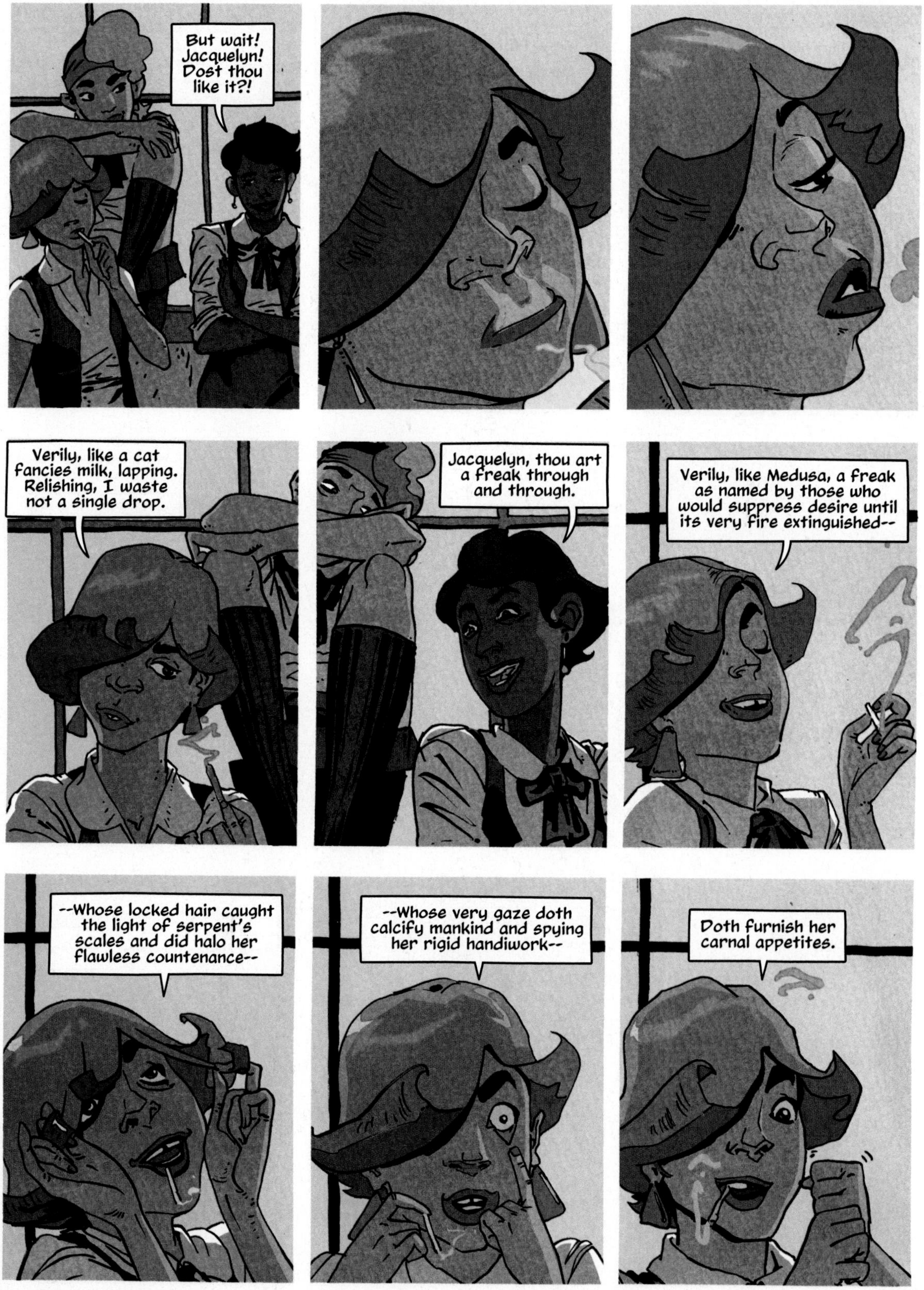
But wait! Jacquelyn! Dost thou like it?!
Verily, like a cat fancies milk, lapping. Relishing, I waste not a single drop.
Jacquelyn, thou art a freak through and through.
Verily, like Medusa, a freak as named by those who would suppress desire until its very fire extinguished--
--Whose locked hair caught the light of serpent's scales and did halo her flawless countenance--
--Whose very gaze doth calcify mankind and spying her rigid handiwork--
Doth furnish her carnal appetites.

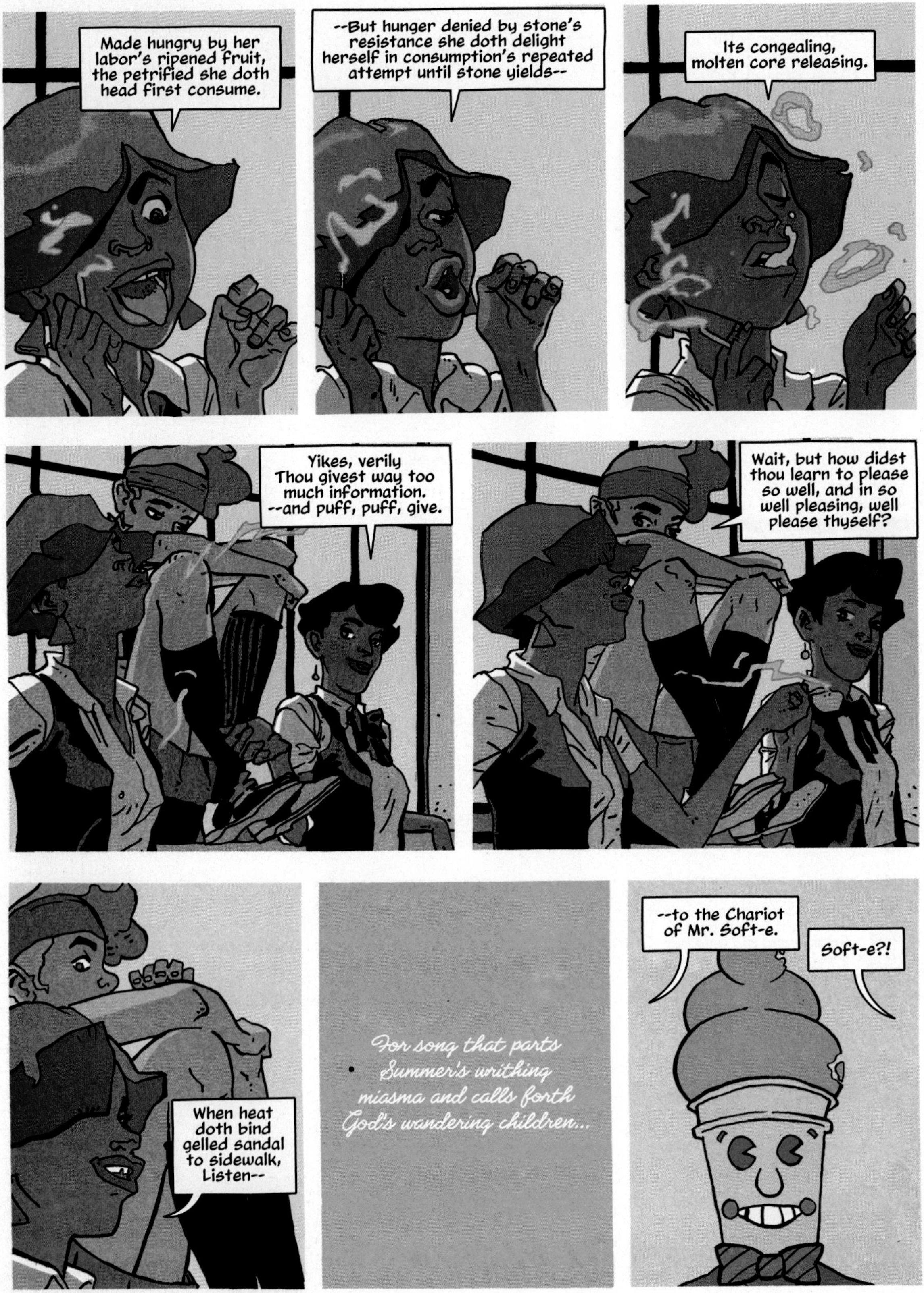
Made hungry by her labor's ripened fruit, the petrified she doth head first consume.
--But hunger denied by stone's resistance she doth delight herself in consumption's repeated attempt until stone yields--
Its congealing, molten core releasing.
Yikes, verily Thou givest way too much information. --and puff, puff, give.
Wait, but how didst thou learn to please so well, and in so well pleasing, well please thyself?
When heat doth bind gelled sandal to sidewalk, Listen--
For song that parts Summer's writhing miasma and calls forth God's wandering children...
--to the Chariot of Mr. Soft-e.
Soft-e?!

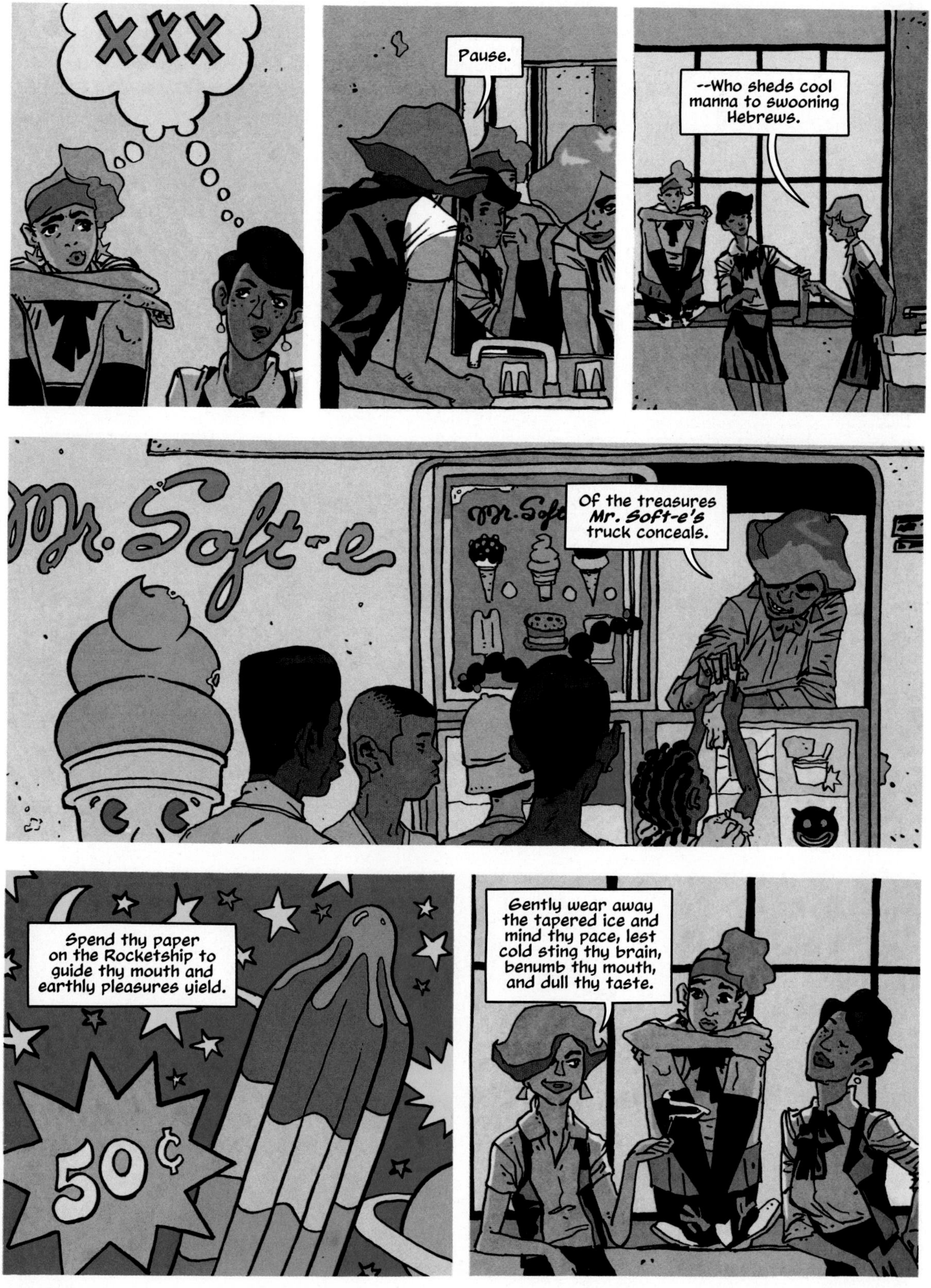
XXX
Pause.
--Who sheds cool manna to swooning Hebrews.
Mr. Soft-e
Of the treasures Mr. Soft-e's truck conceals.
Spend thy paper on the Rocketship to guide thy mouth and earthly pleasures yield.
50¢
Gently wear away the tapered ice and mind thy pace, lest cold sting thy brain, benumb thy mouth, and dull thy taste.

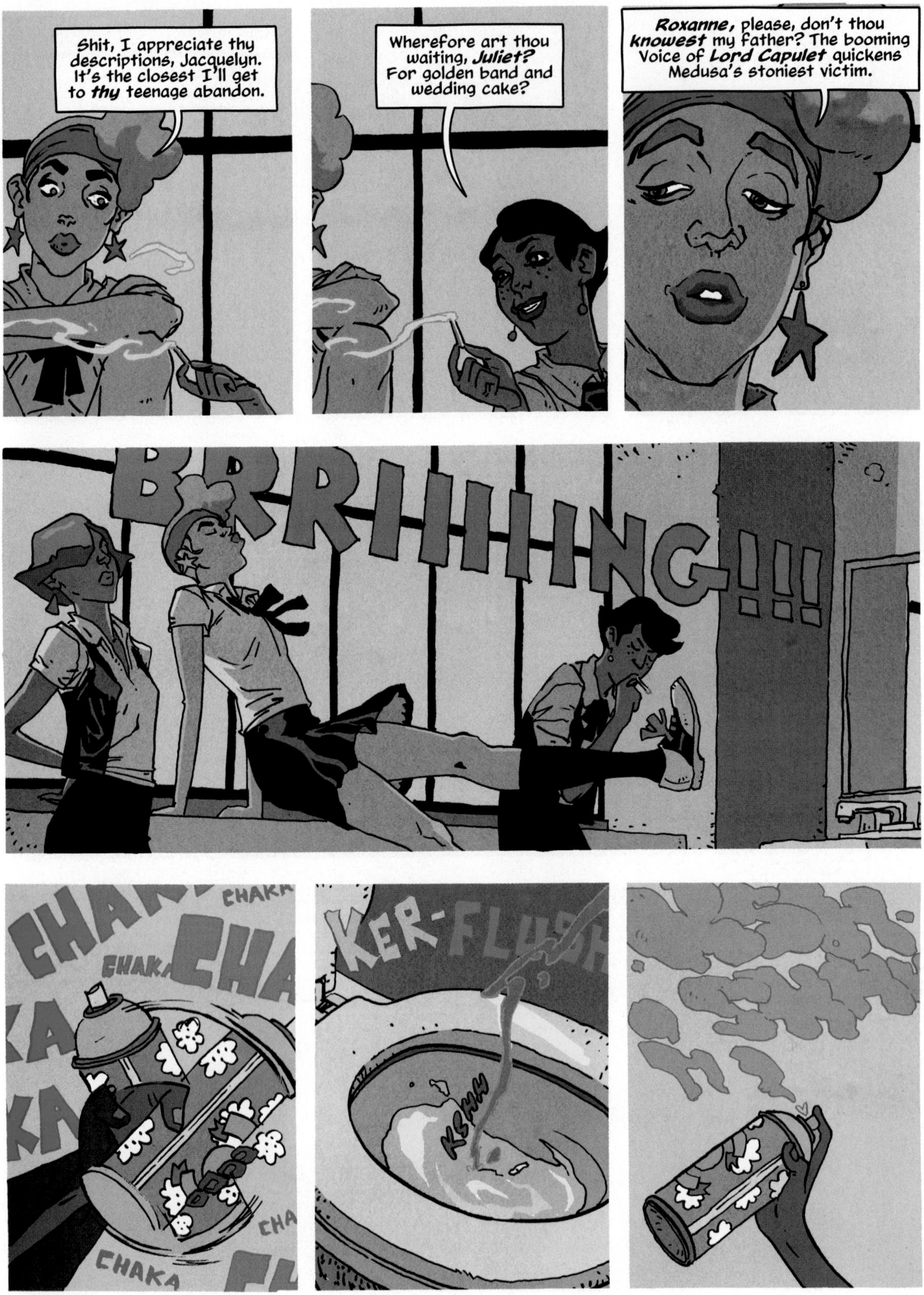

Shit, I appreciate thy descriptions, Jacquelyn. It's the closest I'll get to *thy* teenage abandon.
Wherefore art thou waiting, *Juliet?* For golden band and wedding cake?
Roxanne, please, don't thou *knowest* my father? The booming Voice of *Lord Capulet* quickens Medusa's stoniest victim.
BRRIIIIING!!!
CHAKA
CHAKA
CHAKA
CHAKA
KER-FLUSH
KSHHH

Verily, free at last!

My father's enrolled me in summer school.

Juliet, you failed? A shame you'll miss the Mermaid Parade!

Not failed! My dad, he fears my idle hands, binds them with-- Extracurricular Activities.

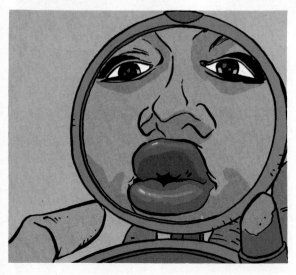

SNAP

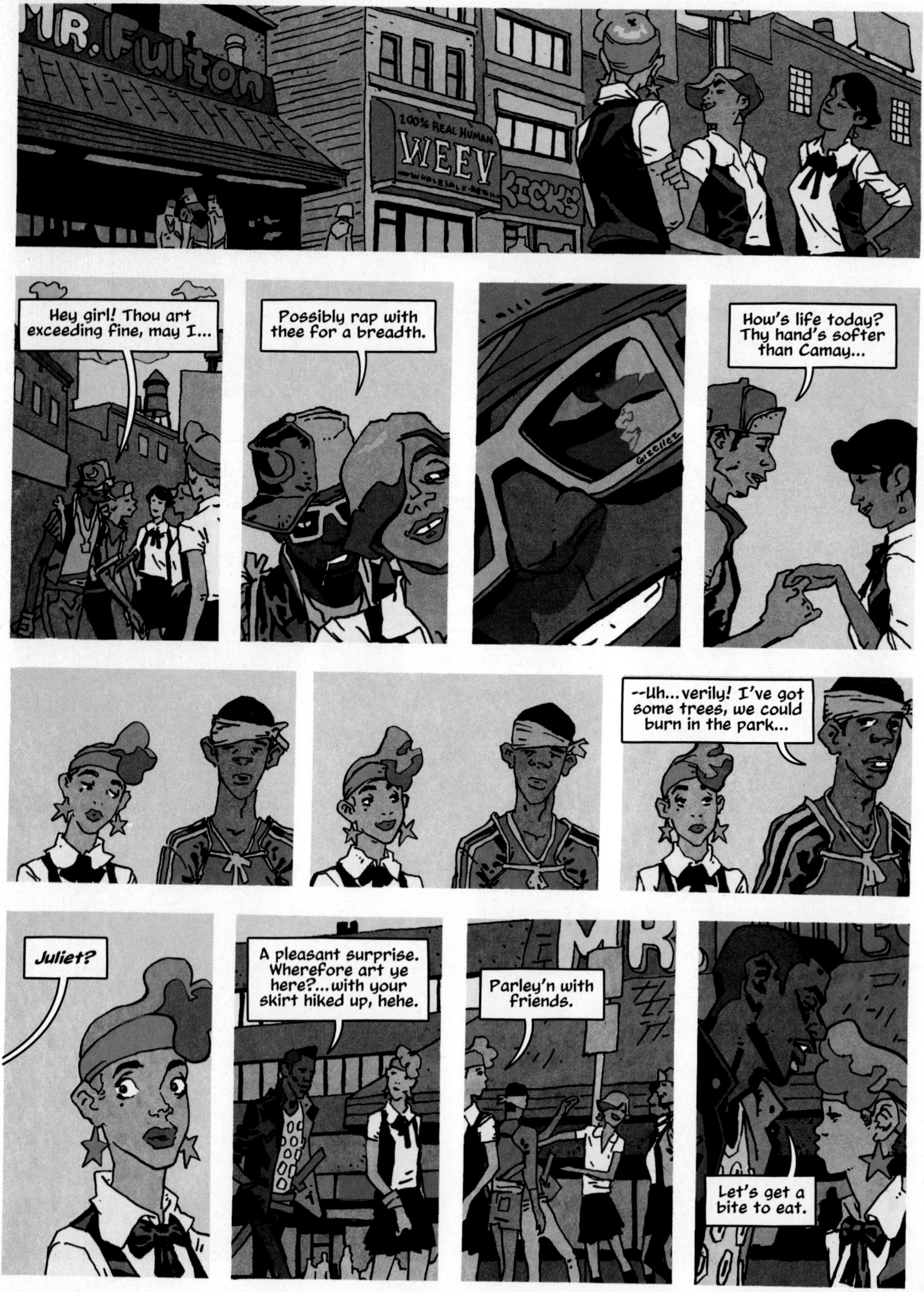
MR. Fulton
100% REAL HUMAN
WEEV
KICKS
Hey girl! Thou art exceeding fine, may I...
Possibly rap with thee for a breadth.
How's life today? Thy hand's softer than Camay...
--Uh...verily! I've got some trees, we could burn in the park...
Juliet?
A pleasant surprise. Wherefore art ye here?...with your skirt hiked up, hehe.
Parley'n with friends.
Let's get a bite to eat.

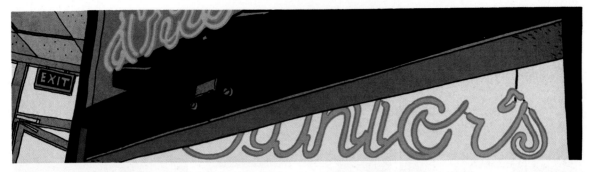

Cheesecake?

Tybalt...

Mm?

Am I cute?

Uh...

Of course! Verily! Why?

≠Sigh≠

Check, please.

See--

Hahaha, ye look so serious!

--Can't give these fools an inch. Here comes the final boss.

Thou never speakest of private school, *Tybalt*, why?

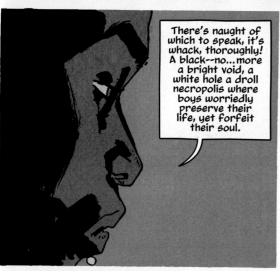

There's naught of which to speak, it's whack, thoroughly! A black--no...more a bright void, a white hole a droll necropolis where boys worriedly preserve their life, yet forfeit their soul.

Surely a better place than this, though.

A place, no better--

--but barren, void of friend and foe alike.

≥Psst≤ Ma, might I have your ear.

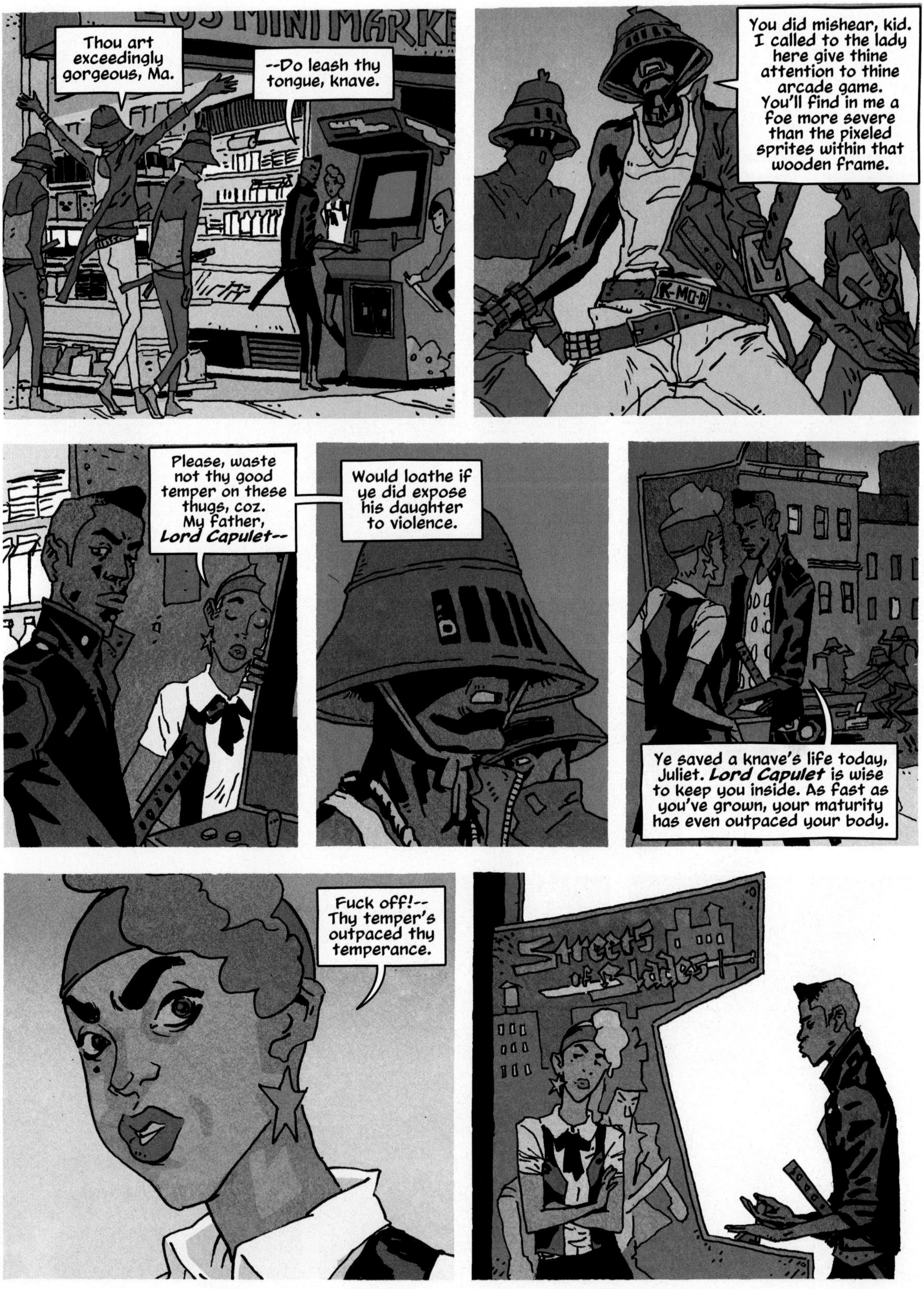
LOS MINI MARKE
Thou art exceedingly gorgeous, Ma.
--Do leash thy tongue, knave.
You did mishear, kid. I called to the lady here give thine attention to thine arcade game. You'll find in me a foe more severe than the pixeled sprites within that wooden frame.
K-MO-D
Please, waste not thy good temper on these thugs, coz. My father, Lord Capulet--
Would loathe if ye did expose his daughter to violence.
Ye saved a knave's life today, Juliet. Lord Capulet is wise to keep you inside. As fast as you've grown, your maturity has even outpaced your body.
Fuck off!--Thy temper's outpaced thy temperance.
Streets of Blades

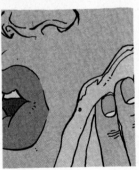

Hi, Daddy.

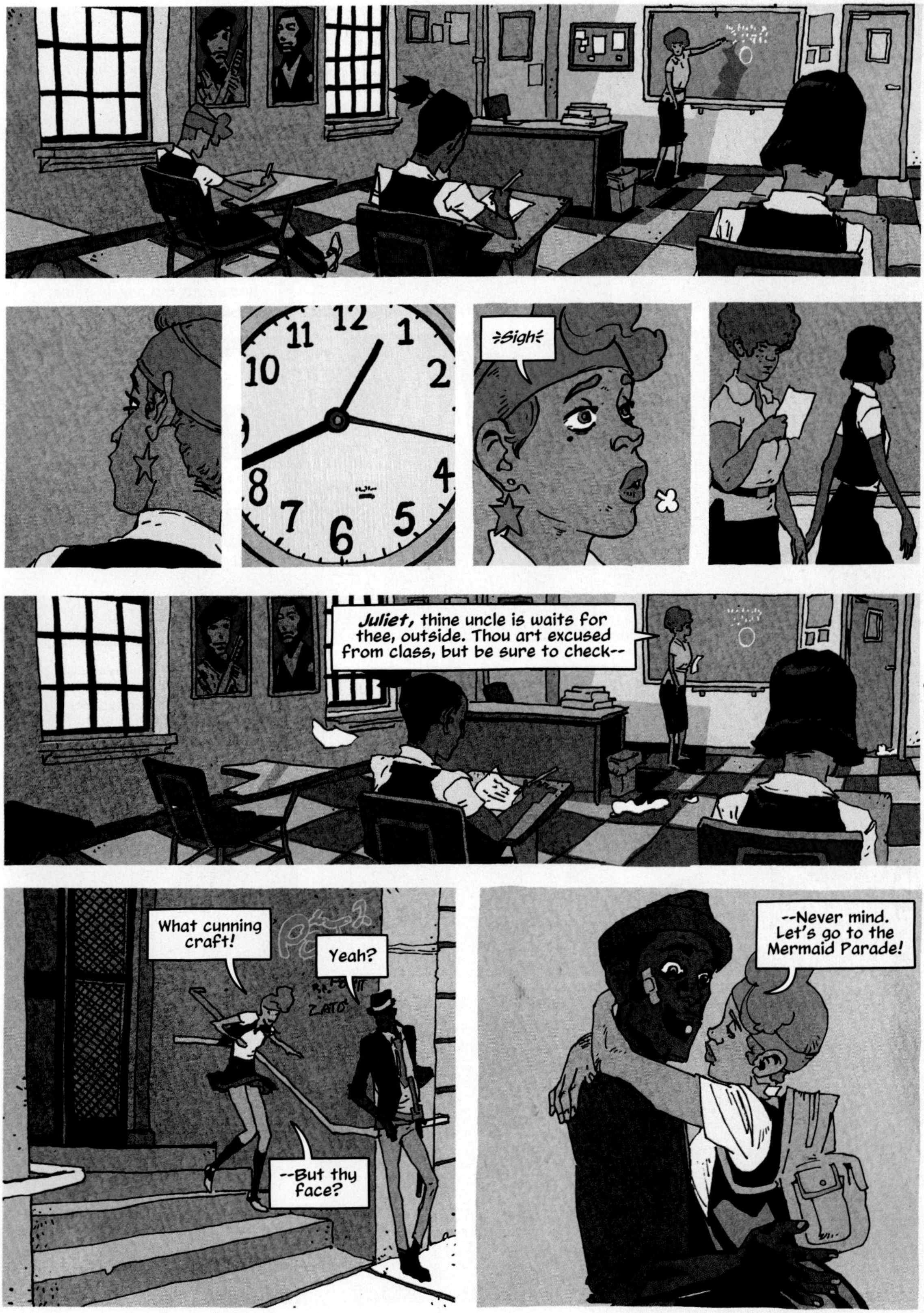

Sigh
Juliet, thine uncle is waits for thee, outside. Thou art excused from class, but be sure to check--
What cunning craft!
Yeah?
--But thy face?
--Never mind. Let's go to the Mermaid Parade!

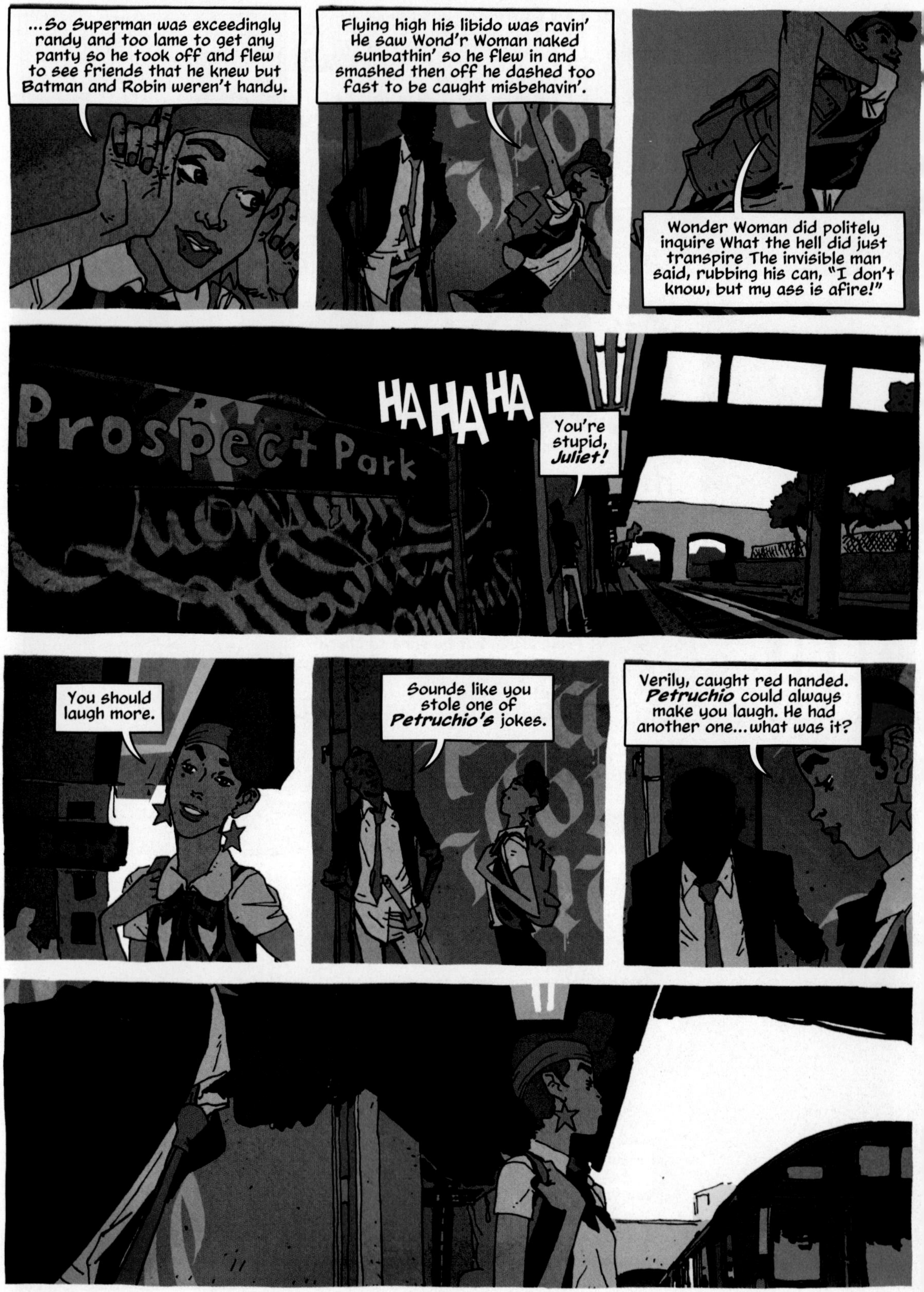

...So Superman was exceedingly randy and too lame to get any panty so he took off and flew to see friends that he knew but Batman and Robin weren't handy.
Flying high his libido was ravin' He saw Wond'r Woman naked sunbathin' so he flew in and smashed then off he dashed too fast to be caught misbehavin'.
Wonder Woman did politely inquire What the hell did just transpire The invisible man said, rubbing his can, "I don't know, but my ass is afire!"
Prospect Park
HA HA HA HA
You're stupid, *Juliet!*
You should laugh more.
Sounds like you stole one of *Petruchio's* jokes.
Verily, caught red handed. *Petruchio* could always make you laugh. He had another one...what was it?

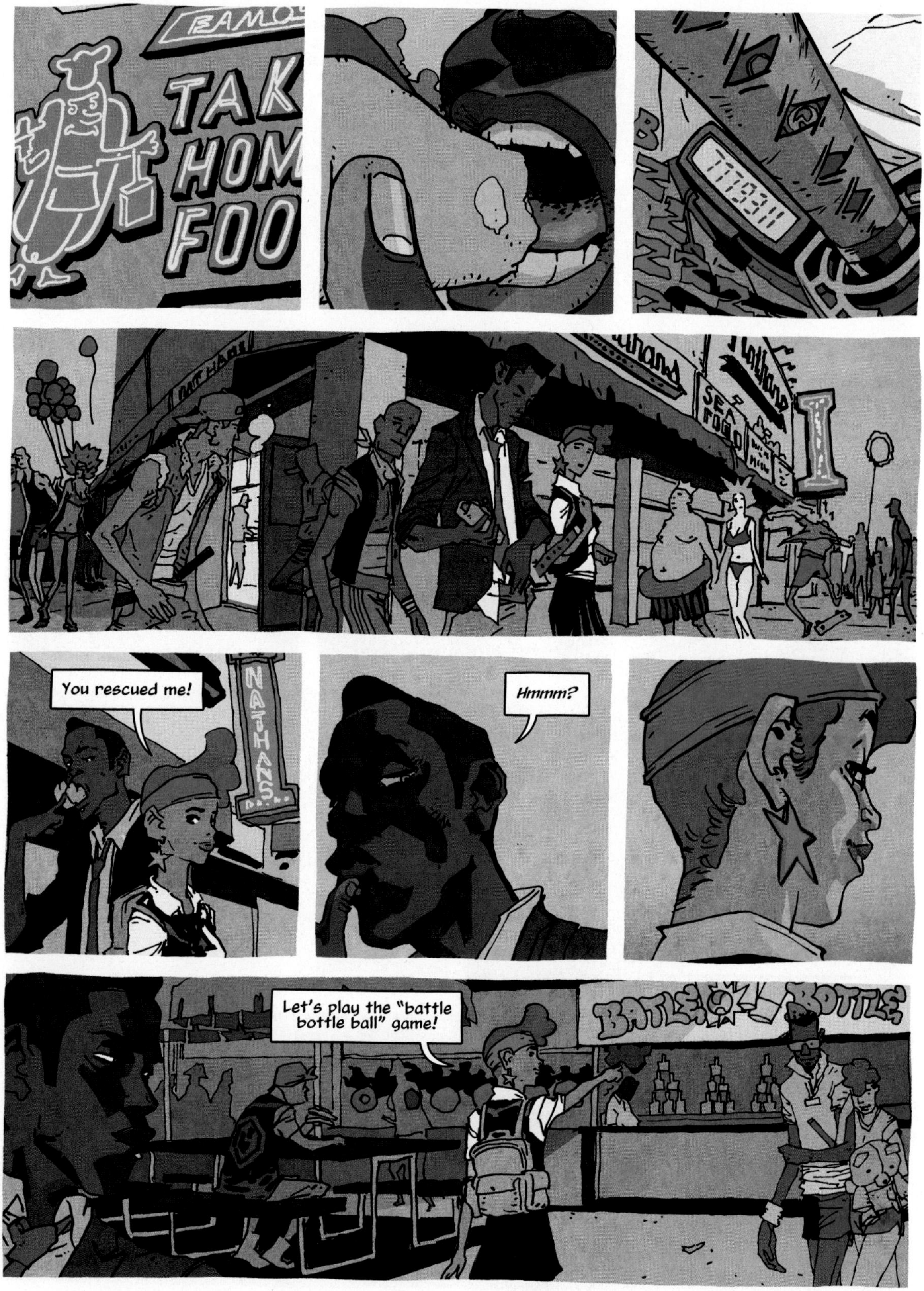

You rescued me!
NATHANS
Hmmm?
Let's play the "battle bottle ball" game!

CRASH

Geez, Kiddo, thou art a professional--at busting my balls, take thy prize and scram.

Which will it be, Sweetheart? Take your pick.

What charms are those beneath the plush?

My wife, she makes these, each one by hand each is a one-of-a-kind love charm.

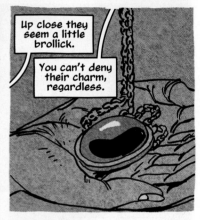
Up close they seem a little brollick.

You can't deny their charm, regardless.

On delicate necks as yours maybe, but on the sturdy neck of your lover, this amulet will rest perfectly, guarding his affections from any other.

Ha, you've no need for trifling trinkets.

I'll take it!

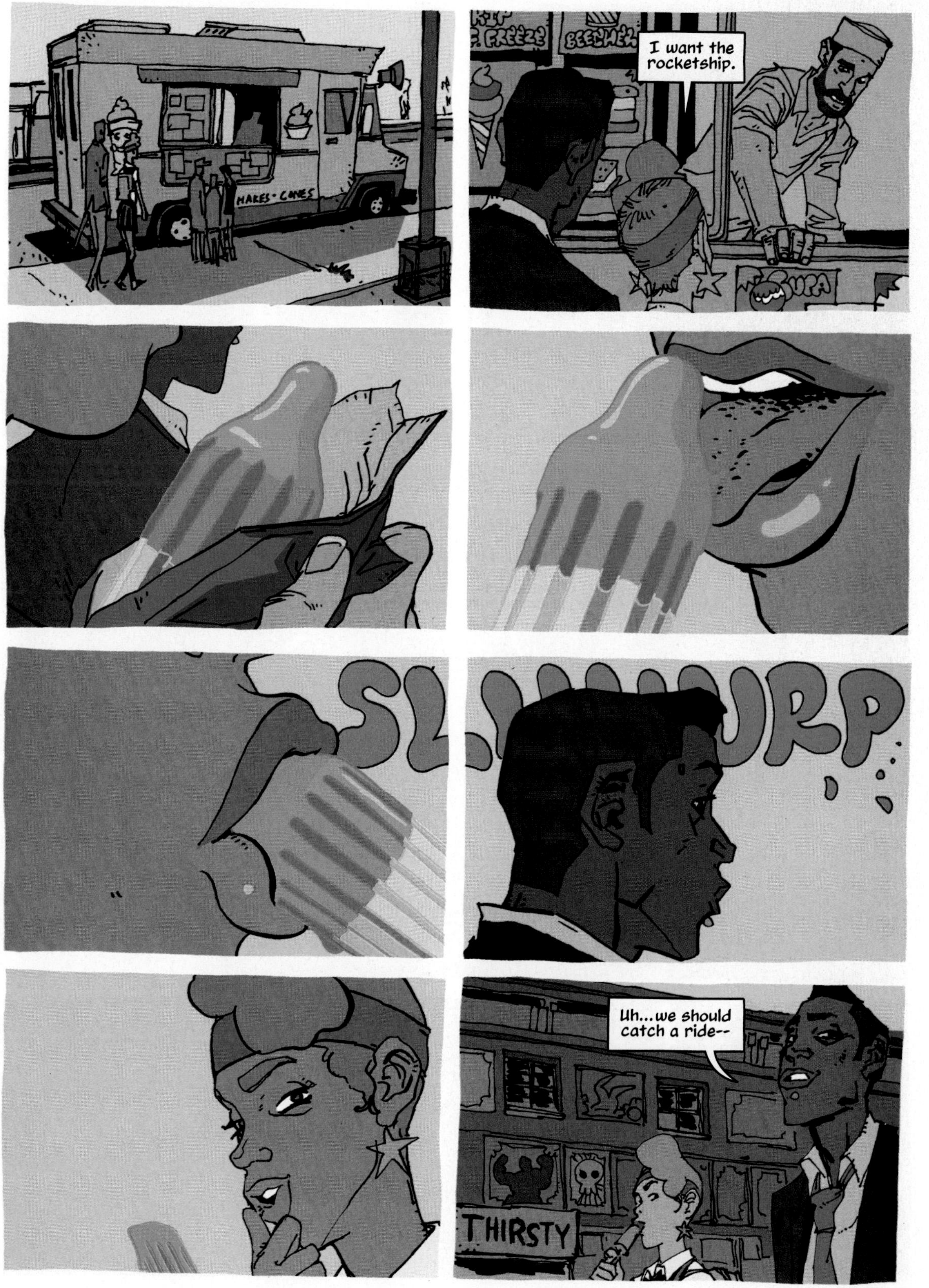
MAKES · CONES
I want the rocketship.
SUPA
SLURP
Uh...we should catch a ride--
THIRSTY

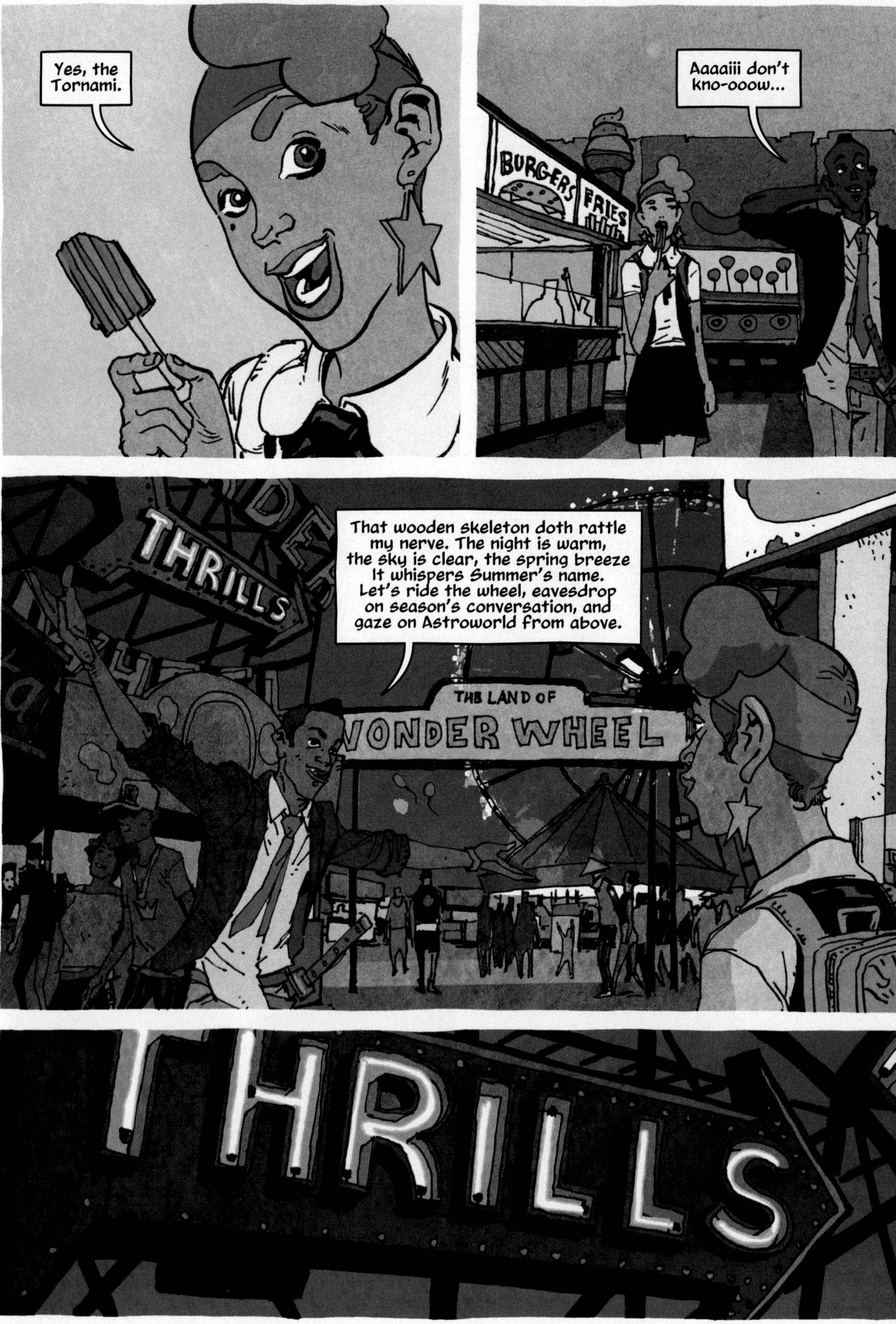
Yes, the Tornami.
Aaaaiii don't kno-ooow...
BURGERS
FRIES
THRILLS
That wooden skeleton doth rattle my nerve. The night is warm, the sky is clear, the spring breeze It whispers Summer's name. Let's ride the wheel, eavesdrop on season's conversation, and gaze on Astroworld from above.
THE LAND OF
WONDER WHEEL
THRILLS

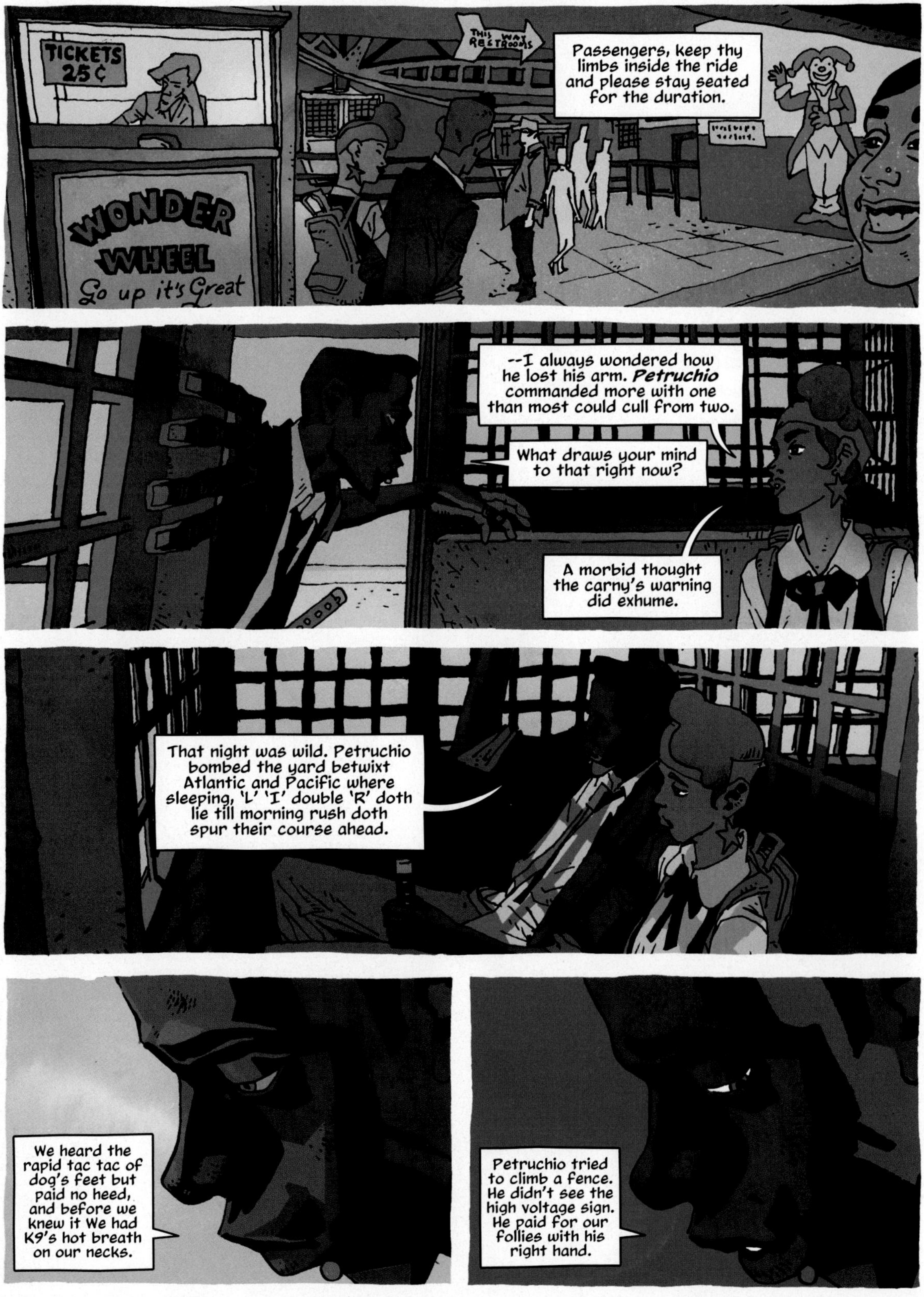
TICKETS 25¢
WONDER WHEEL Go up it's Great
THIS WAY RESTROOMS
Passengers, keep thy limbs inside the ride and please stay seated for the duration.
--I always wondered how he lost his arm. Petruchio commanded more with one than most could cull from two.
What draws your mind to that right now?
A morbid thought the carny's warning did exhume.
That night was wild. Petruchio bombed the yard betwixt Atlantic and Pacific where sleeping, 'L' 'I' double 'R' doth lie till morning rush doth spur their course ahead.
We heard the rapid tac tac of dog's feet but paid no heed, and before we knew it We had K9's hot breath on our necks.
Petruchio tried to climb a fence. He didn't see the high voltage sign. He paid for our follies with his right hand.

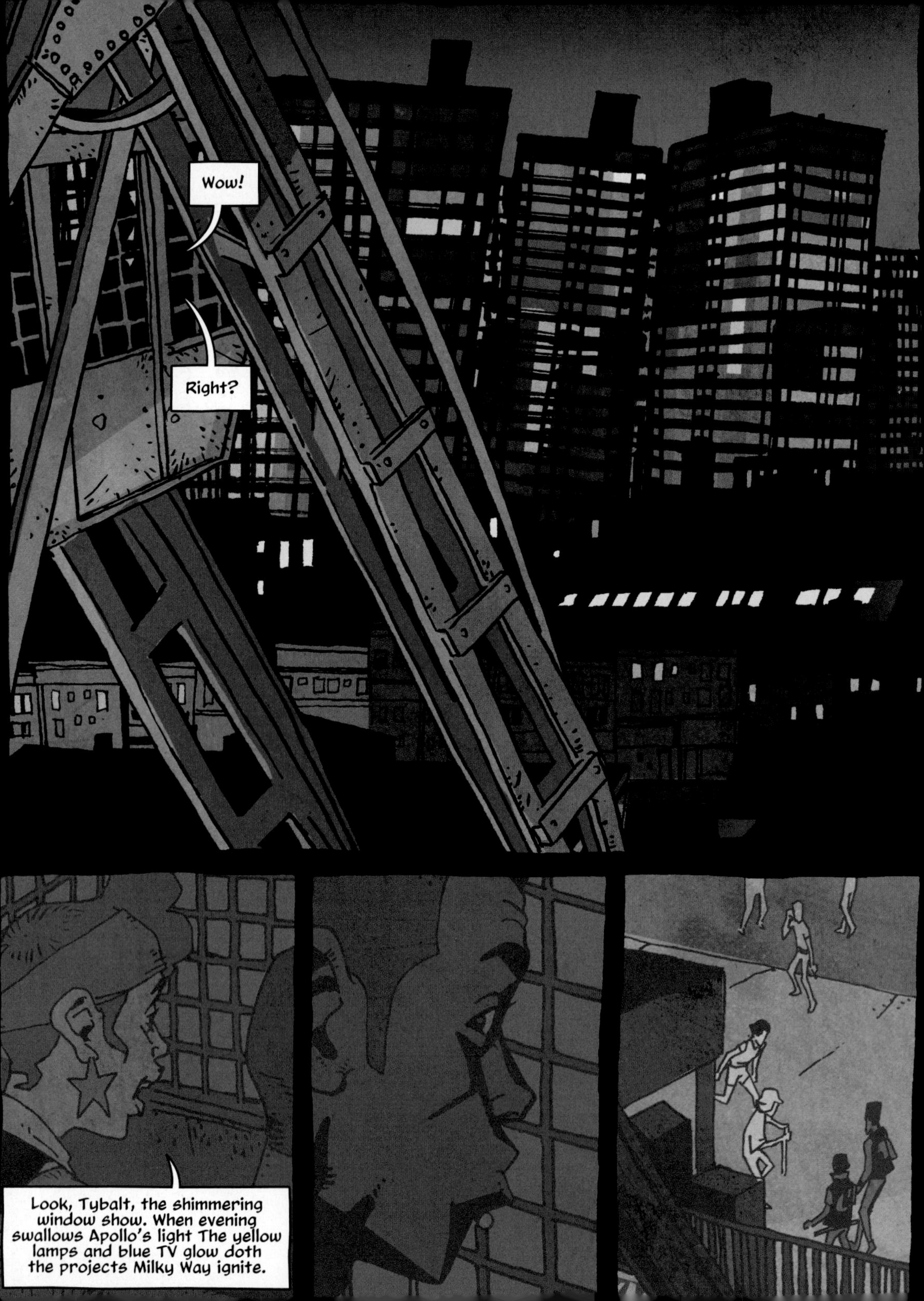
Wow!
Right?
Look, Tybalt, the shimmering window show. When evening swallows Apollo's light The yellow lamps and blue TV glow doth the projects Milky Way ignite.

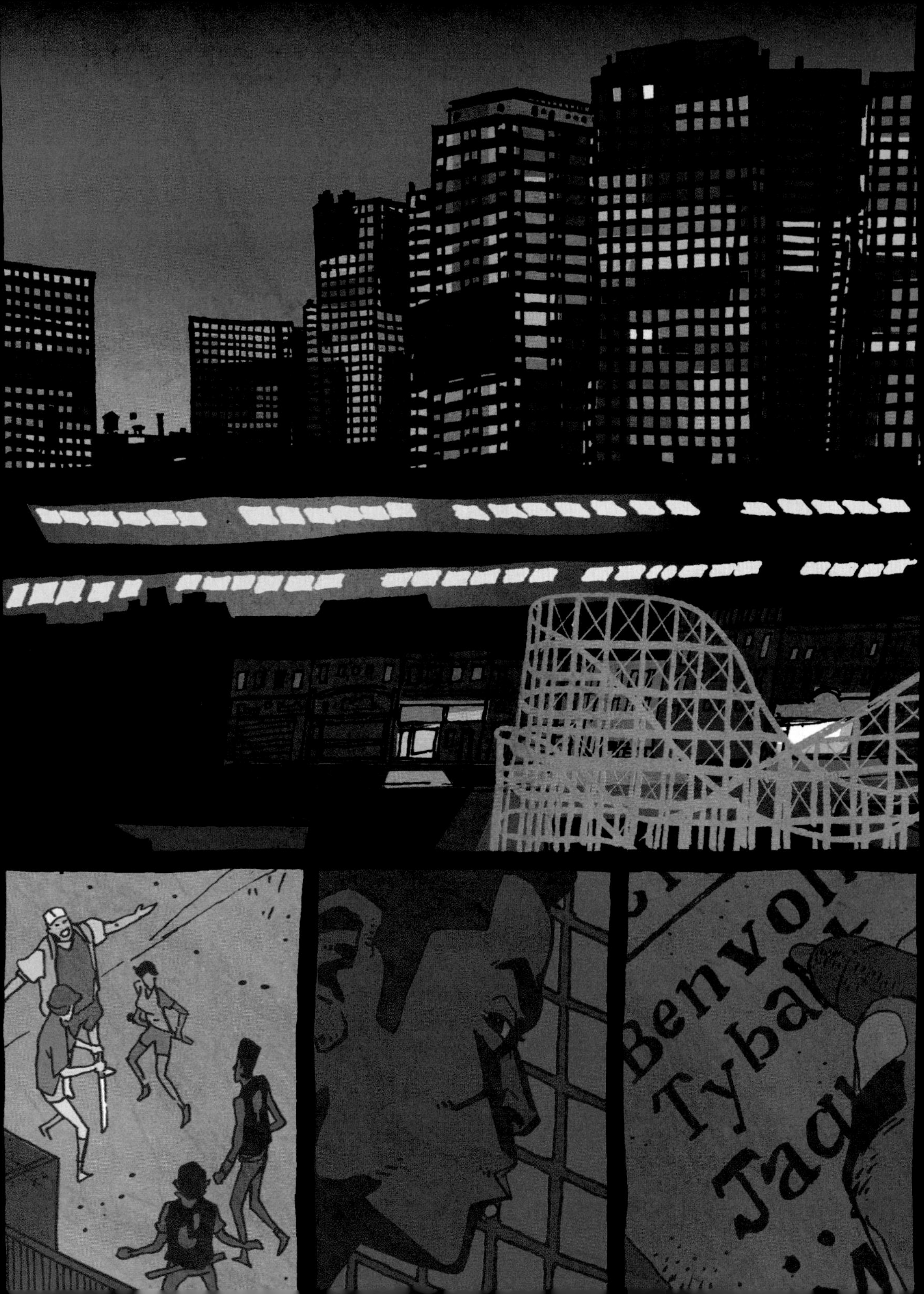

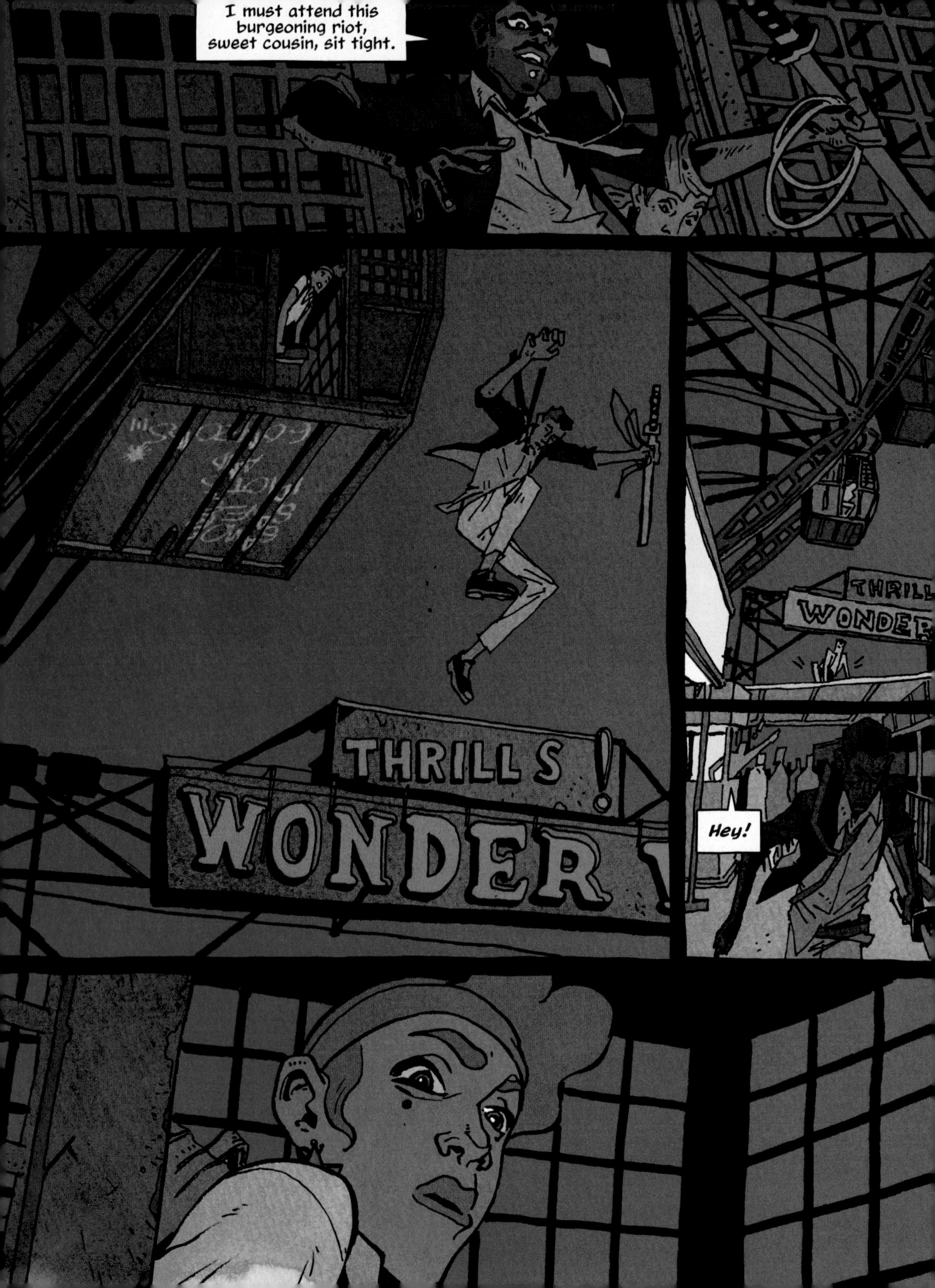
I must attend this burgeoning riot, sweet cousin, sit tight.
THRILLS!
WONDER
THRILL
WONDER
Hey!

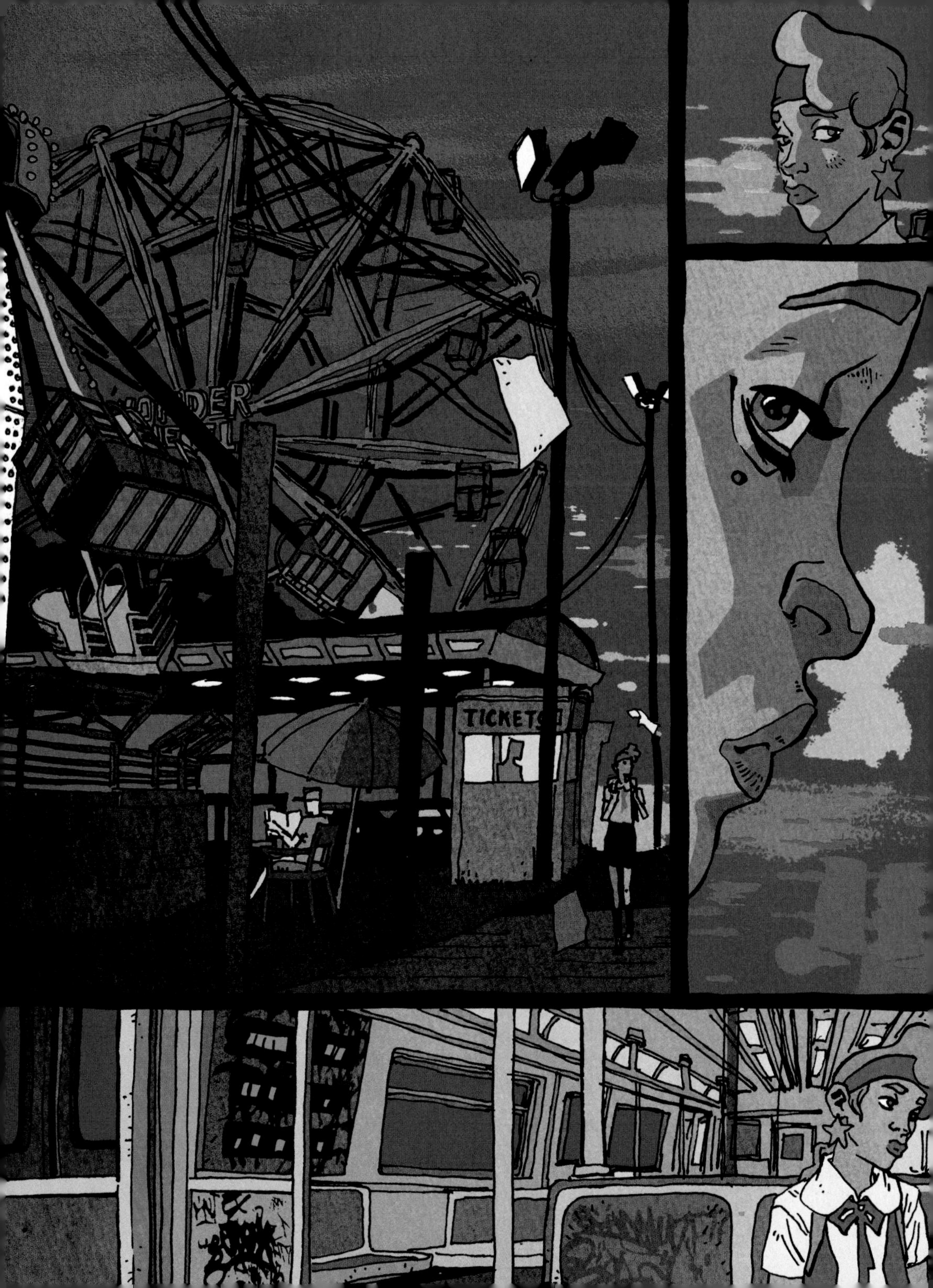
TICKETS

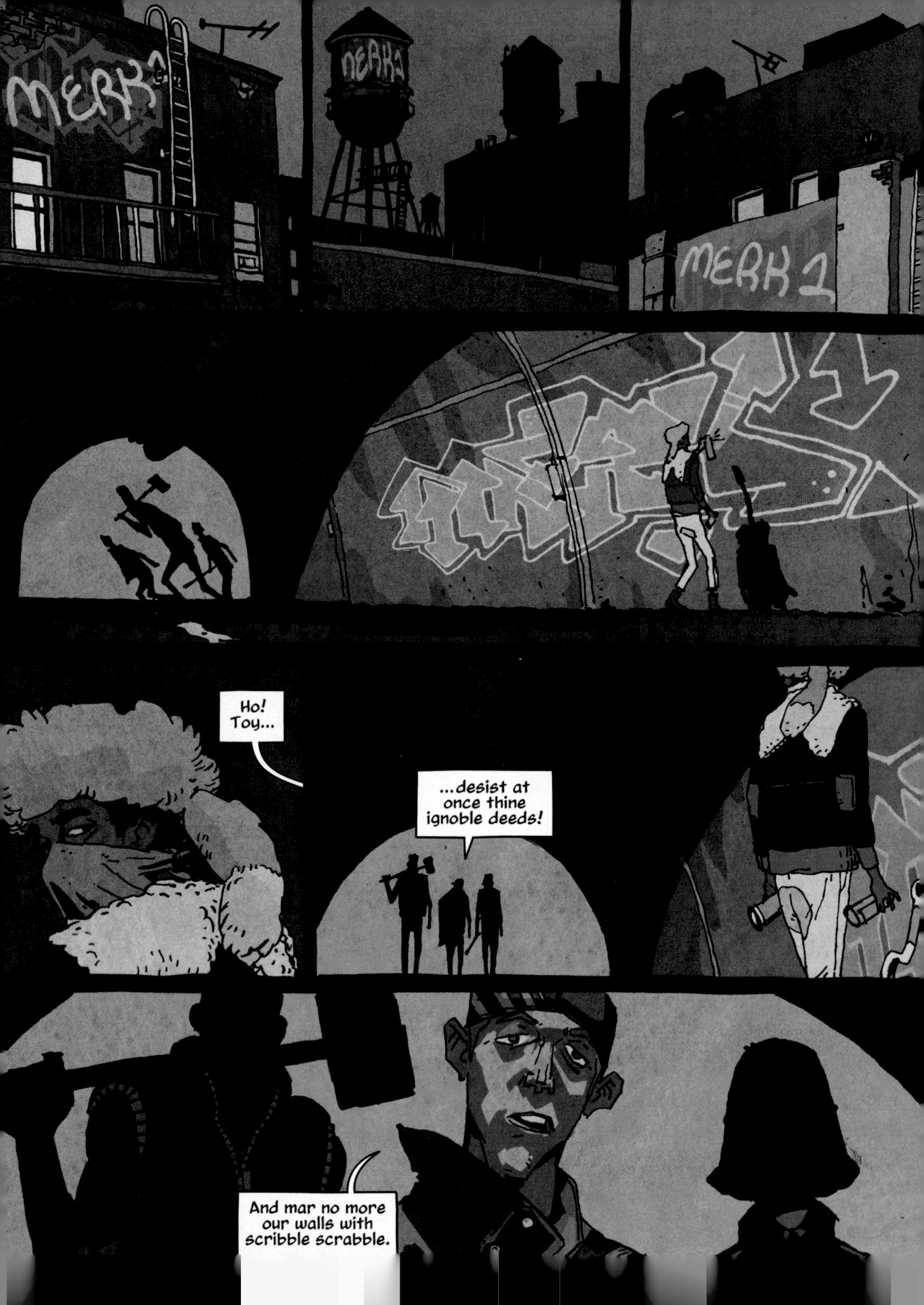
MERK
MERK
MERK 1
Ho! Toy...
...desist at once thine ignoble deeds!
And mar no more our walls with scribble scrabble.

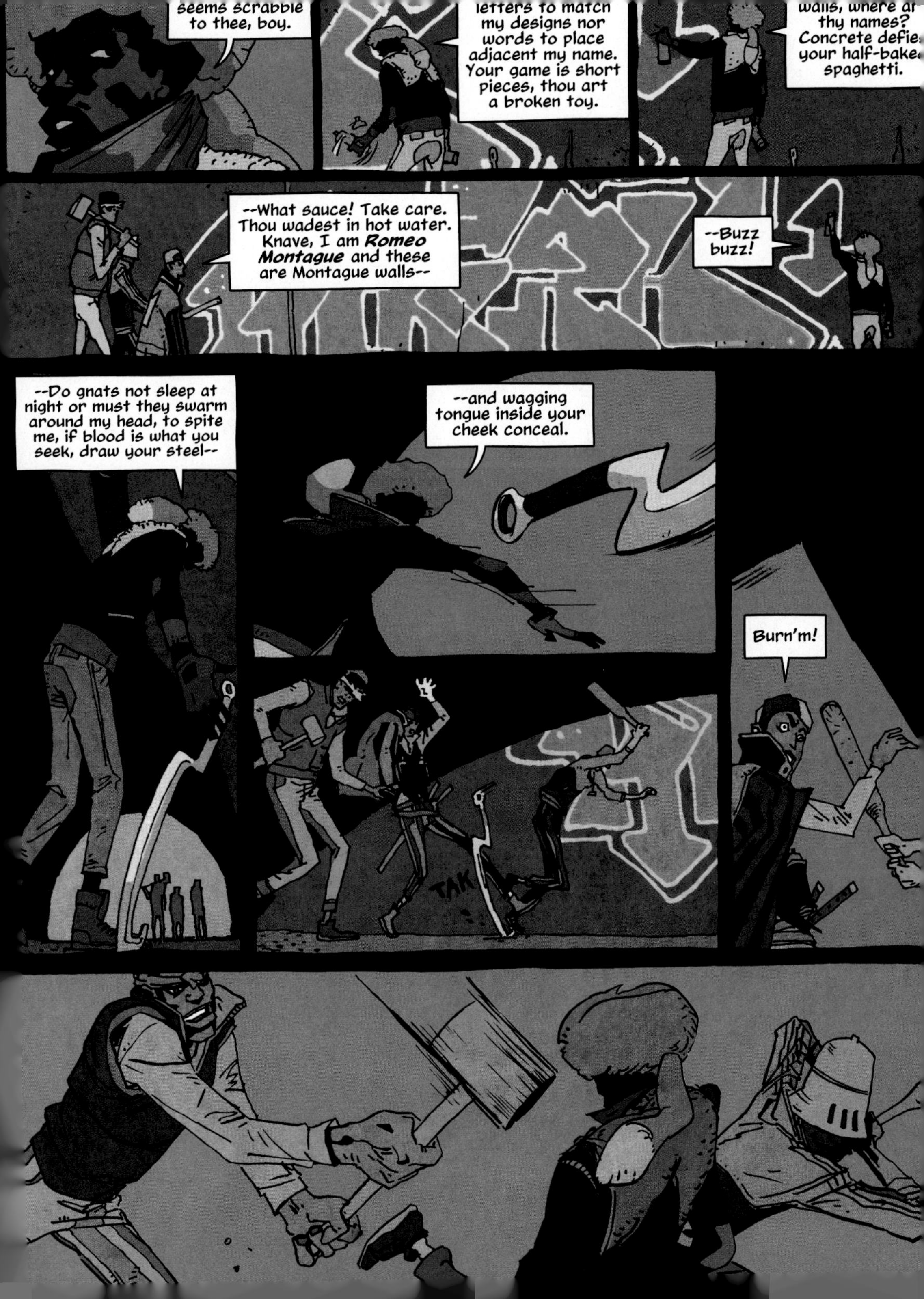

seems scrabble to thee, boy.
letters to match my designs nor words to place adjacent my name. Your game is short pieces, thou art a broken toy.
walls, where ar thy names? Concrete defie your half-bake spaghetti.
--What sauce! Take care. Thou wadest in hot water. Knave, I am **Romeo Montague** and these are Montague walls--
--Buzz buzz!
--Do gnats not sleep at night or must they swarm around my head, to spite me, if blood is what you seek, draw your steel--
--and wagging tongue inside your cheek conceal.
Burn'm!
TAK

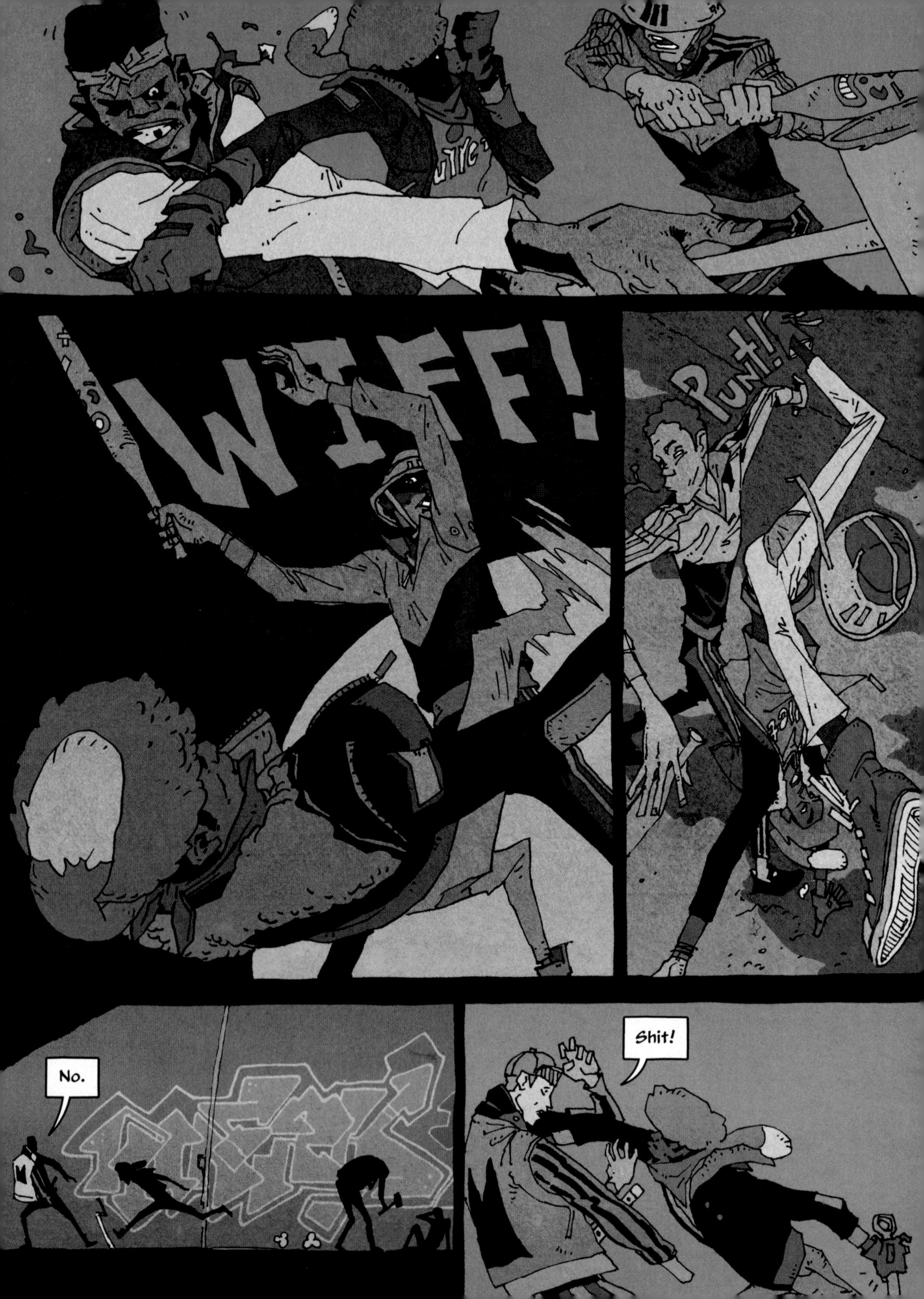
WIFF!
Punt!
No.
Shit!

ACT 3

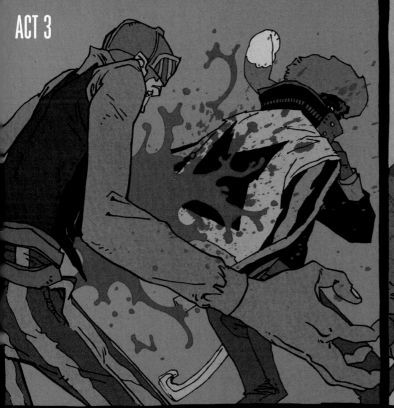

Oh.

Romeo

HA HA
HA HA
HA HA
HA
HA

Shit.

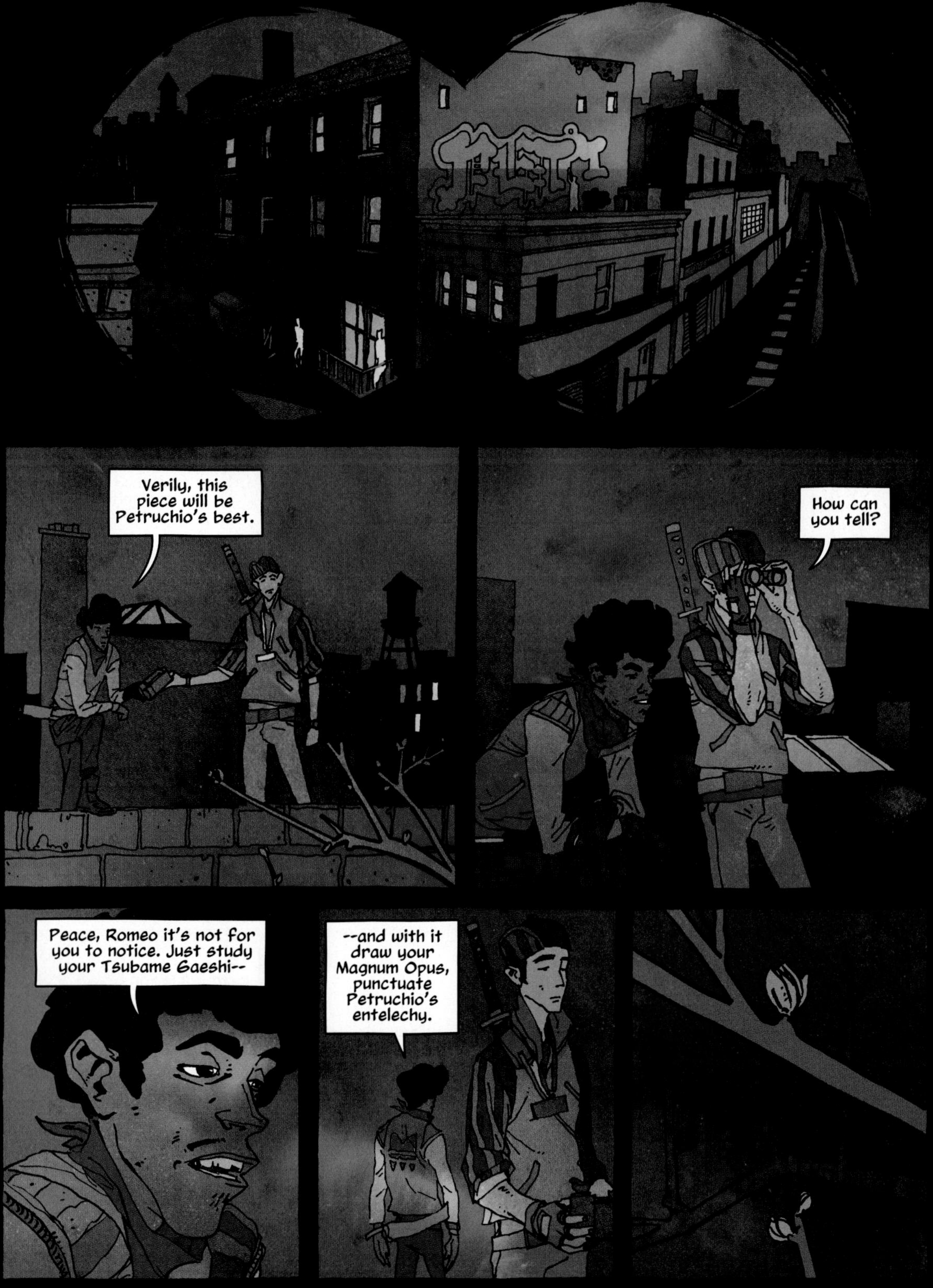
Verily, this piece will be Petruchio's best.
How can you tell?
Peace, Romeo it's not for you to notice. Just study your Tsubame Gaeshi--
--and with it draw your Magnum Opus, punctuate Petruchio's entelechy.

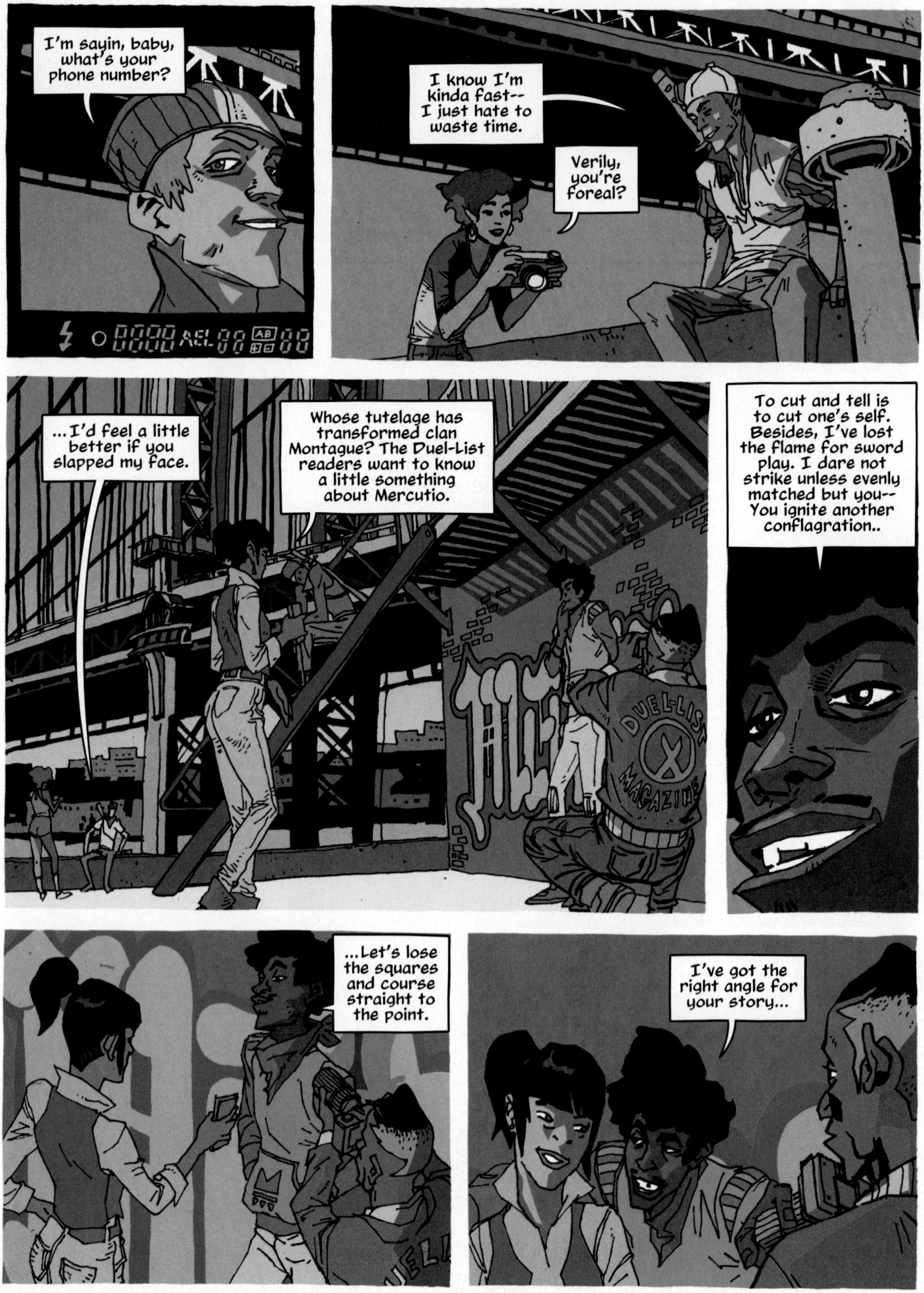
I'm sayin, baby, what's your phone number?
I know I'm kinda fast-- I just hate to waste time.
Verily, you're foreal?
...I'd feel a little better if you slapped my face.
Whose tutelage has transformed clan Montague? The Duel-List readers want to know a little something about Mercutio.
DUEL-LIST MAGAZINE
To cut and tell is to cut one's self. Besides, I've lost the flame for sword play. I dare not strike unless evenly matched but you-- You ignite another conflagration..
...Let's lose the squares and course straight to the point.
I've got the right angle for your story...

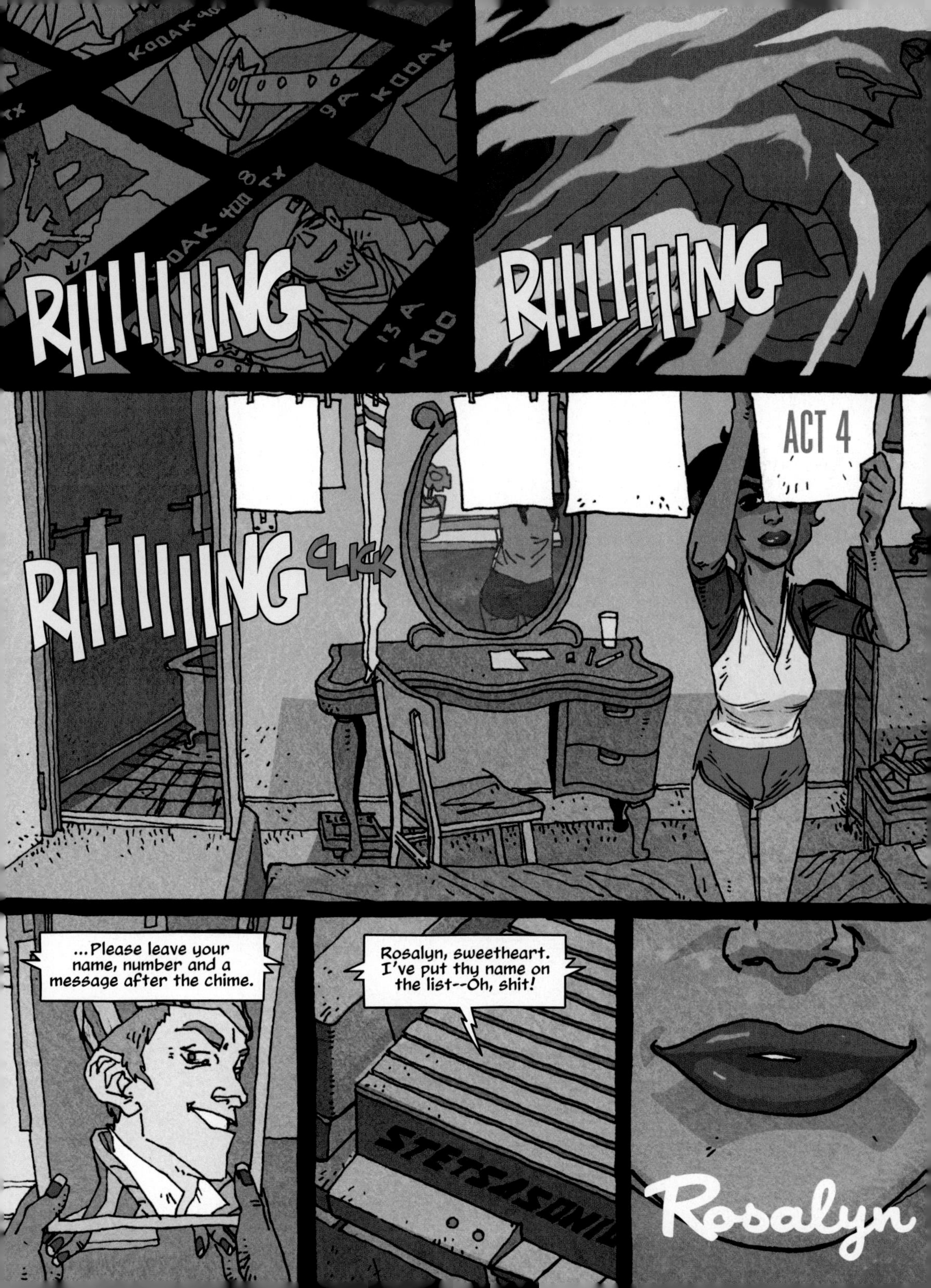
RIIIIIING
RIIIIIING
ACT 4
RIIIIIING
CLICK
...Please leave your name, number and a message after the chime.
Rosalyn, sweetheart. I've put thy name on the list--Oh, shit!
STETSASONIC
Rosalyn

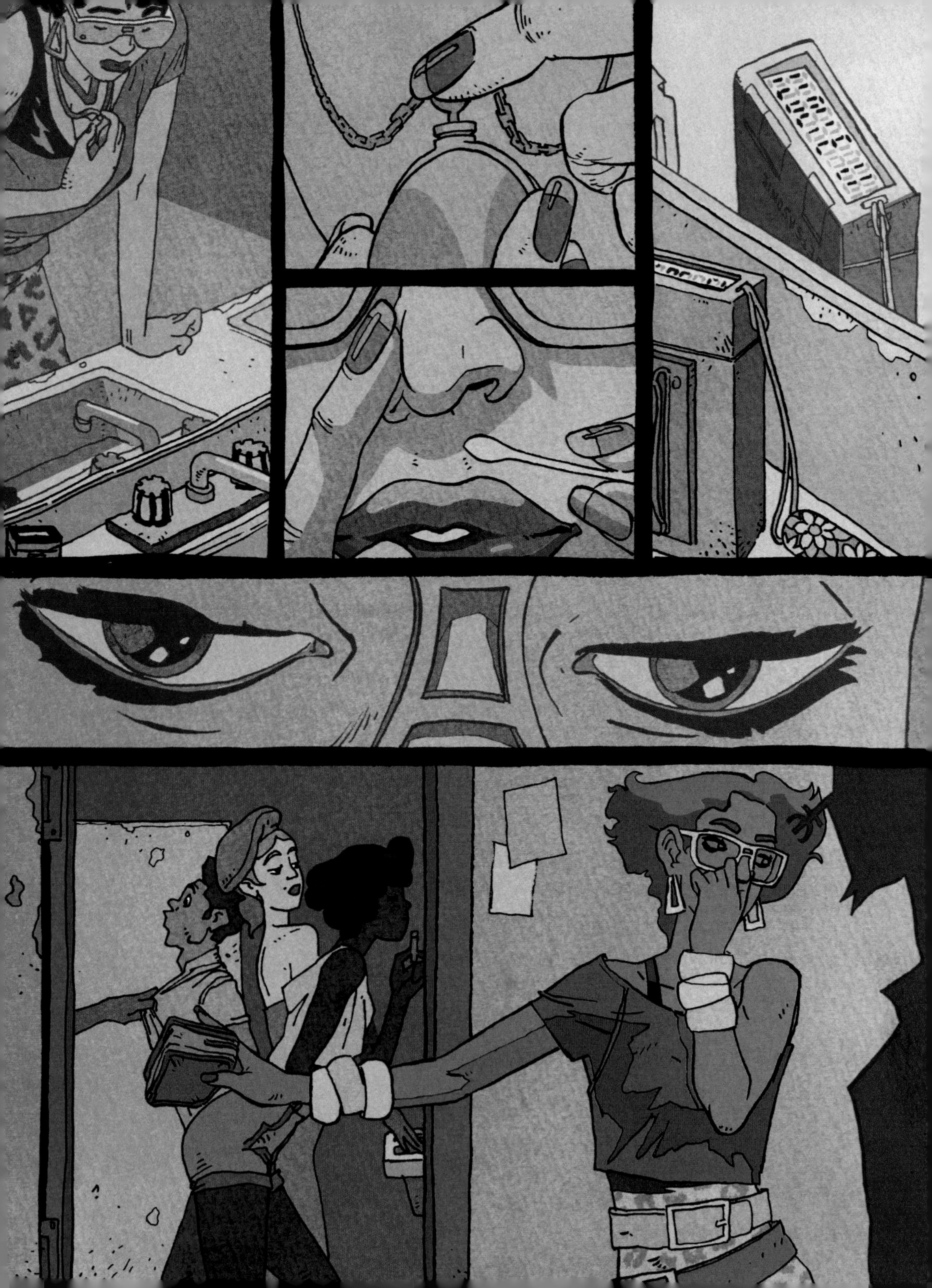

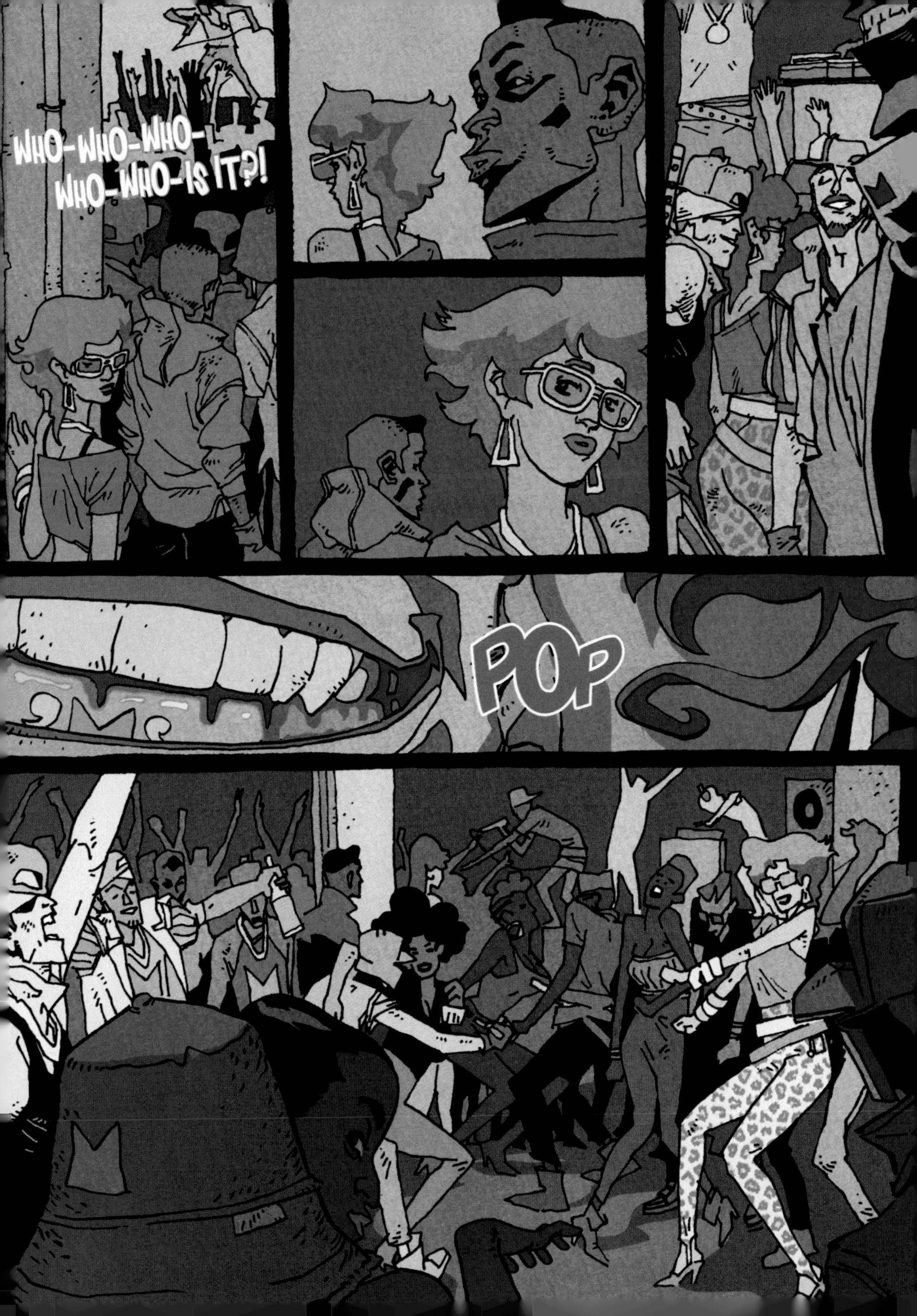
WHO-WHO-WHO-
WHO-WHO-IS IT?!
POP

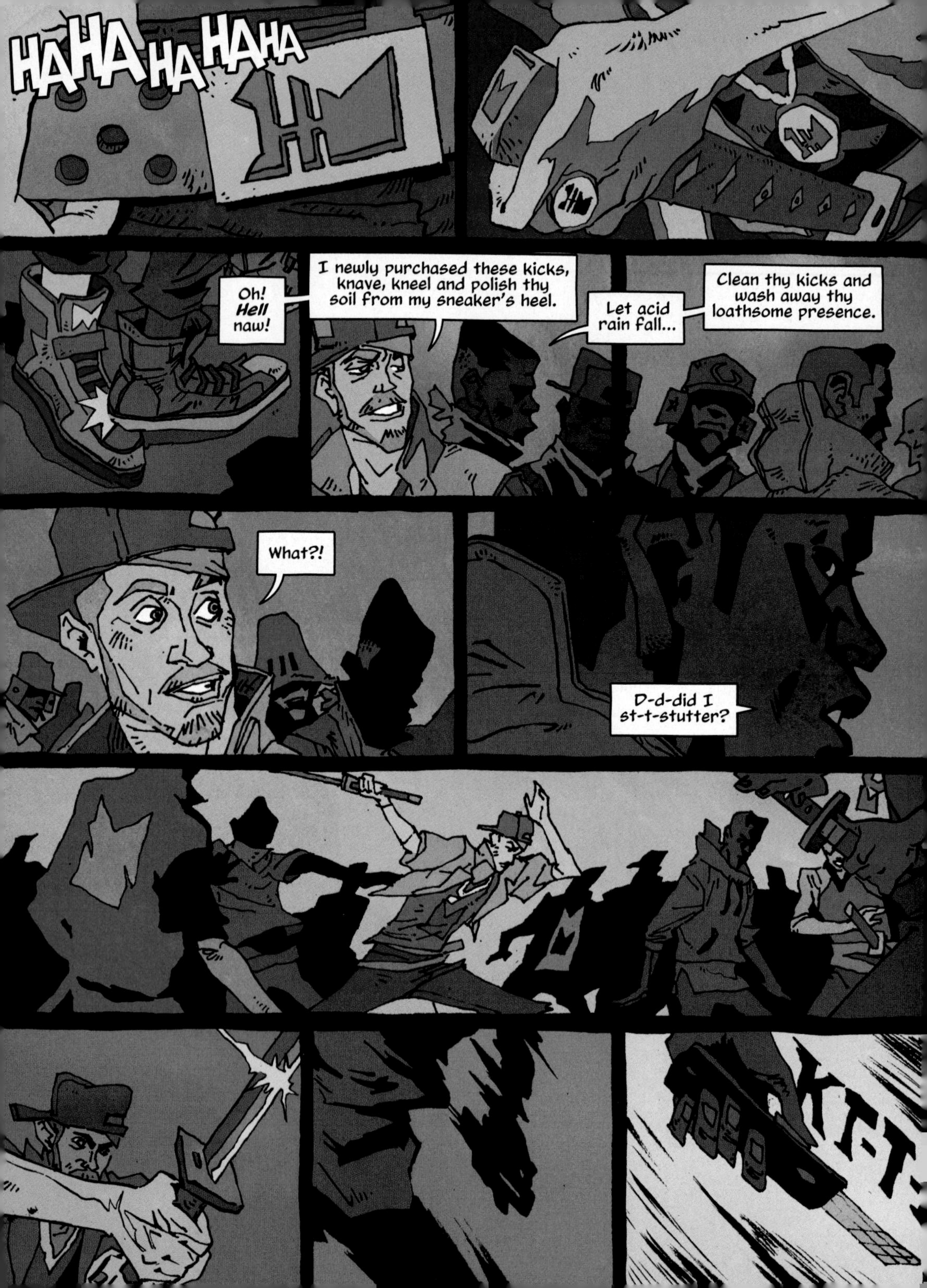
HAHA HAHA HA HAHA
Oh! Hell naw!
I newly purchased these kicks, knave, kneel and polish thy soil from my sneaker's heel.
Let acid rain fall...
Clean thy kicks and wash away thy loathsome presence.
What?!
D-d-did I st-t-stutter?
KT-T-

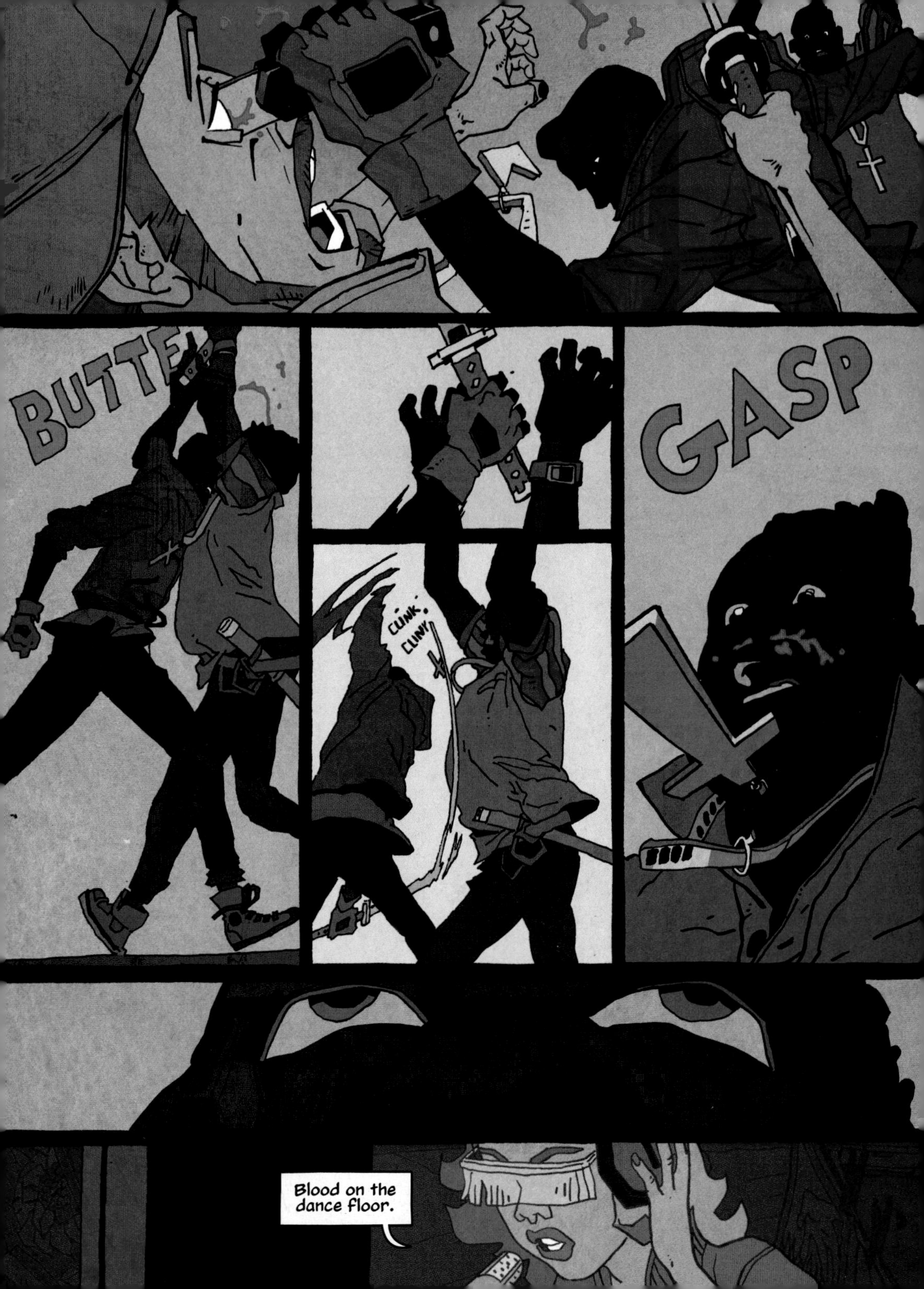
BUTTE
CLINK CLINK
GASP
Blood on the dance floor.

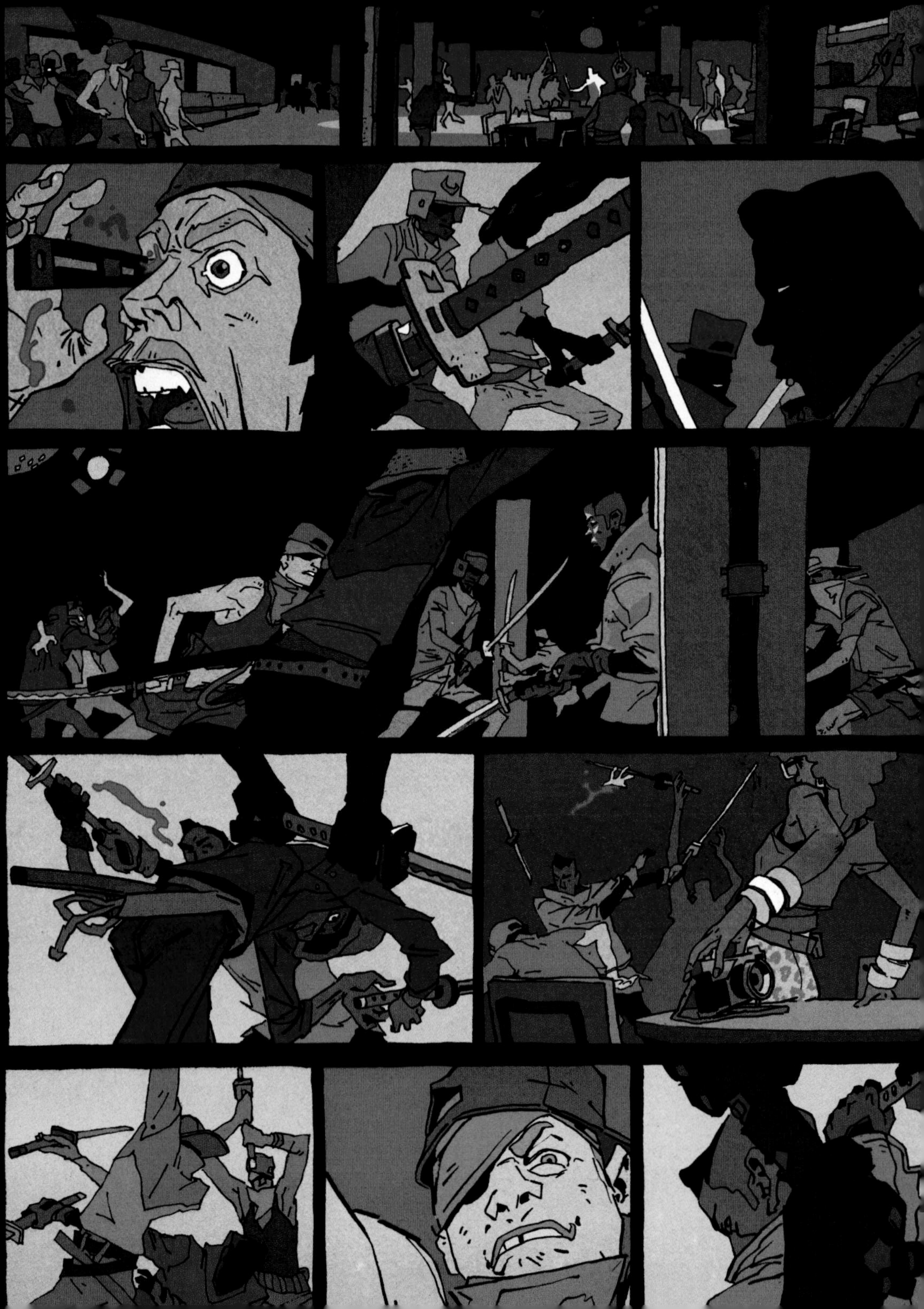

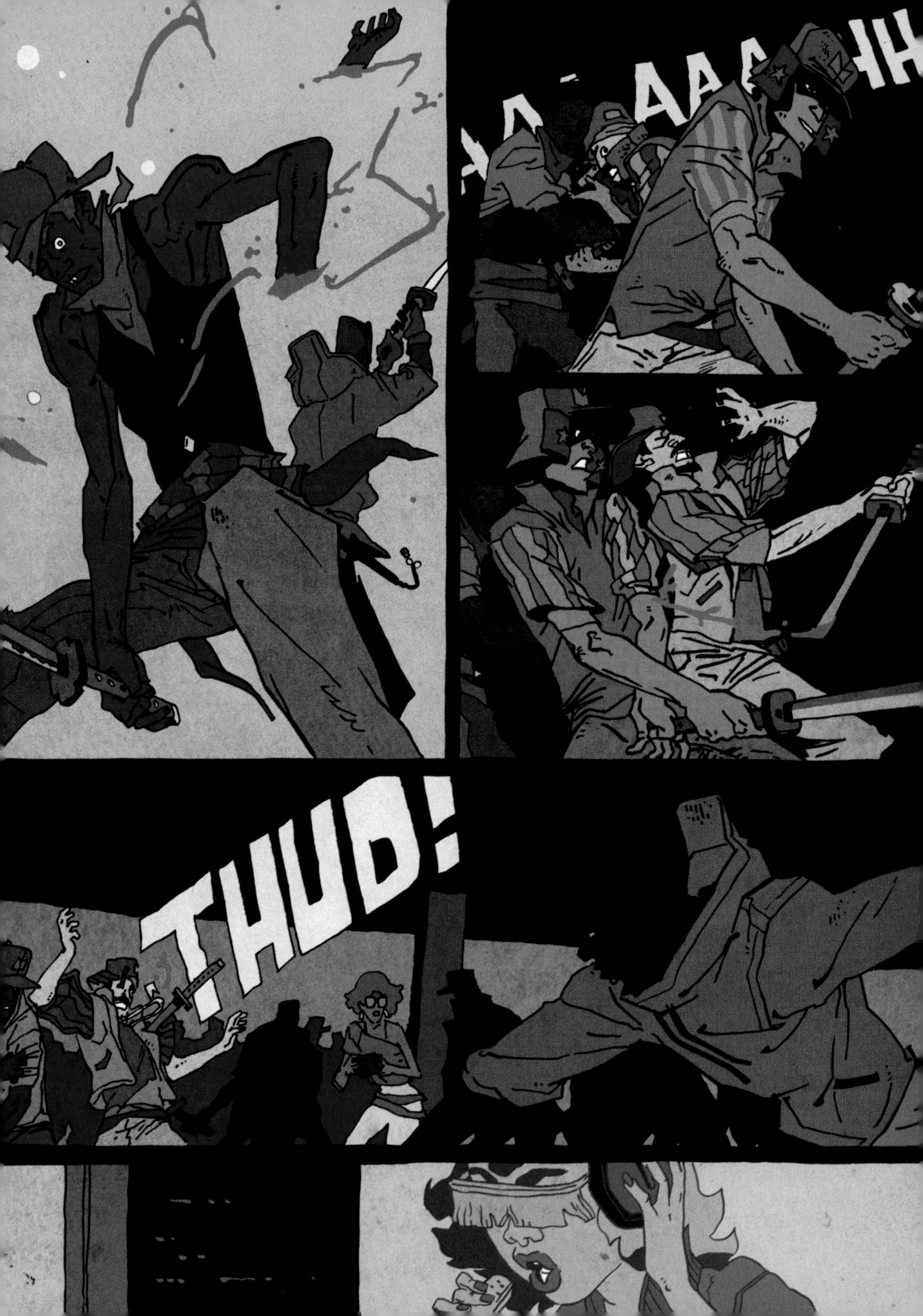
THUD!

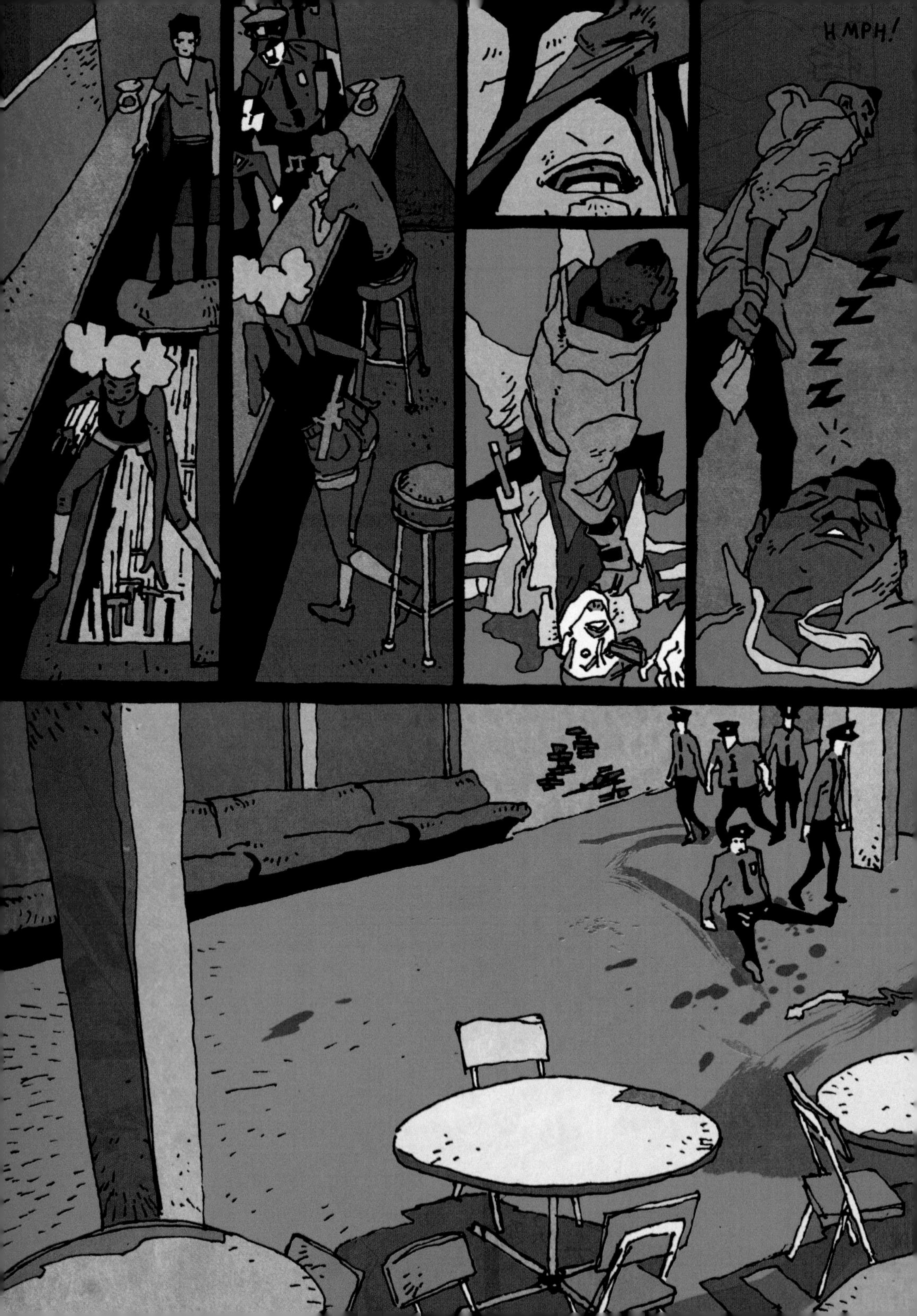
HMPH!
ZZZZ

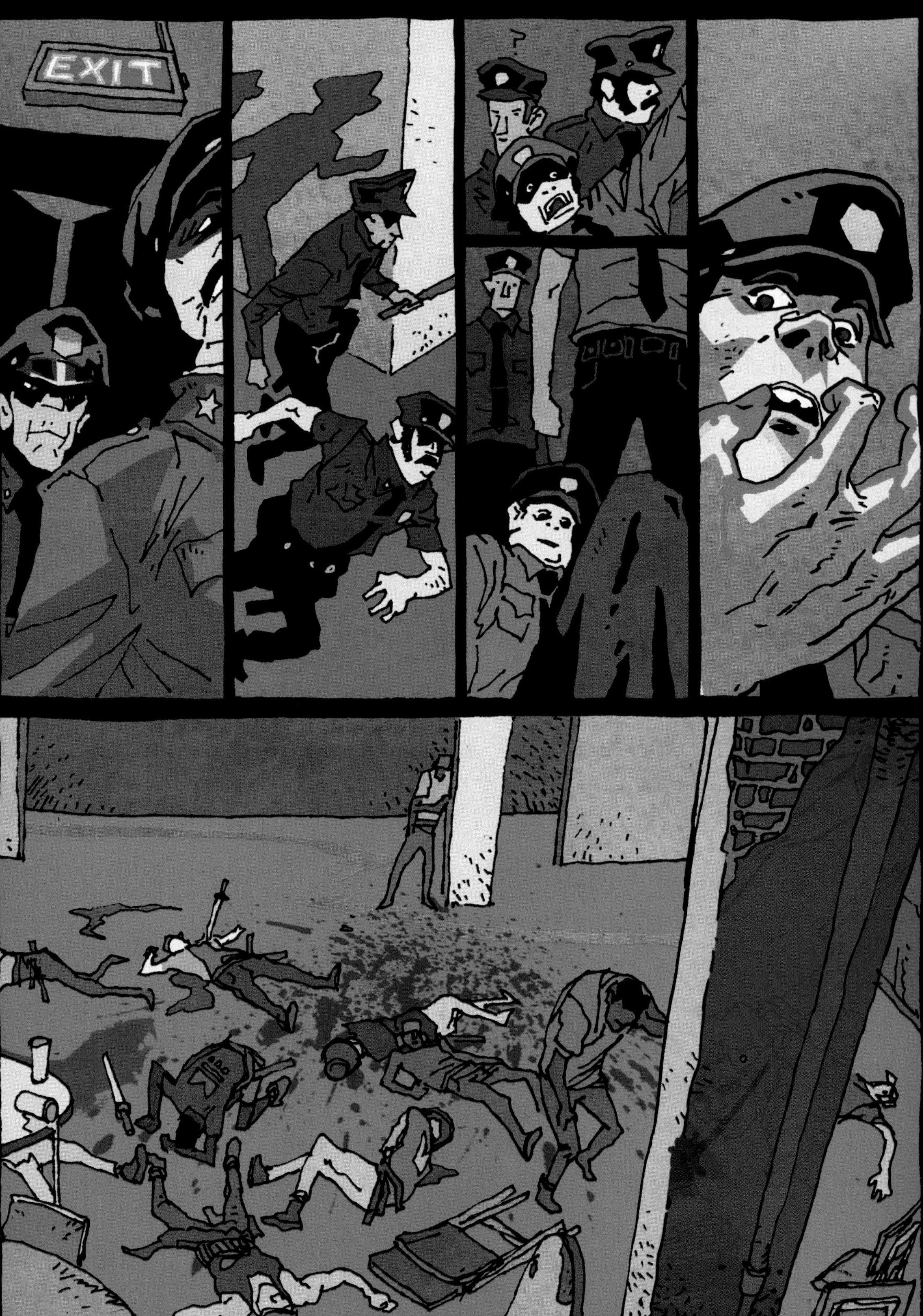
EXIT

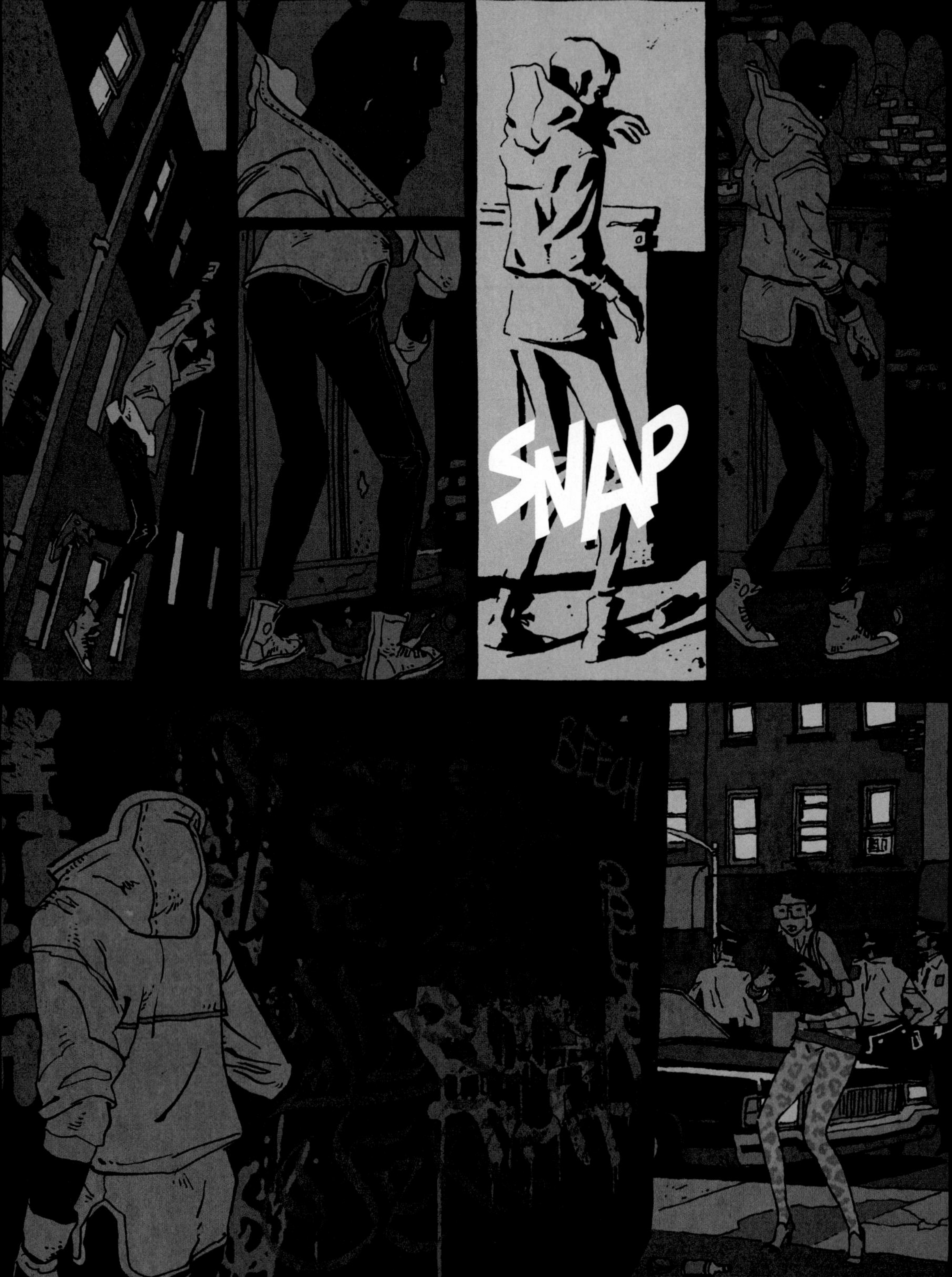
SNAP

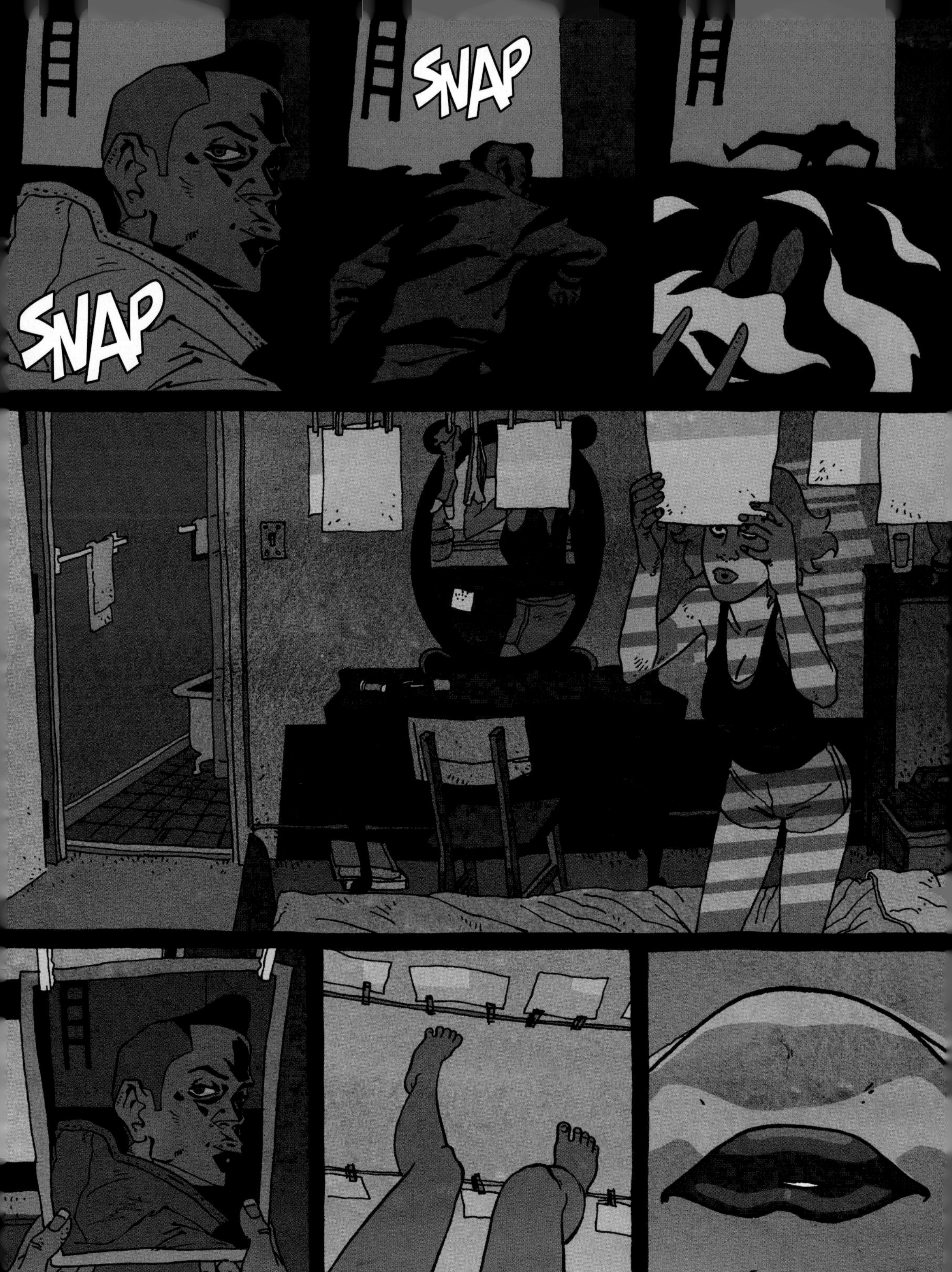
SNAP
SNAP

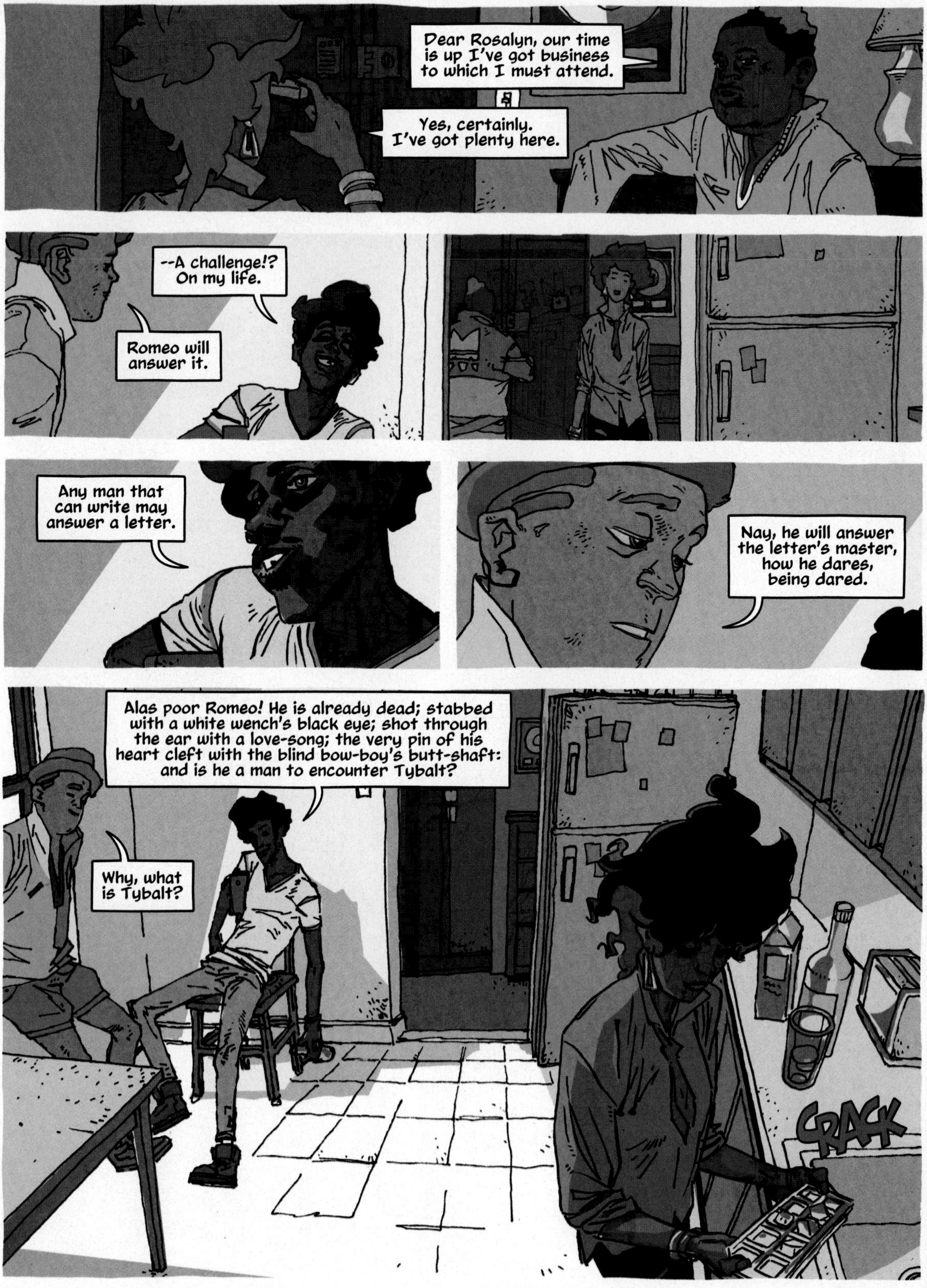

Dear Rosalyn, our time is up I've got business to which I must attend.
Yes, certainly. I've got plenty here.
--A challenge!? On my life.
Romeo will answer it.
Any man that can write may answer a letter.
Nay, he will answer the letter's master, how he dares, being dared.
Alas poor Romeo! He is already dead; stabbed with a white wench's black eye; shot through the ear with a love-song; the very pin of his heart cleft with the blind bow-boy's butt-shaft: and is he a man to encounter Tybalt?
Why, what is Tybalt?
CRACK

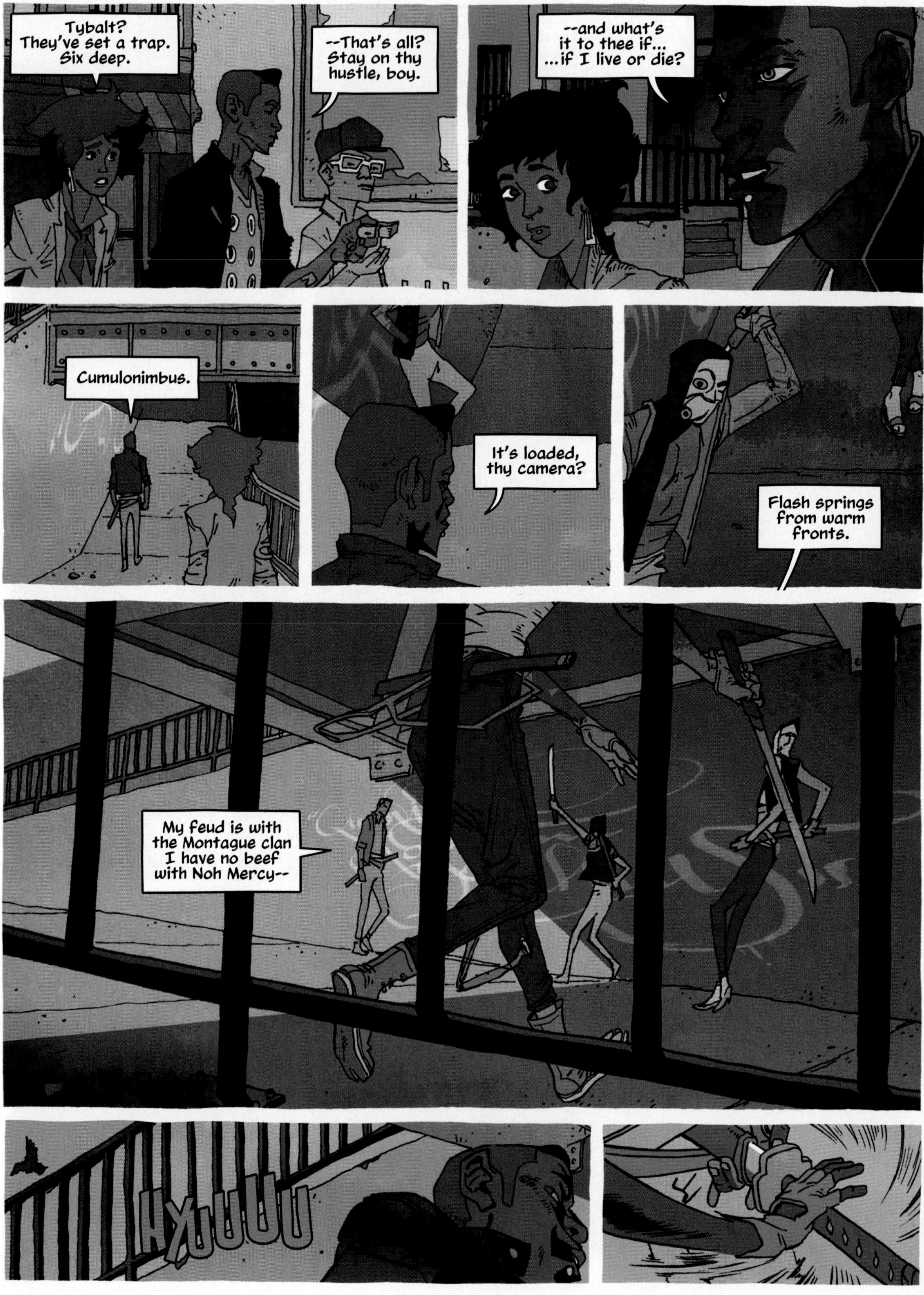
Tybalt? They've set a trap. Six deep.
--That's all? Stay on thy hustle, boy.
--and what's it to thee if... ...if I live or die?
Cumulonimbus.
It's loaded, thy camera?
Flash springs from warm fronts.
My feud is with the Montague clan I have no beef with Noh Mercy--
HYUUUU

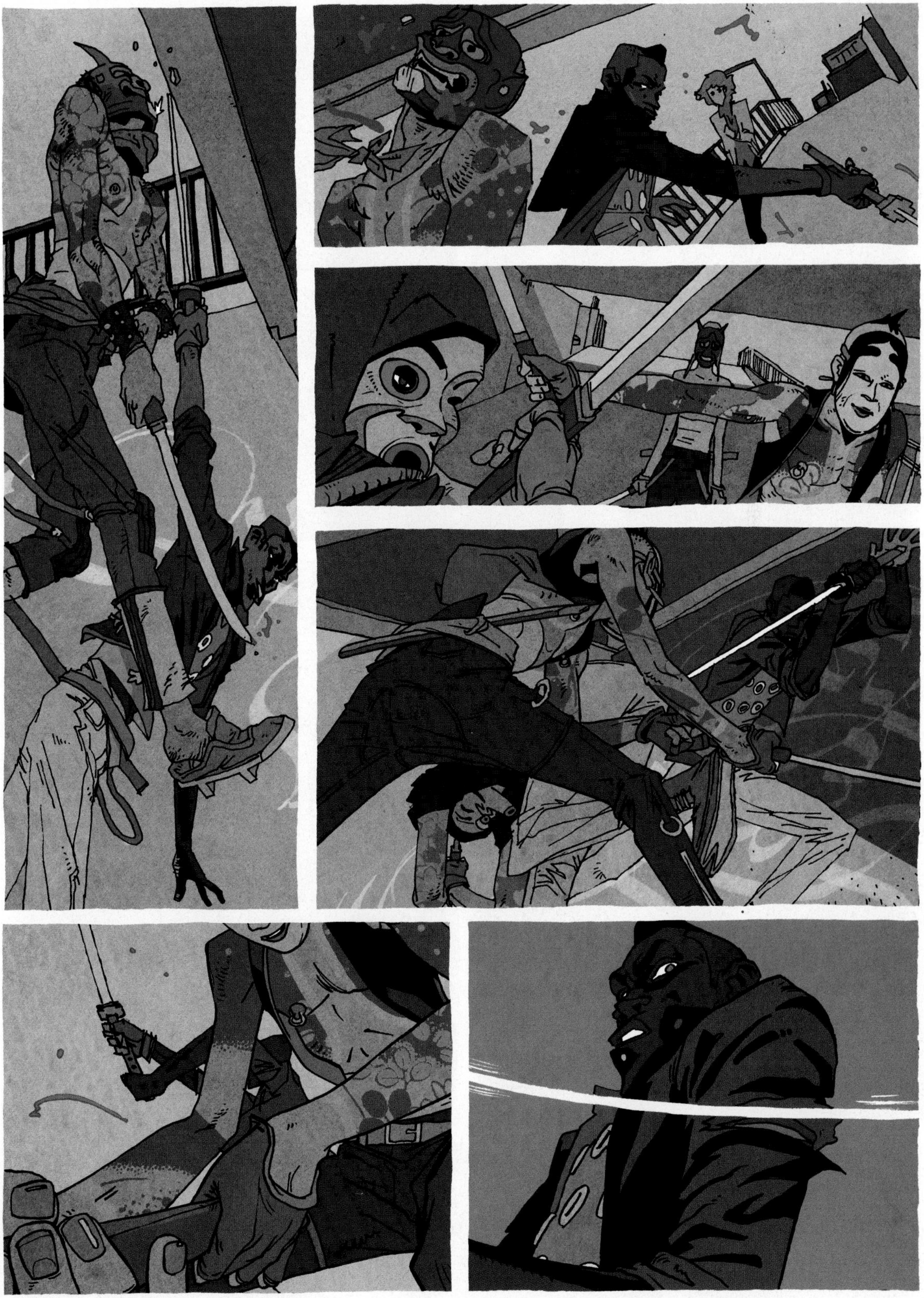

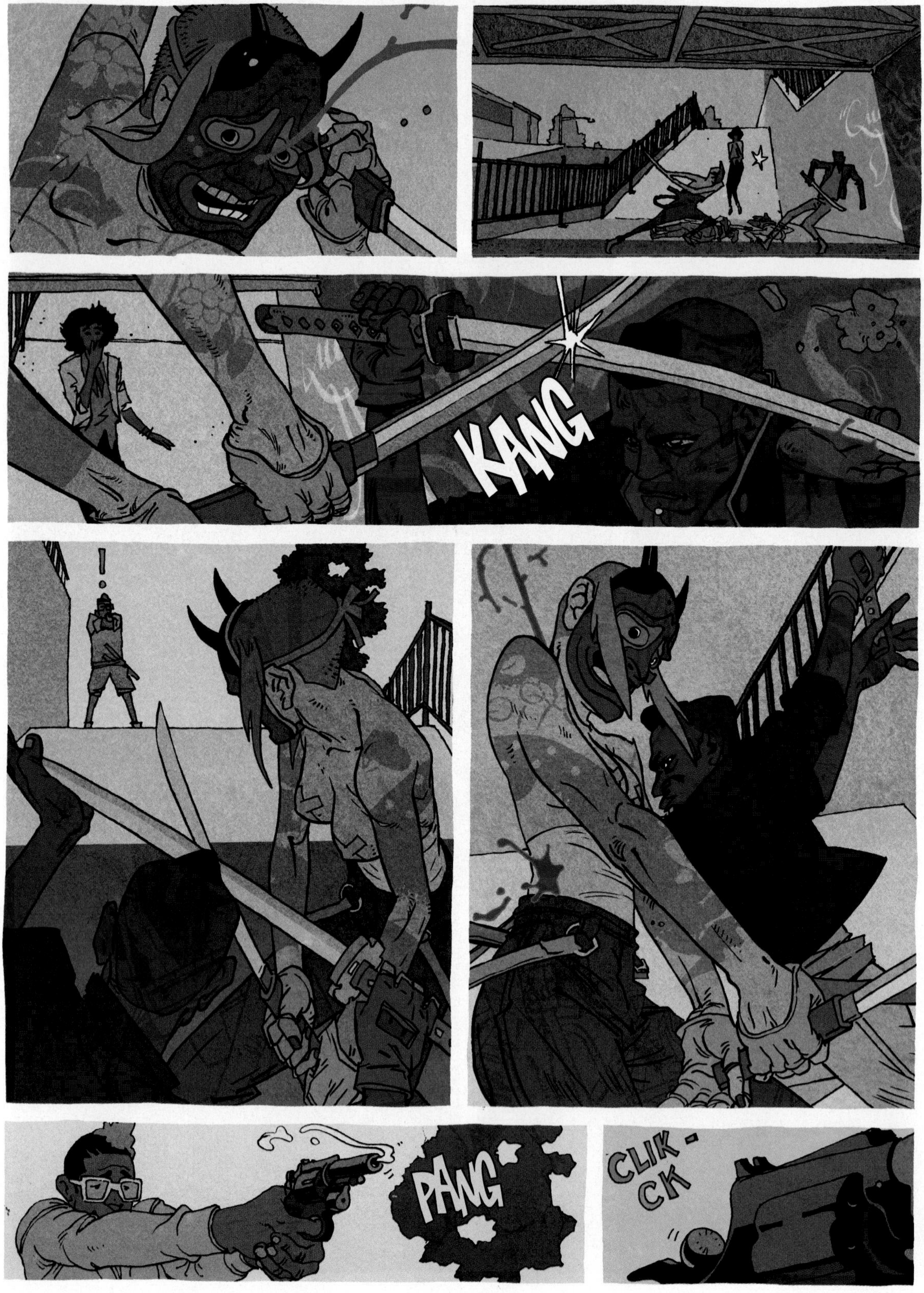
KANG
!
PANG
CLIK-
CK

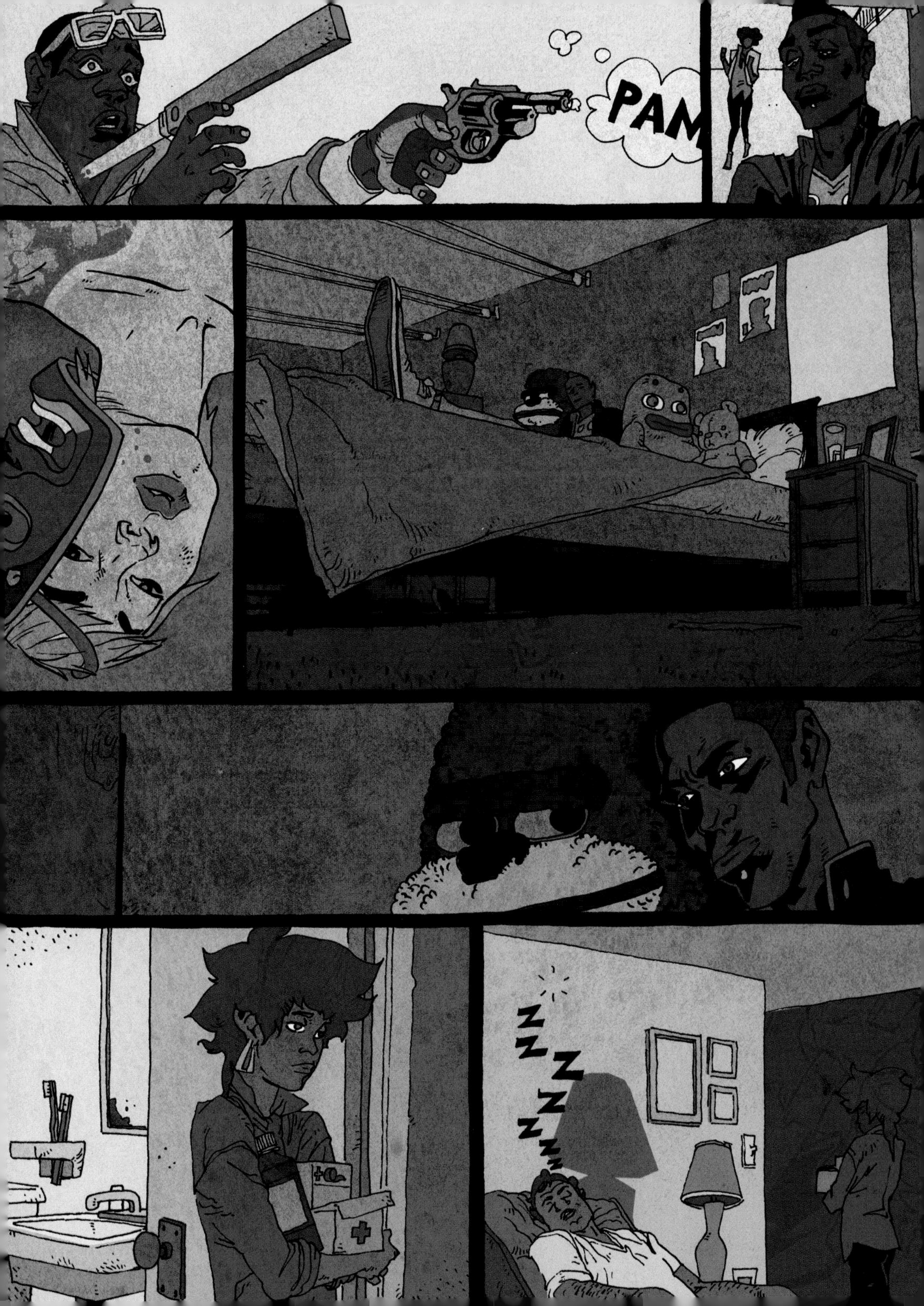
PAM
ZZZZZZ

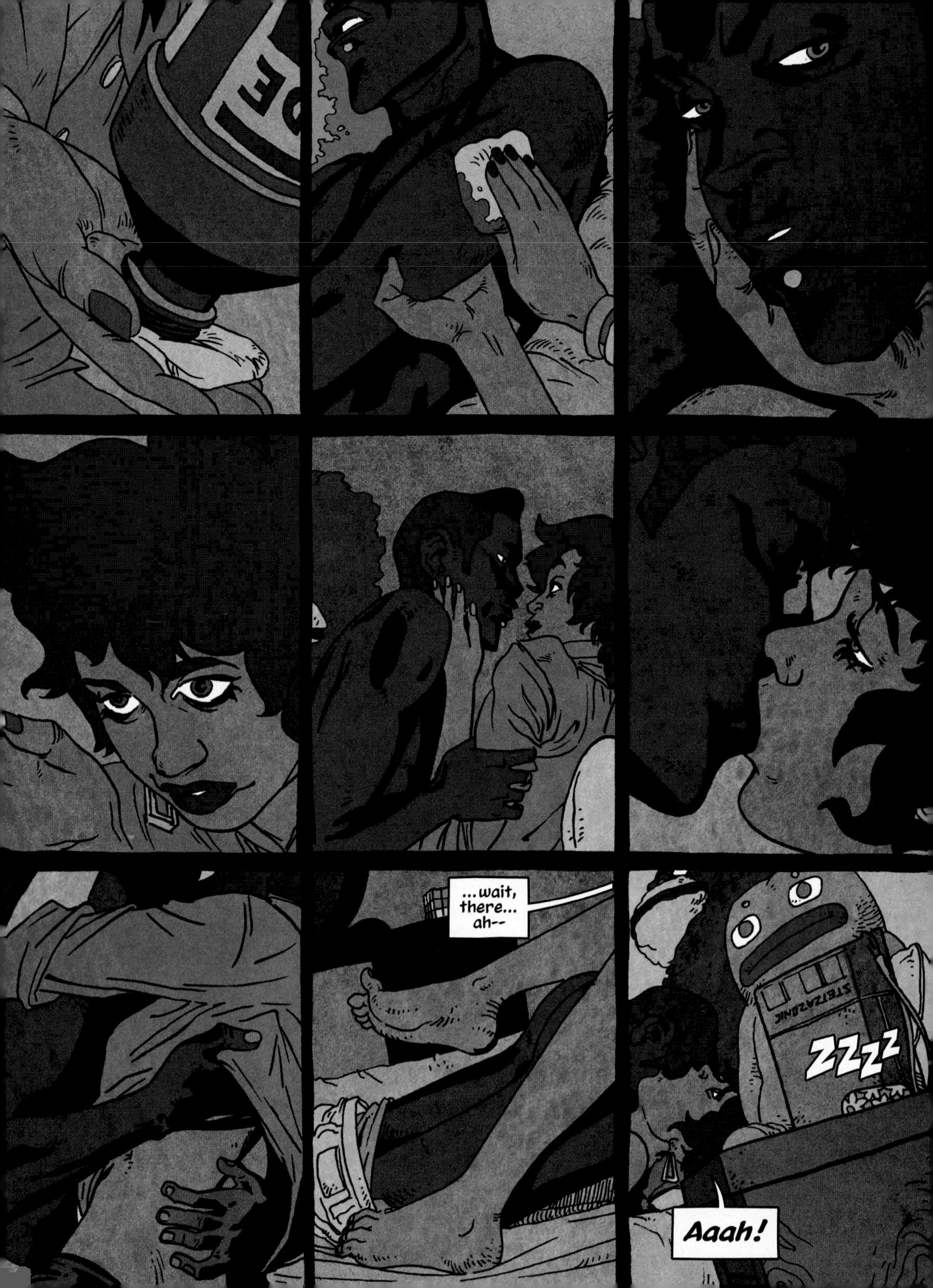
...wait, there... ah--
ZZzz
Aaah!

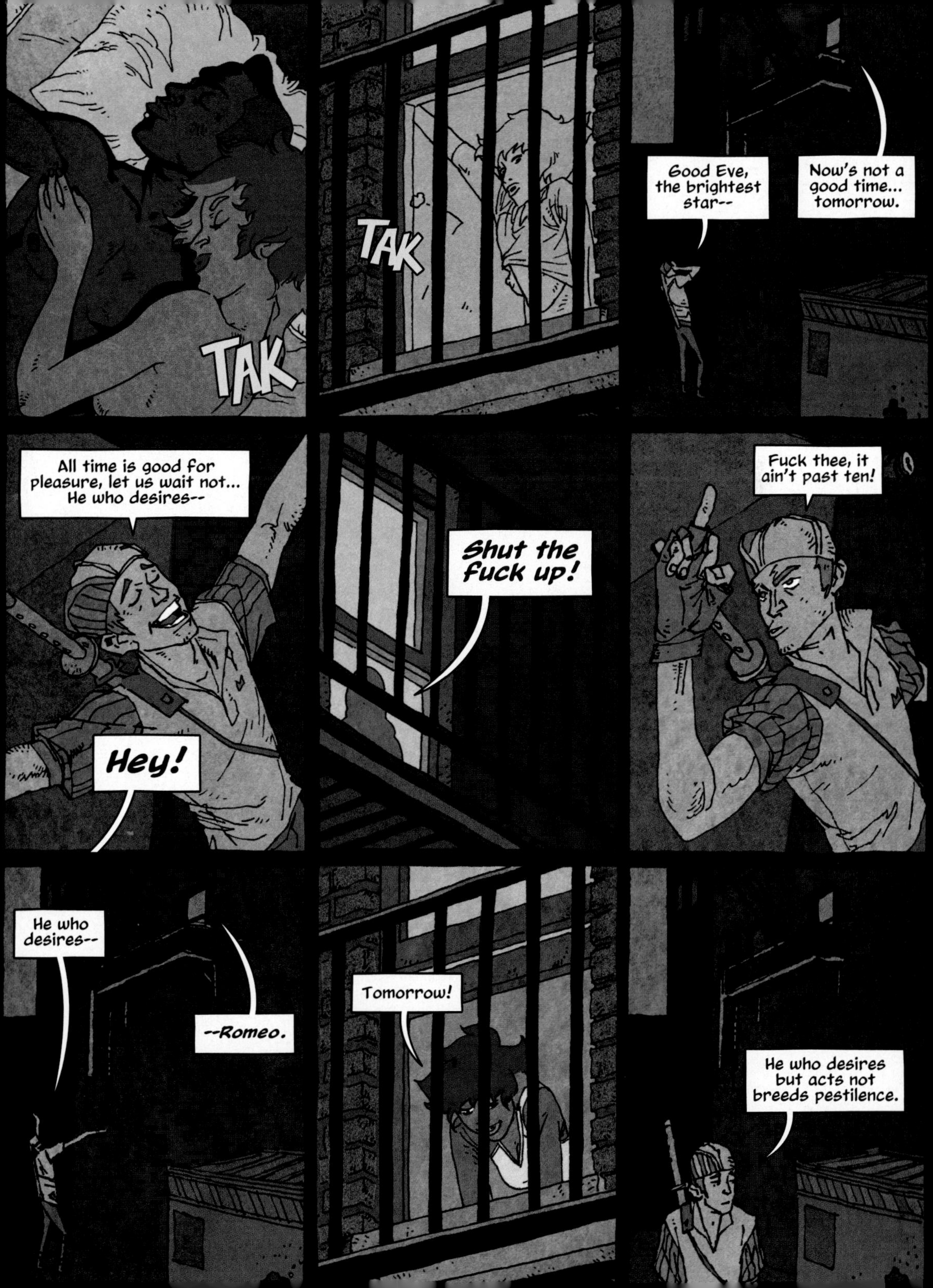
TAK
TAK
Good Eve, the brightest star--
Now's not a good time... tomorrow.
All time is good for pleasure, let us wait not... He who desires--
Shut the fuck up!
Hey!
Fuck thee, it ain't past ten!
He who desires--
--Romeo.
Tomorrow!
He who desires but acts not breeds pestilence.

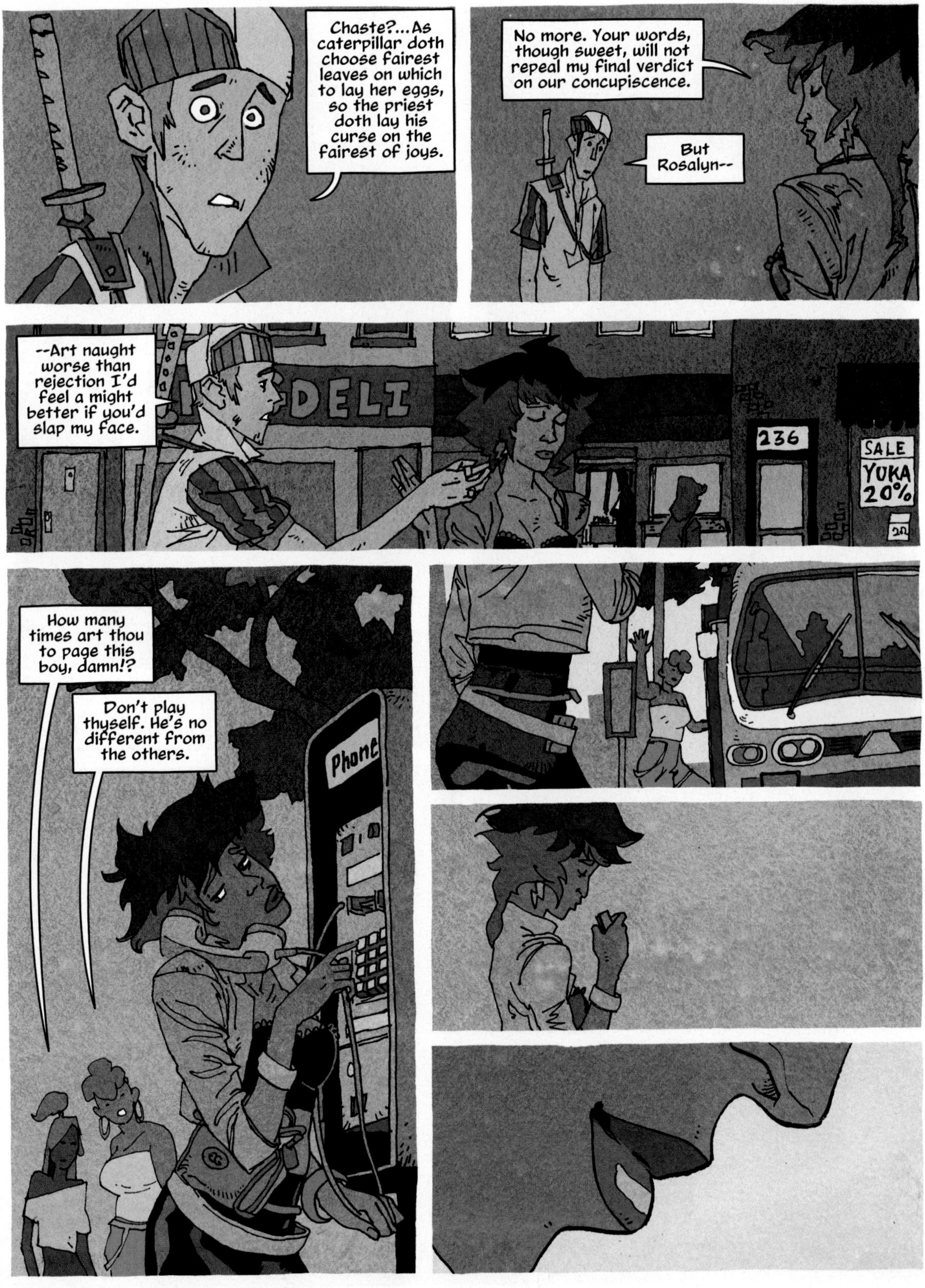
Chaste?...As caterpillar doth choose fairest leaves on which to lay her eggs, so the priest doth lay his curse on the fairest of joys.
No more. Your words, though sweet, will not repeal my final verdict on our concupiscence.
But Rosalyn--
--Art naught worse than rejection I'd feel a might better if you'd slap my face.
DELI
236
SALE
YUKA
20%
How many times art thou to page this boy, damn!?
Don't play thyself. He's no different from the others.
Phone

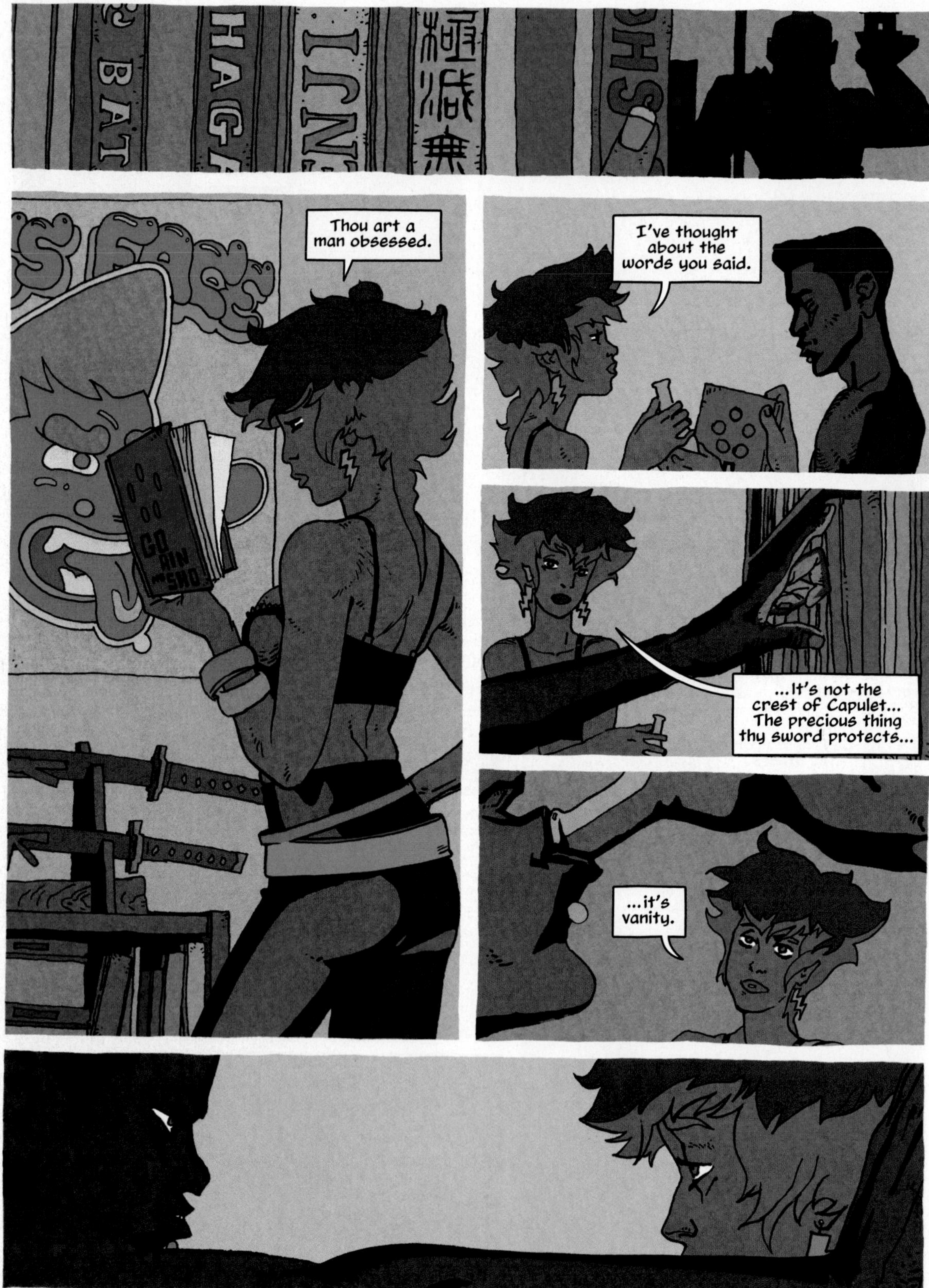
Thou art a man obsessed.
I've thought about the words you said.
...It's not the crest of Capulet... The precious thing thy sword protects...
...it's vanity.

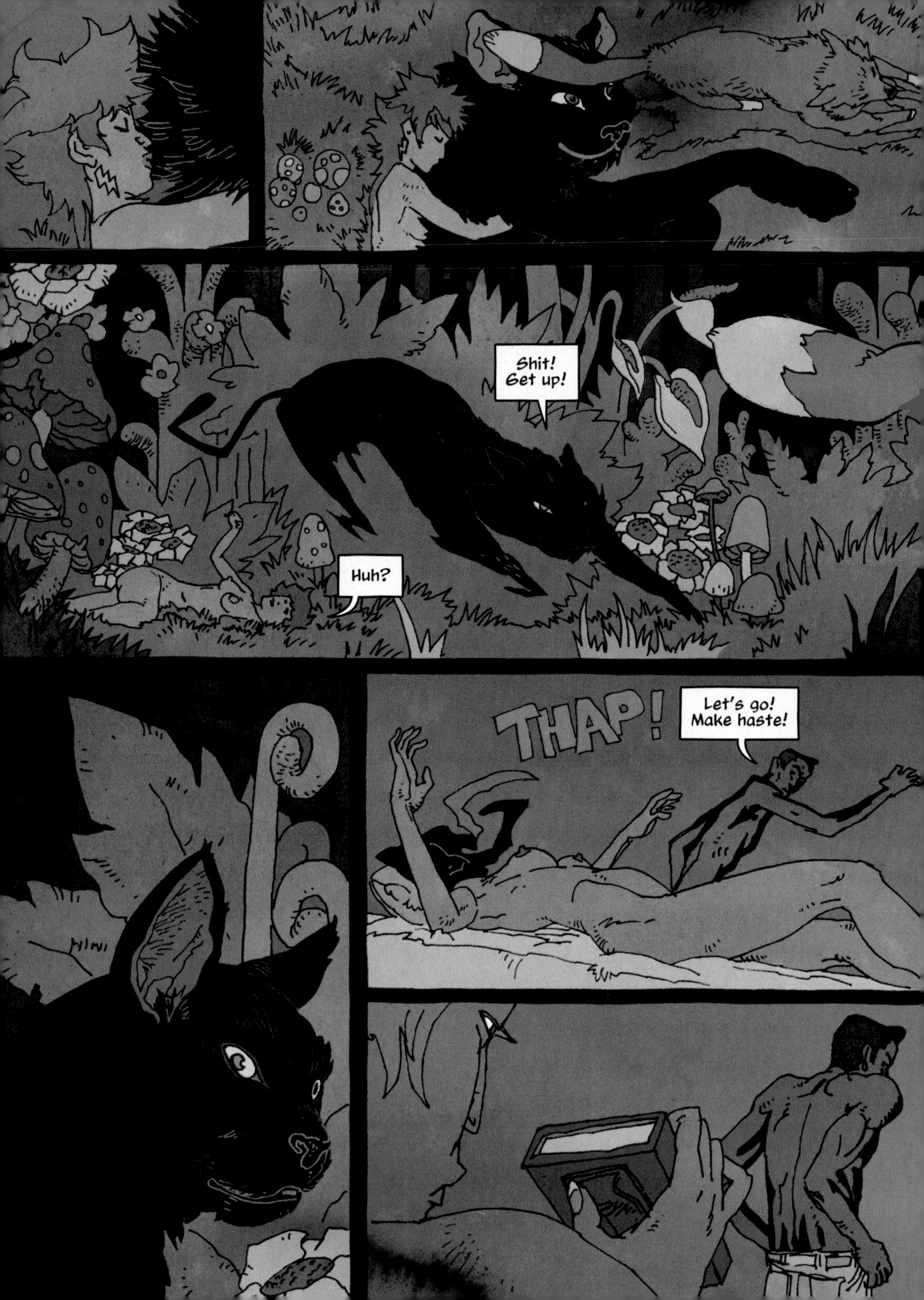
Shit! Get up!
Huh?
THAP!
Let's go! Make haste!

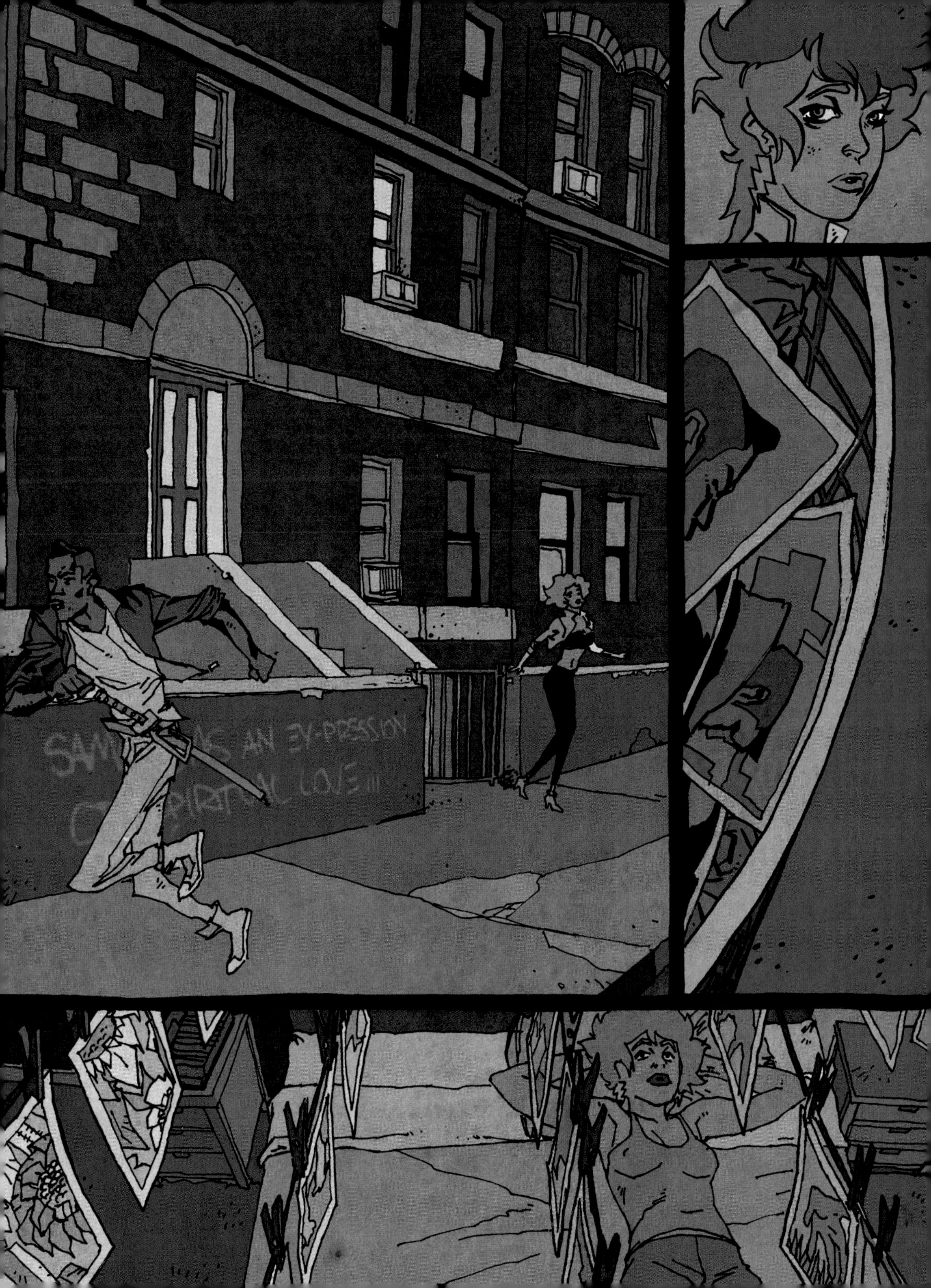
AN EX-PRESSION
LOVE!!!

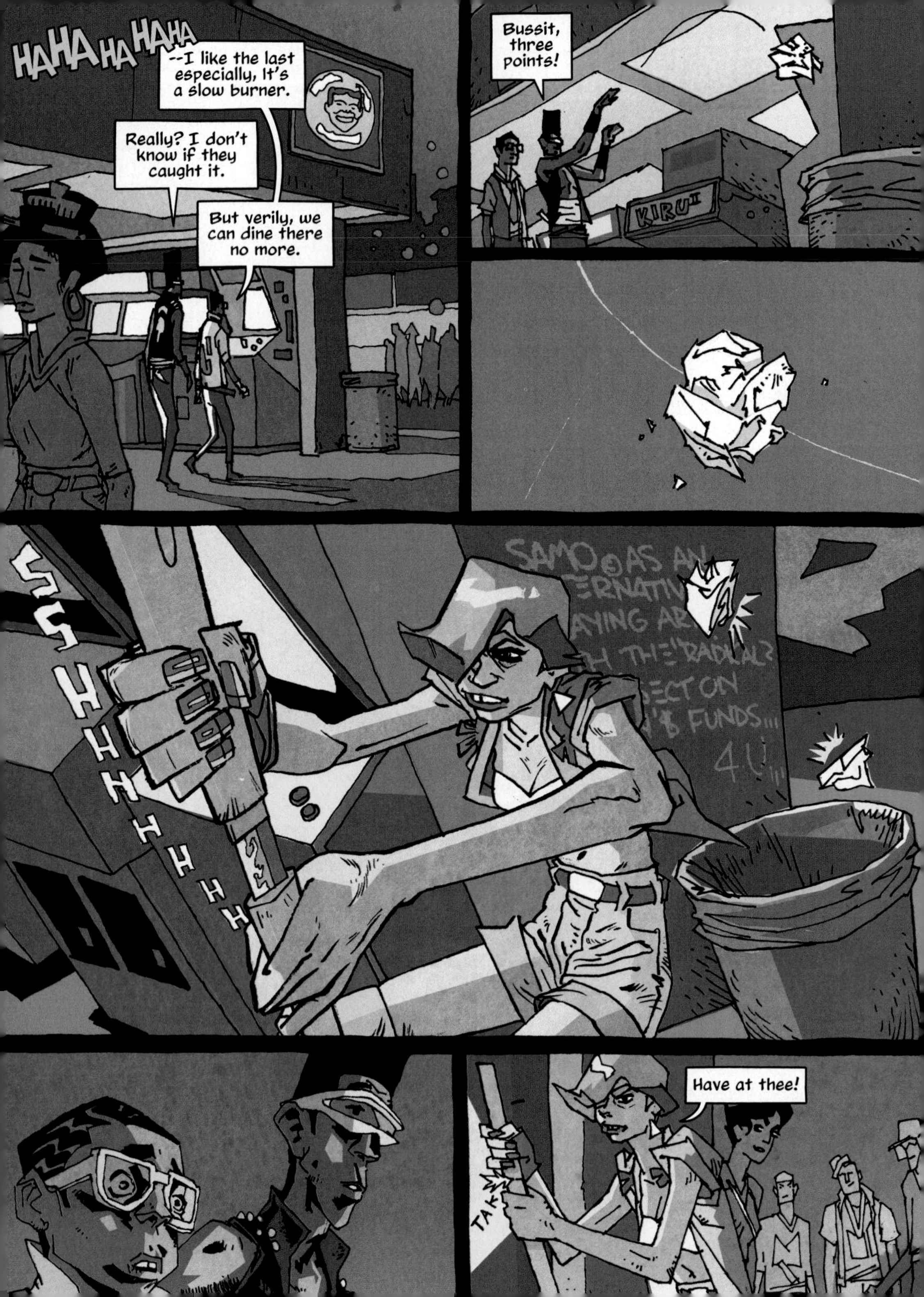
HAHAHAHAHA
--I like the last especially, It's a slow burner.
Really? I don't know if they caught it.
But verily, we can dine there no more.
Bussit, three points!
KIRU
SSHHHHHHHH
TAK
Have at thee!

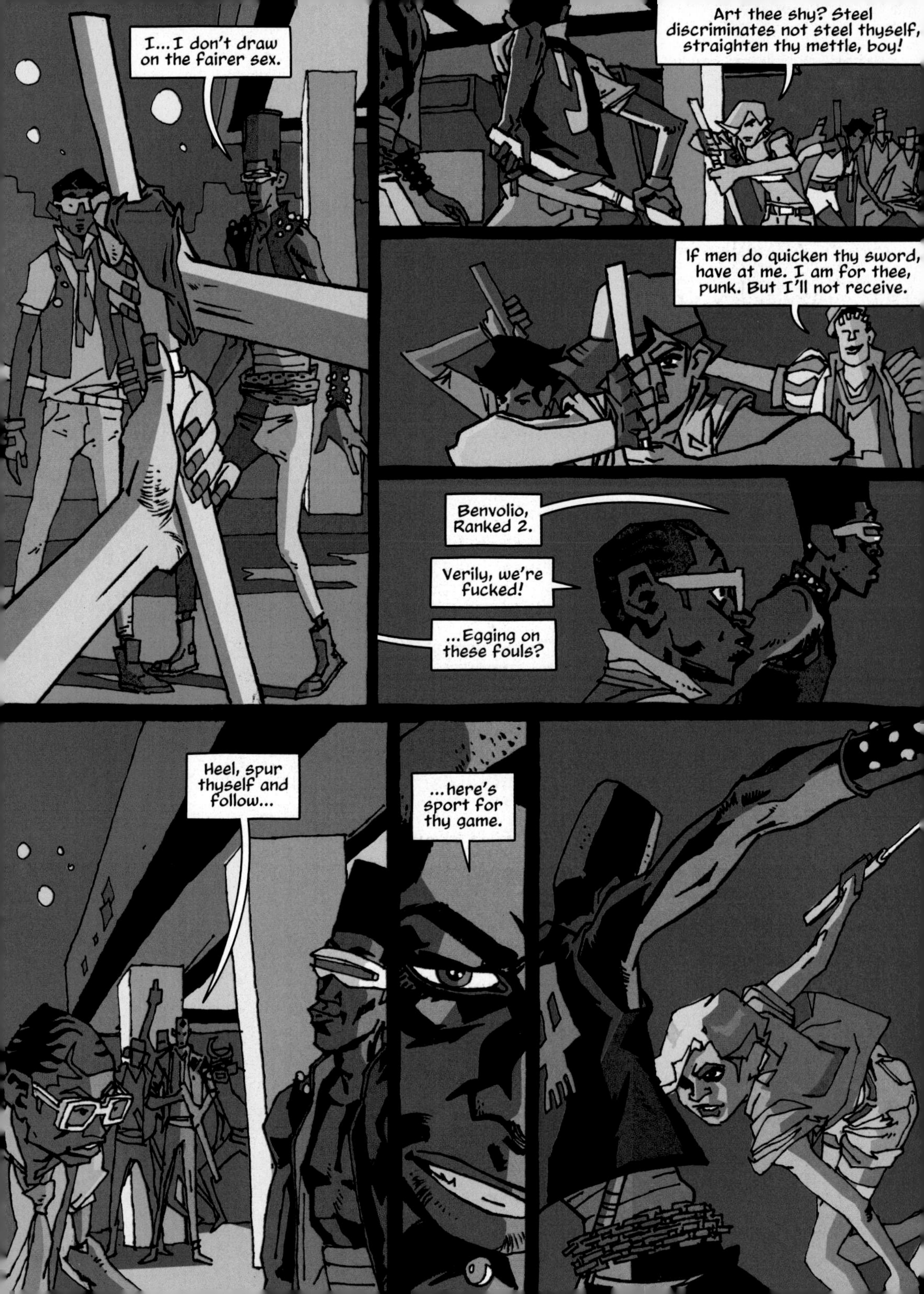
I...I don't draw on the fairer sex.
Art thee shy? Steel discriminates not steel thyself, straighten thy mettle, boy!
If men do quicken thy sword, have at me. I am for thee, punk. But I'll not receive.
Benvolio, Ranked 2.
Verily, we're fucked!
...Egging on these fouls?
Heel, spur thyself and follow...
...here's sport for thy game.

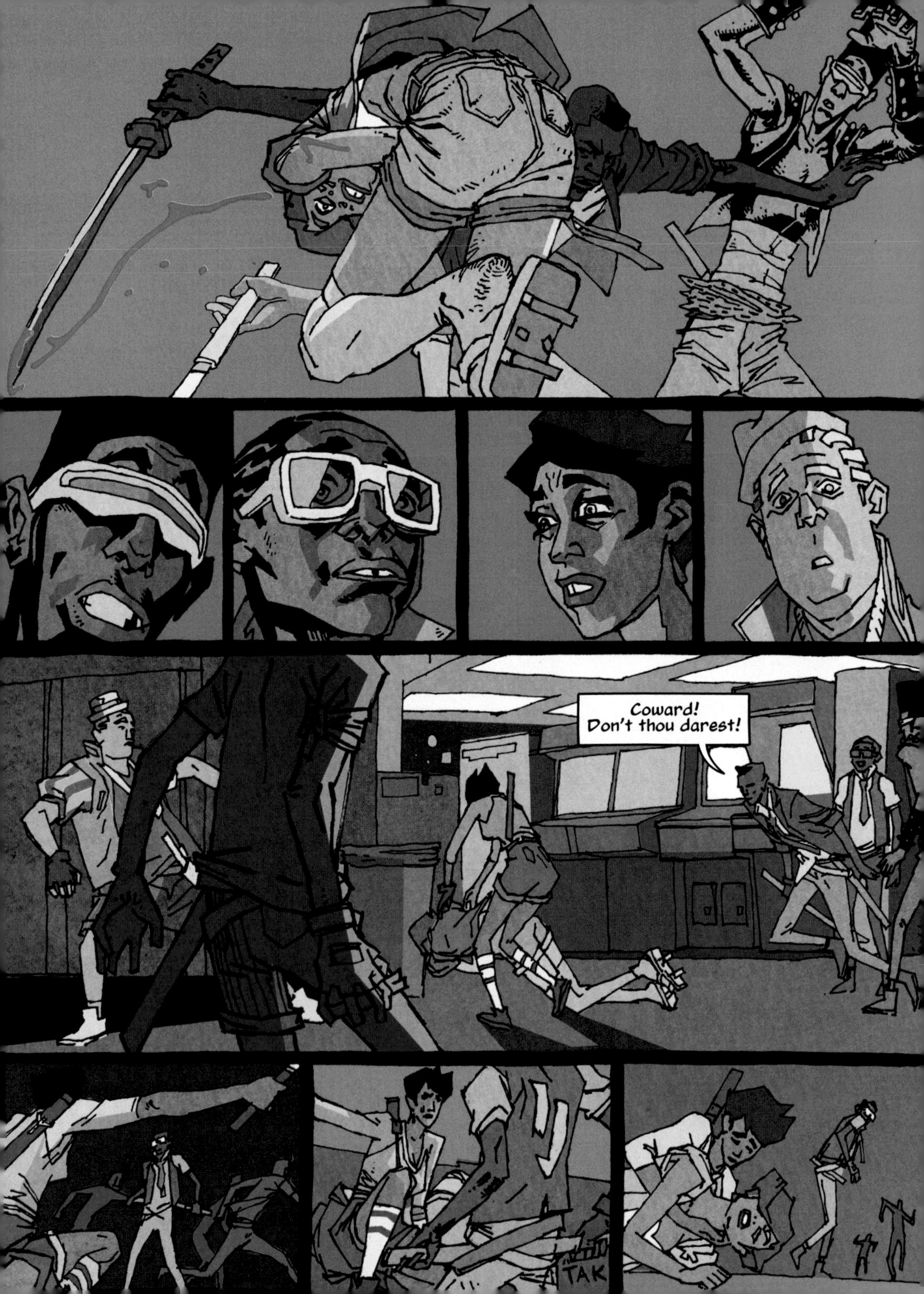
Coward! Don't thou darest!
TAK

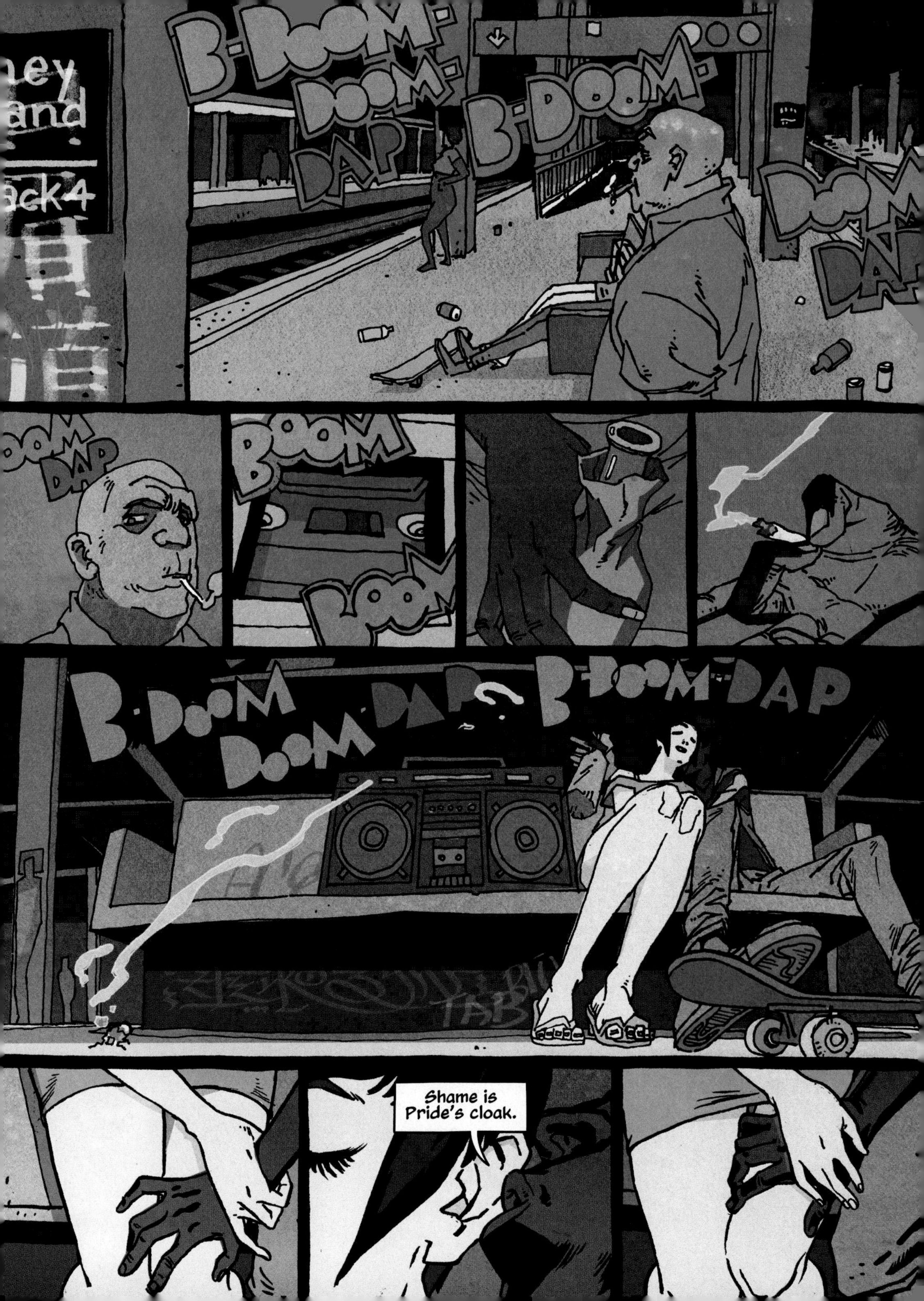
B-DOOM-DOOM-DAP
B-DOOM-
DOOM-DAP
DOOM DAP
BOOM
BOOM
B-DOOM-DOOM-DAP
B-DOOM-DAP
Shame is Pride's cloak.

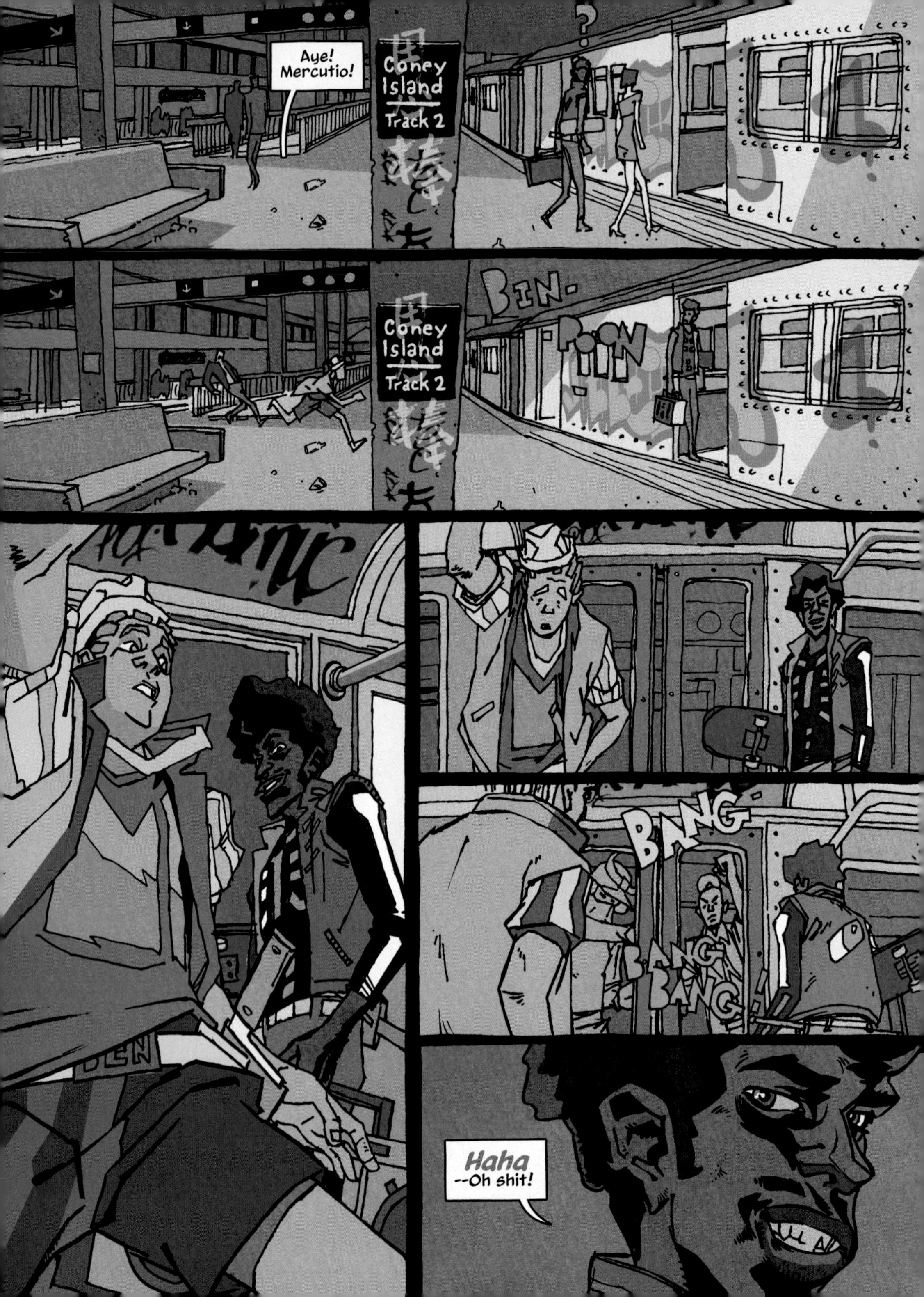
Aye! Mercutio!
Coney Island
Track 2
Coney Island
Track 2
BIN-
BANG-
BANG-
BANG!
Haha
--Oh shit!

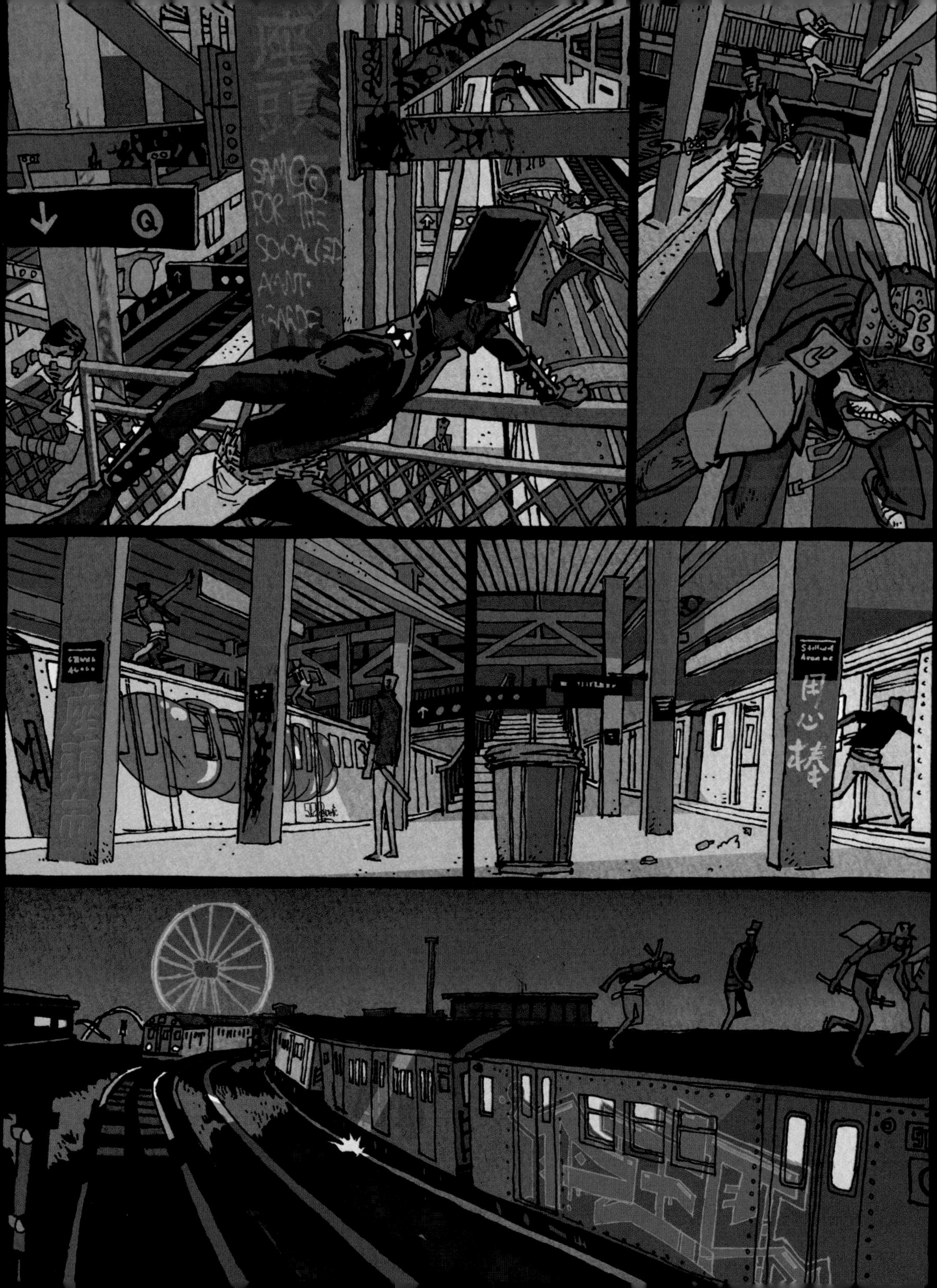

Q
SAMO©
FOR THE
SO-CALLED
AVANT-
GARDE
用心棒

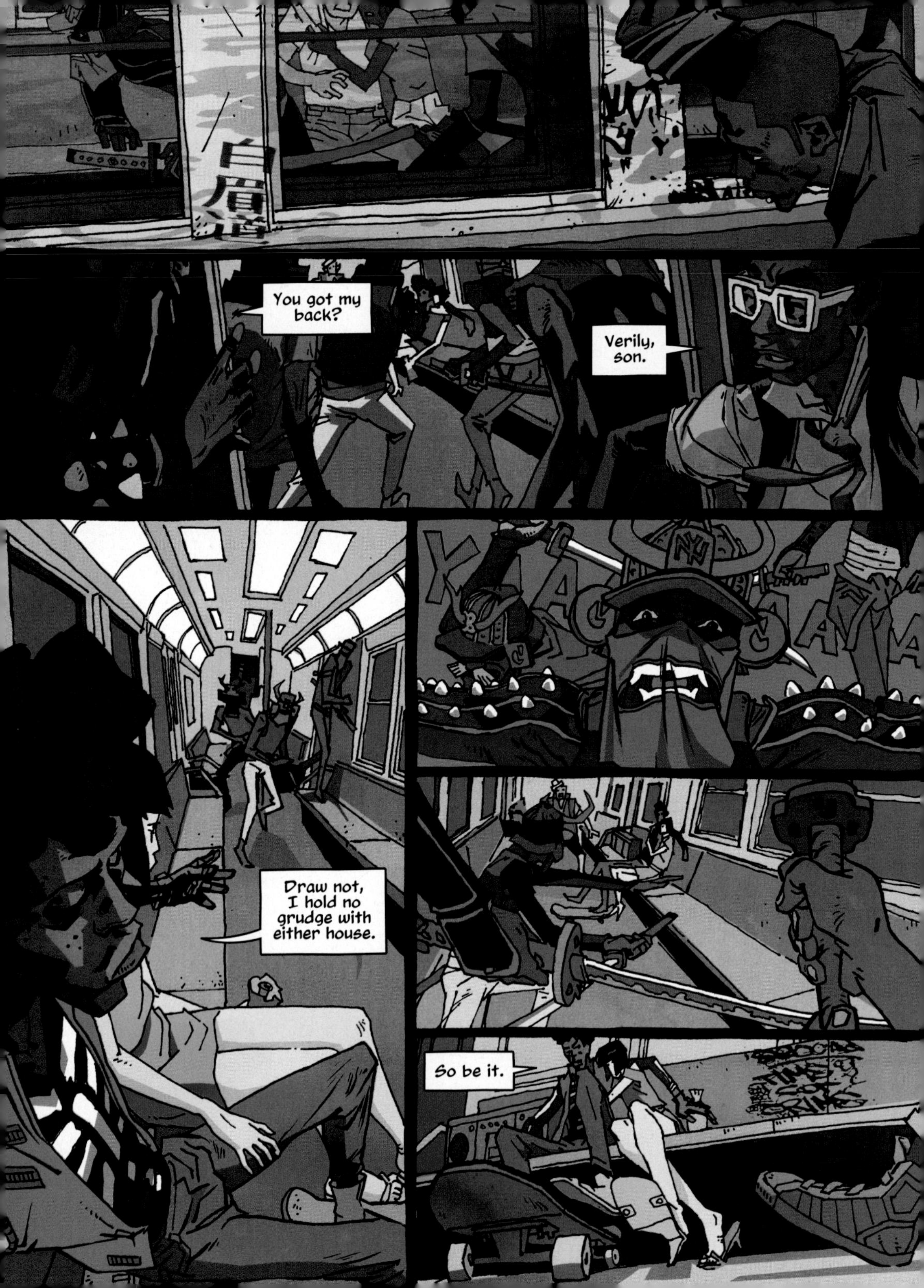
You got my back?
Verily, son.
Draw not, I hold no grudge with either house.
So be it.

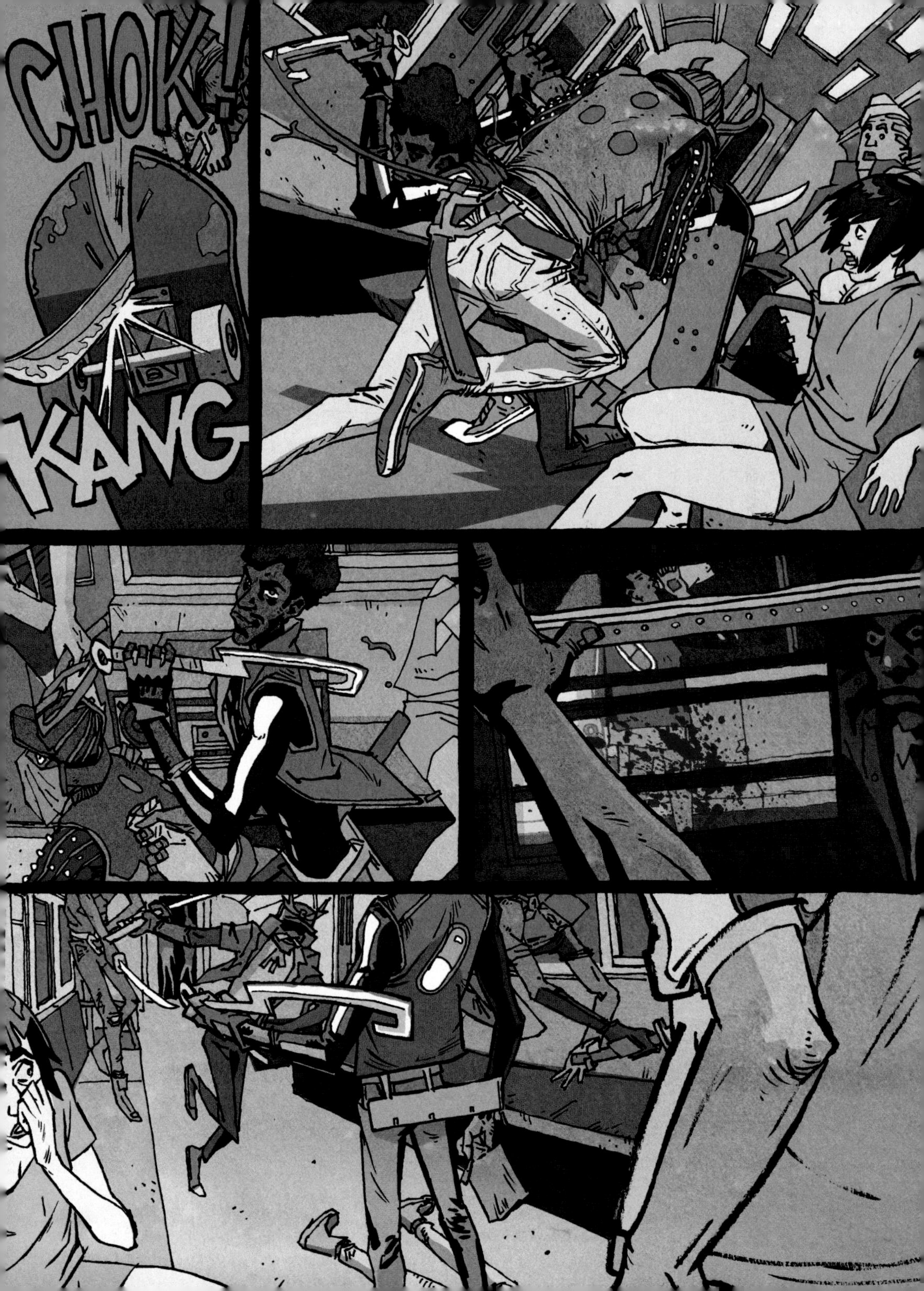
CHOK!
KANG

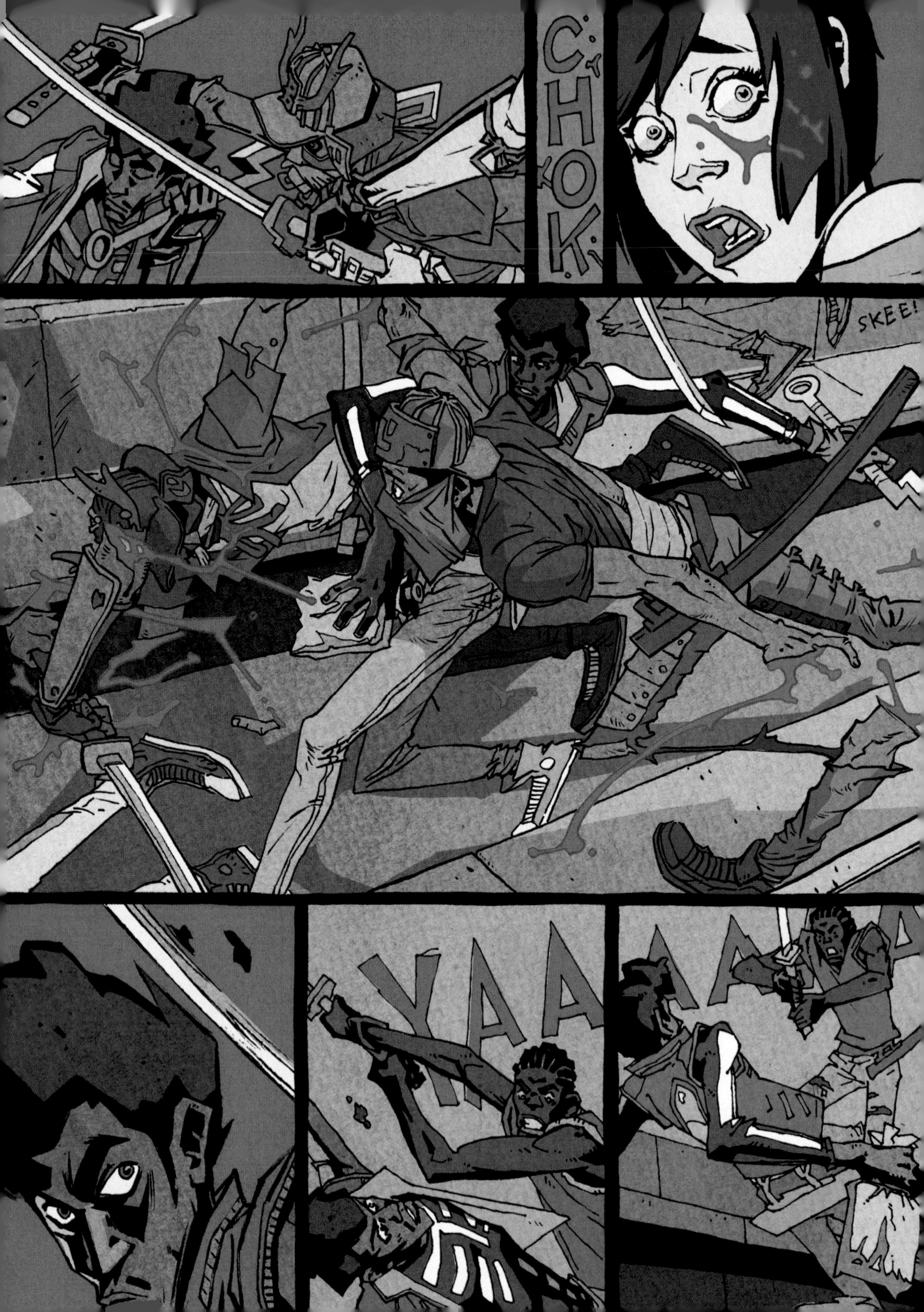
CHOK
SKEE!
YAA
AAA

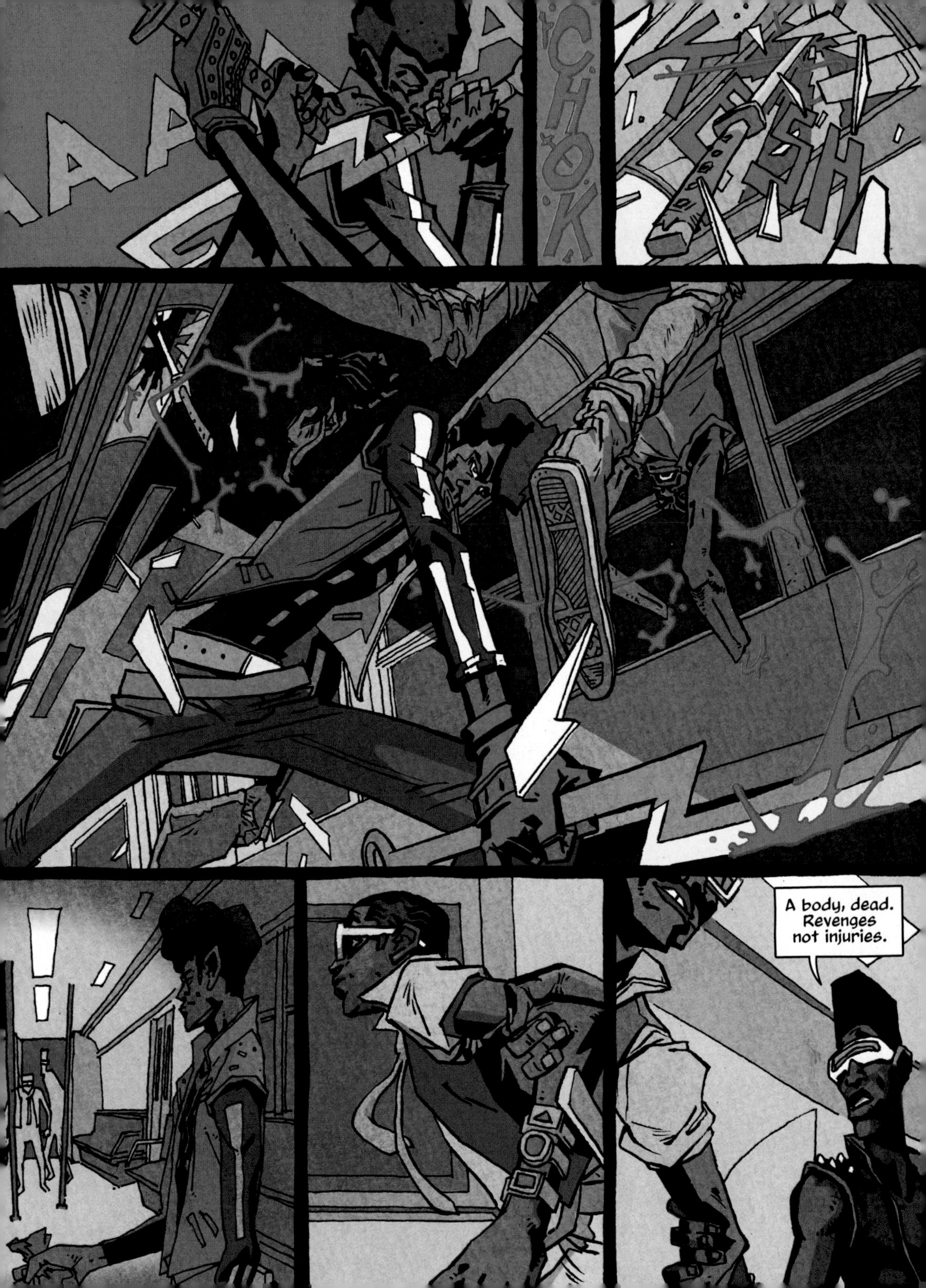
CHOK
A body, dead. Revenges not injuries.

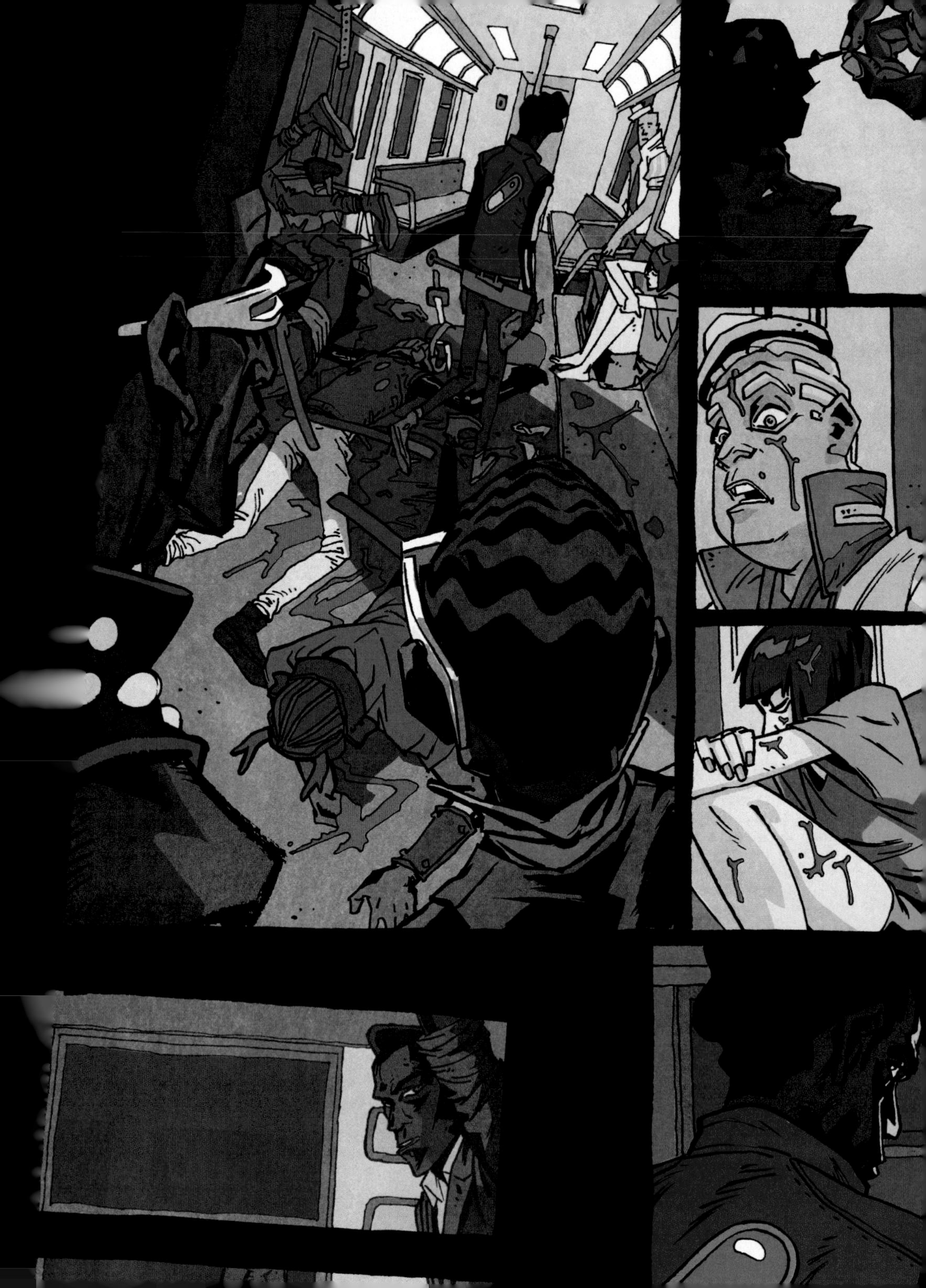

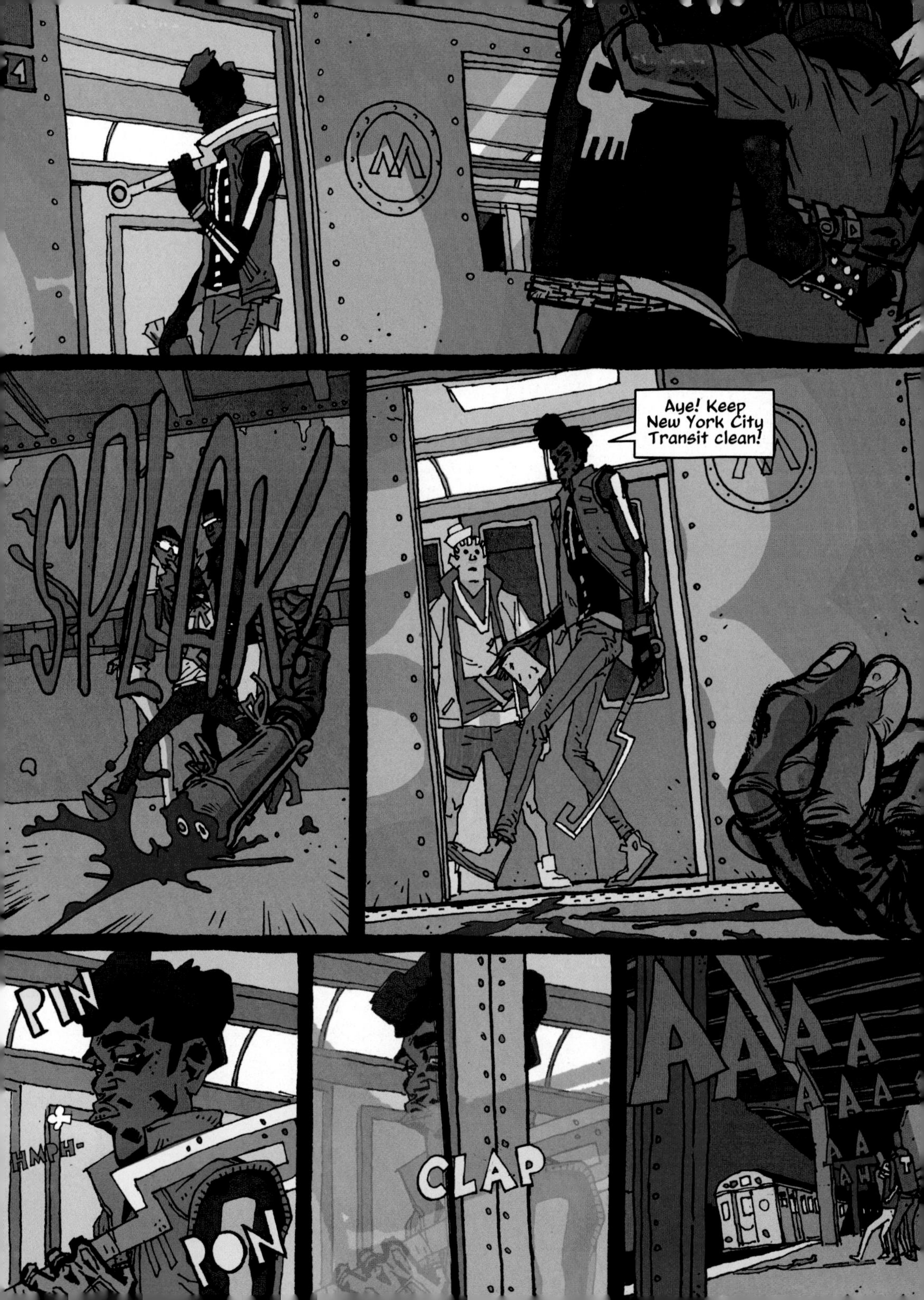
SPLAK!
Aye! Keep New York City Transit clean!
PIN
HMPH-
PON
CLAP
AAAAAAAAAAHH

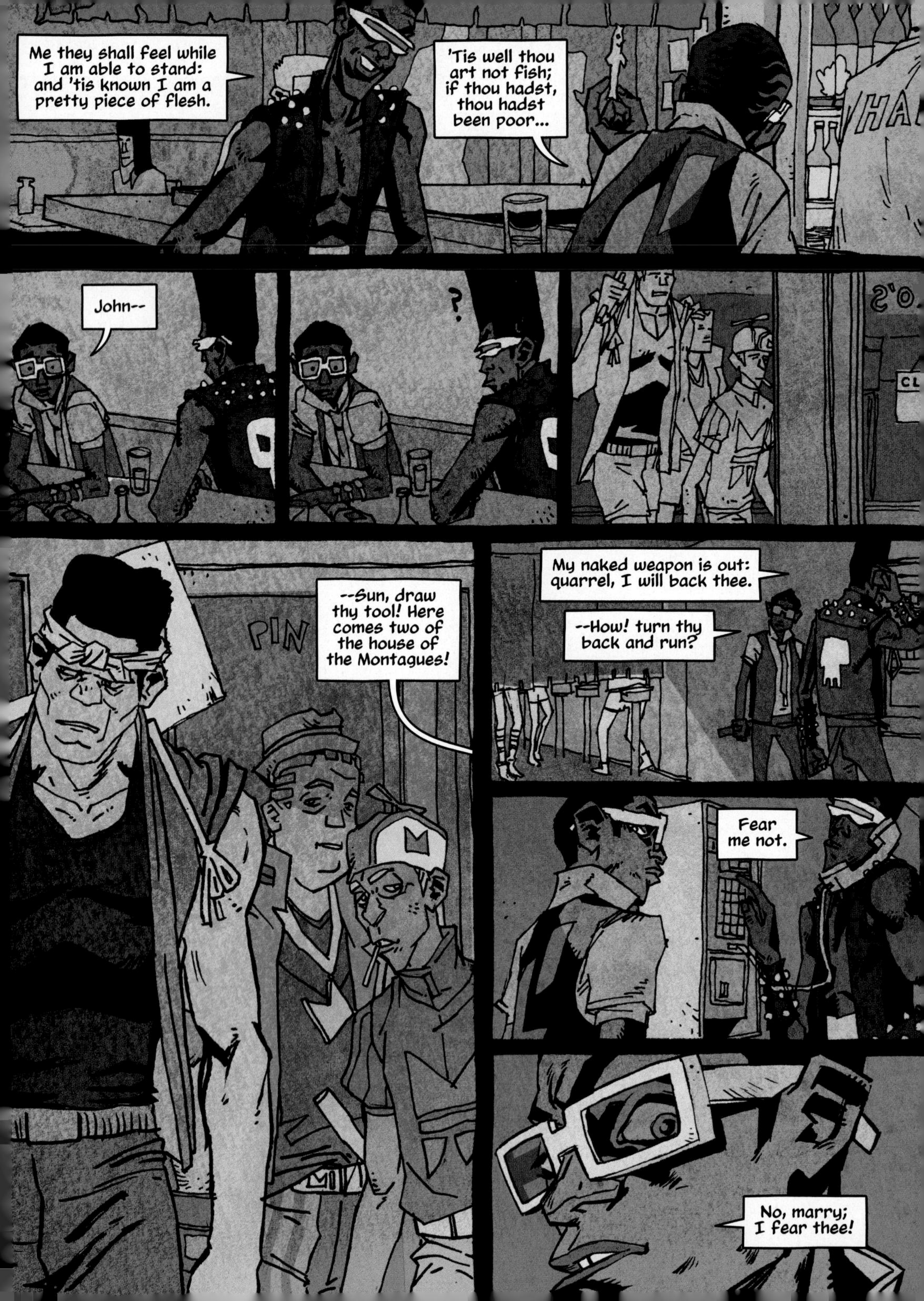
Me they shall feel while I am able to stand: and 'tis known I am a pretty piece of flesh.
'Tis well thou art not fish; if thou hadst, thou hadst been poor...
John--
?
--Sun, draw thy tool! Here comes two of the house of the Montagues!
My naked weapon is out: quarrel, I will back thee.
--How! turn thy back and run?
Fear me not.
No, marry; I fear thee!

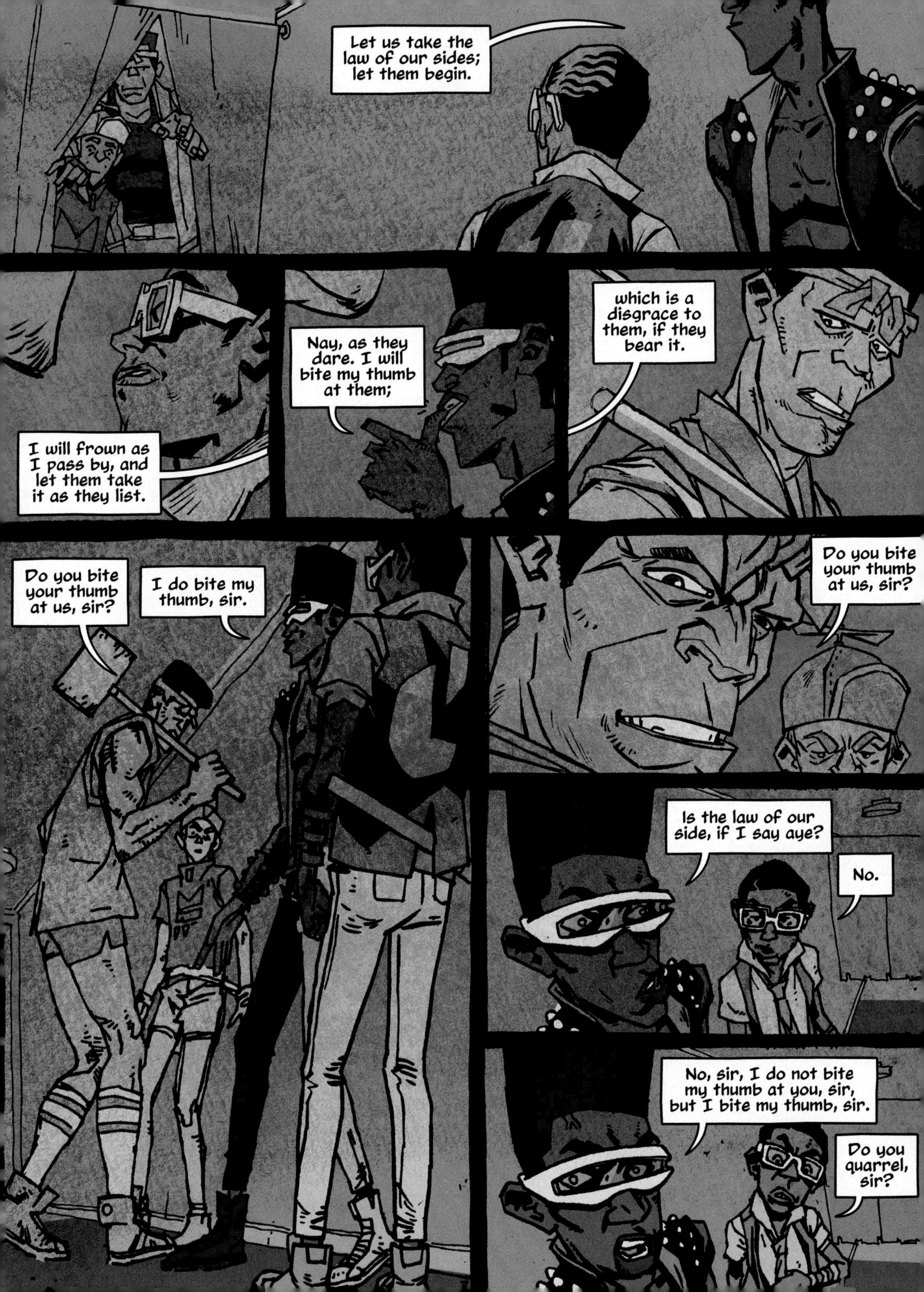

Let us take the law of our sides; let them begin.
I will frown as I pass by, and let them take it as they list.
Nay, as they dare. I will bite my thumb at them;
which is a disgrace to them, if they bear it.
Do you bite your thumb at us, sir?
I do bite my thumb, sir.
Do you bite your thumb at us, sir?
Is the law of our side, if I say aye?
No.
No, sir, I do not bite my thumb at you, sir, but I bite my thumb, sir.
Do you quarrel, sir?

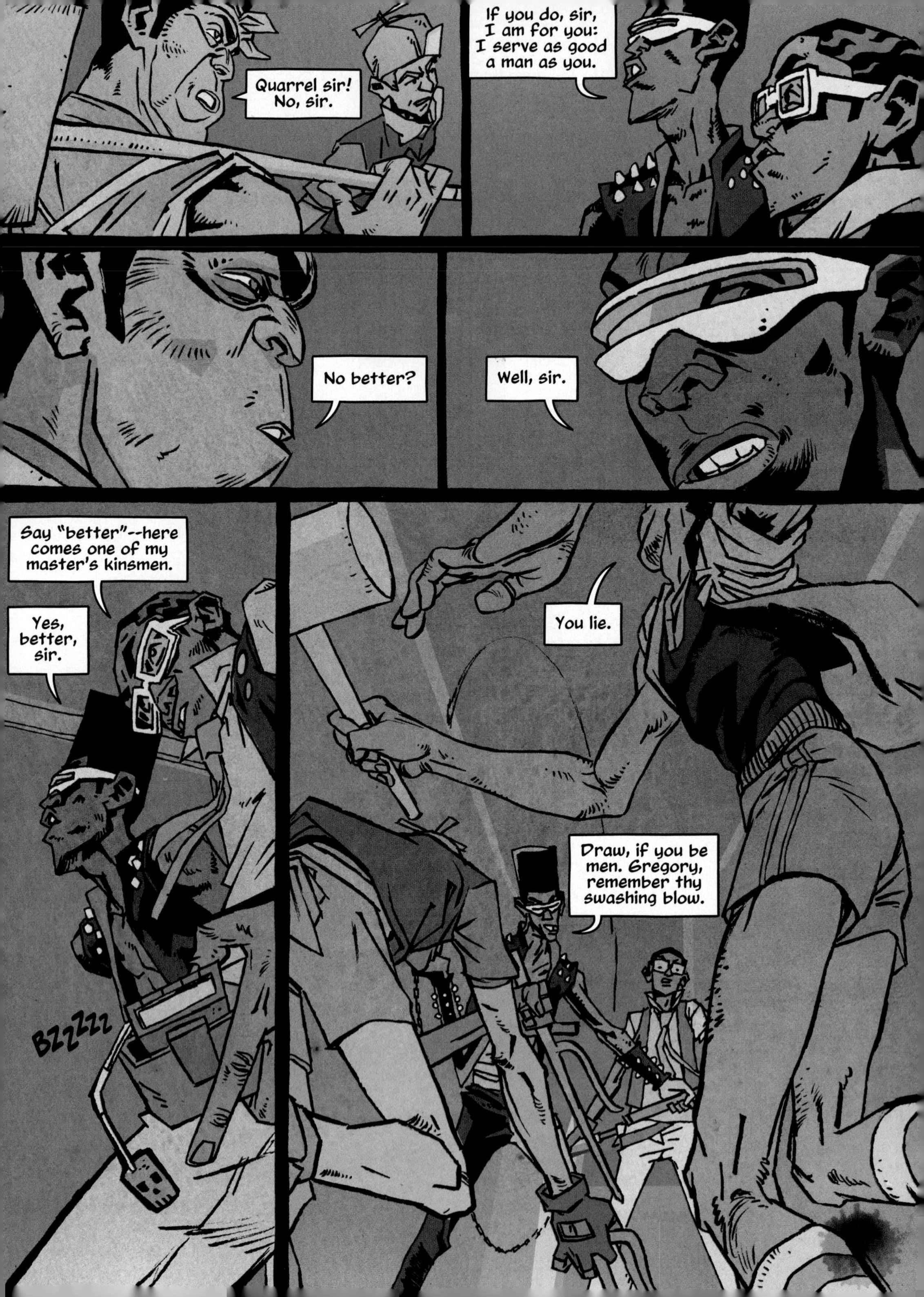
Quarrel sir! No, sir.
If you do, sir, I am for you: I serve as good a man as you.
No better?
Well, sir.
Say "better"--here comes one of my master's kinsmen.
Yes, better, sir.
You lie.
Draw, if you be men. Gregory, remember thy swashing blow.
BZZZZZ

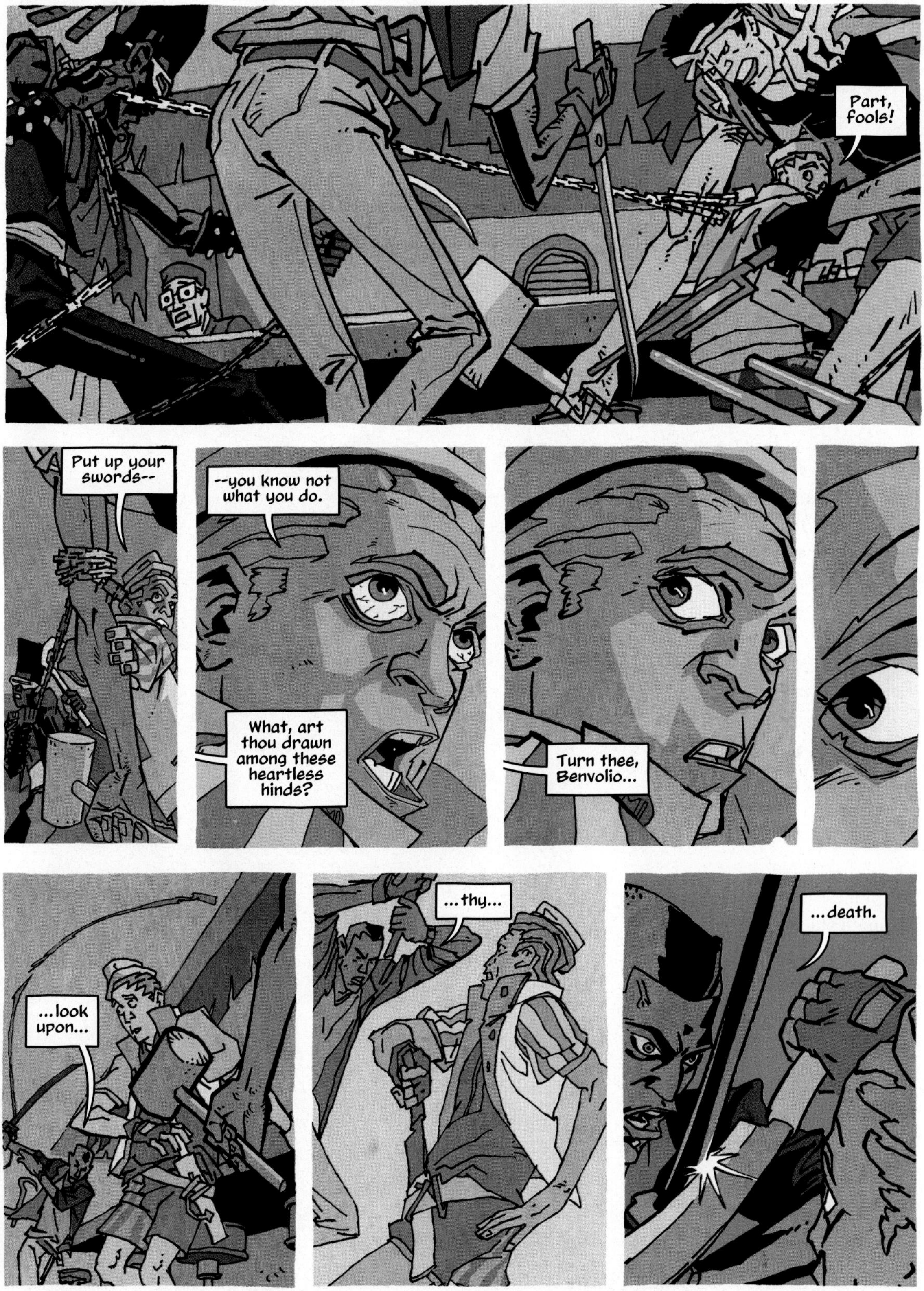
Part, fools!
Put up your swords--
--you know not what you do.
What, art thou drawn among these heartless hinds?
Turn thee, Benvolio...
...look upon...
...thy...
...death.

A Thrice Disturbed Pea

-Edward de Vere

A Thrice Disturbed Peace
Gang violence again did make
A peaceful haunt a battlefield
yesterday
As Montague and Capulet
crossed blades
Over a sushi bar in crown
heights.

Three civil brawls, bred of an airy
word,
Have thrice disturb'd the quiet of
our streets.
Our Mayor, Escalus had this to
say:
Rebellious subjects, enemies to
peace,

Profaners of this neighbour-
stained steel,--
Throw your mistemper'd weapons to the ground,
And hear the sentence of your
moved mayor.
If ever you disturb our streets
again,
Your lives shall pay the forfeit of
the peace.

contd. on page 3a.

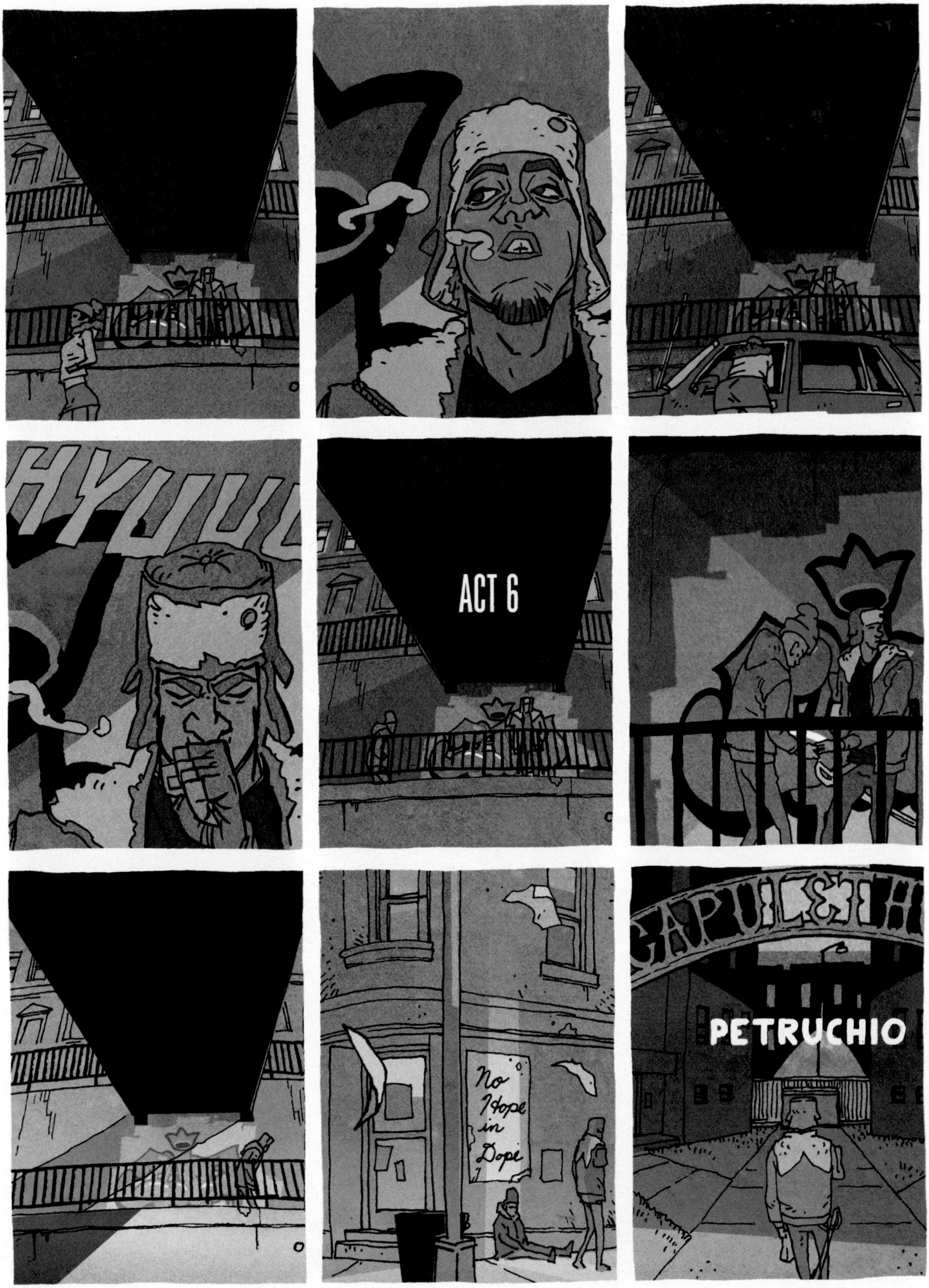
ACT 6
No Hope in Dope
PETRUCHIO

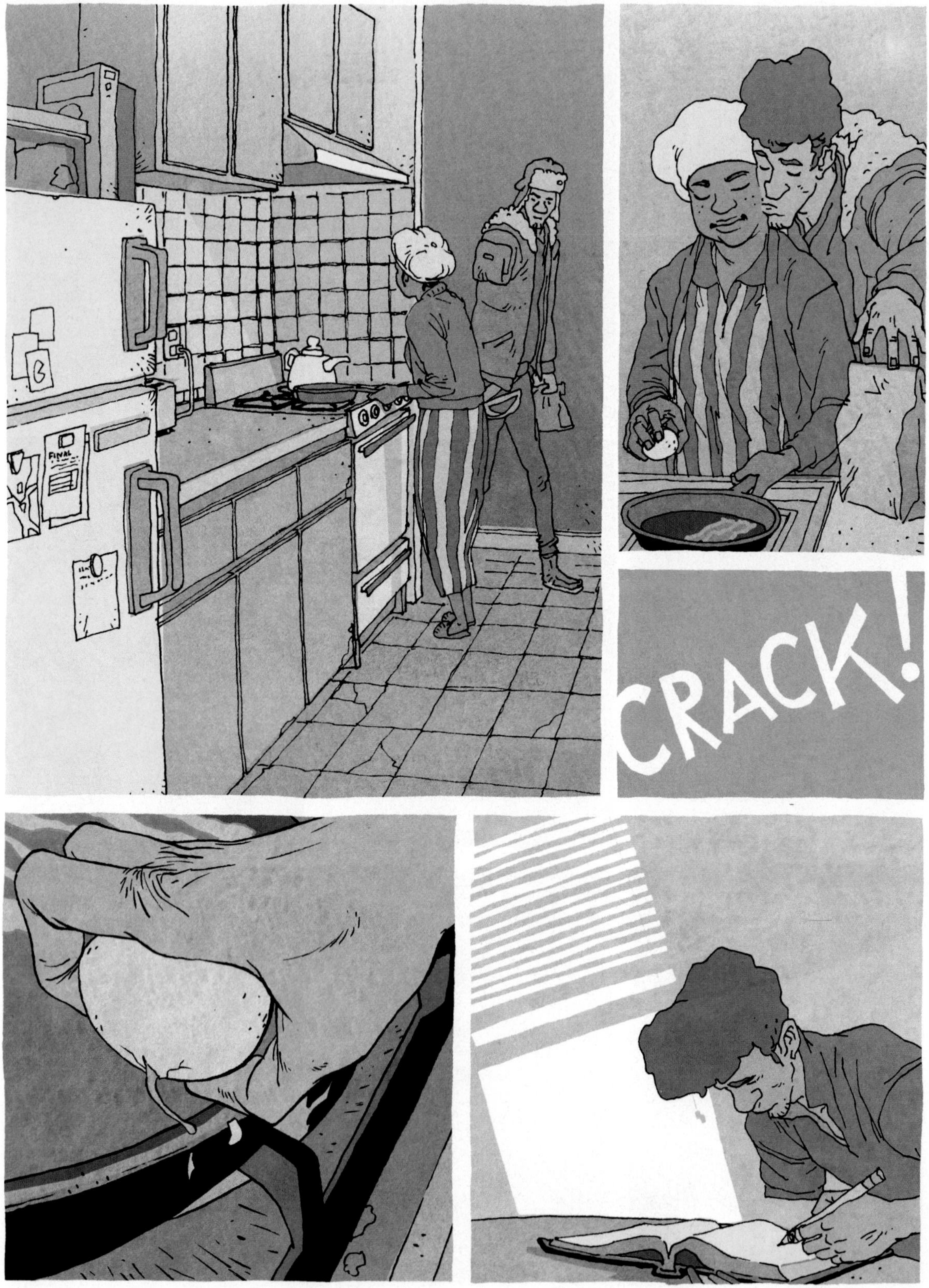
FINAL
CRACK!

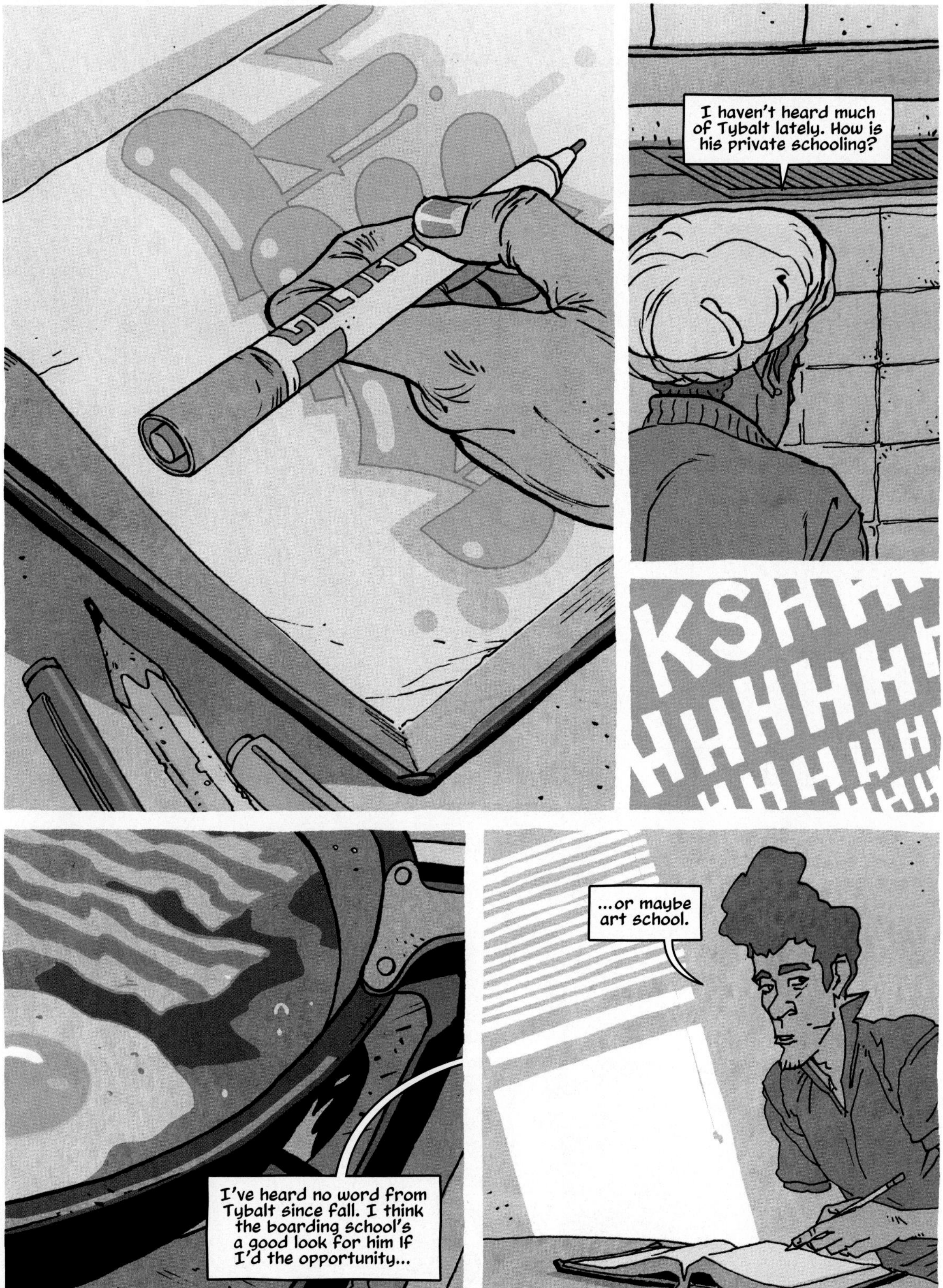
I haven't heard much of Tybalt lately. How is his private schooling?
KSHHHHHHHHHHHHHHHHHHHHH
I've heard no word from Tybalt since fall. I think the boarding school's a good look for him If I'd the opportunity...
...or maybe art school.

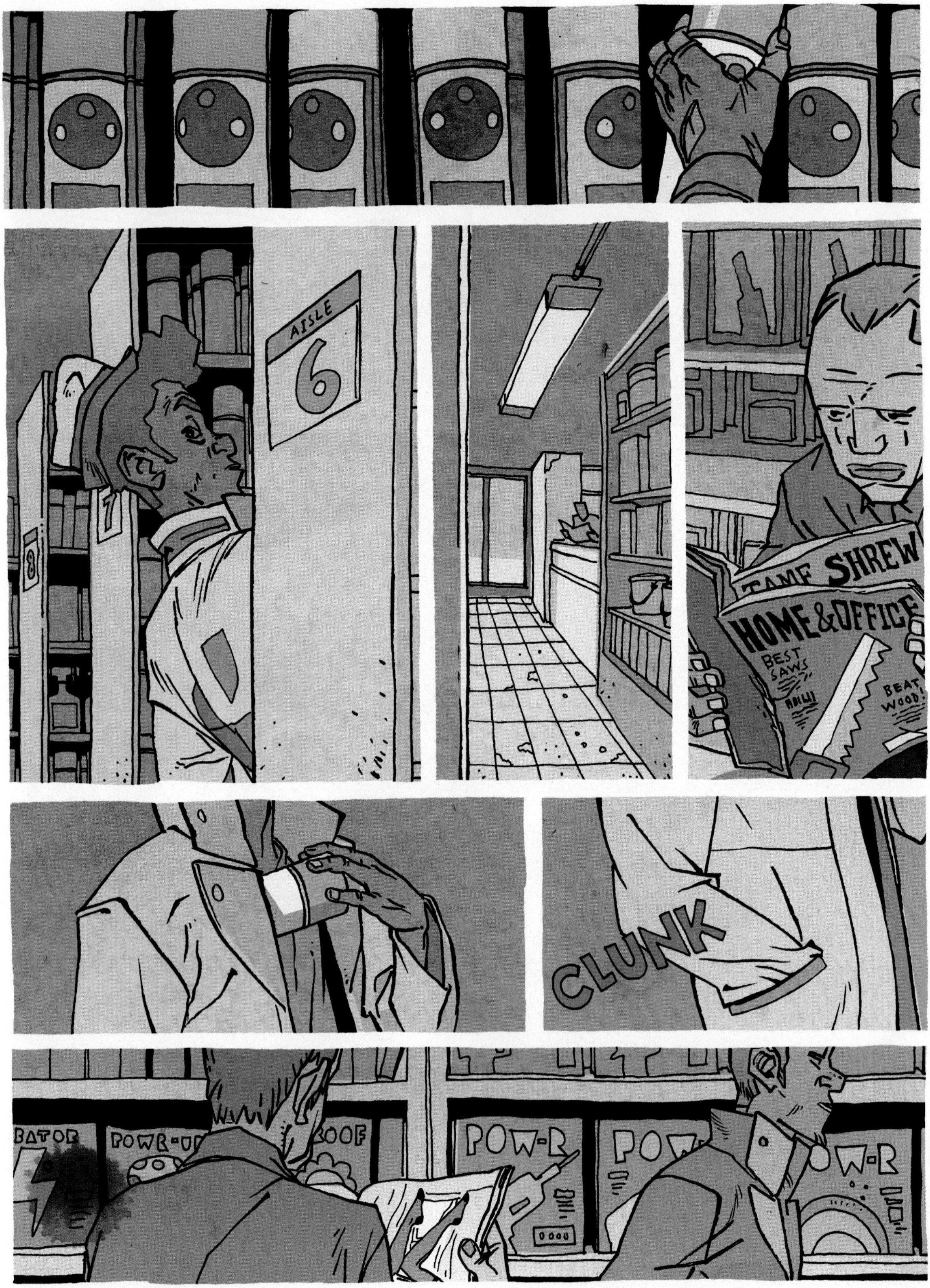
AISLE
6
TAME SHREW
HOME&OFFICE
BEST SAWS
BEAT WOOD!
CLUNK
POW-R

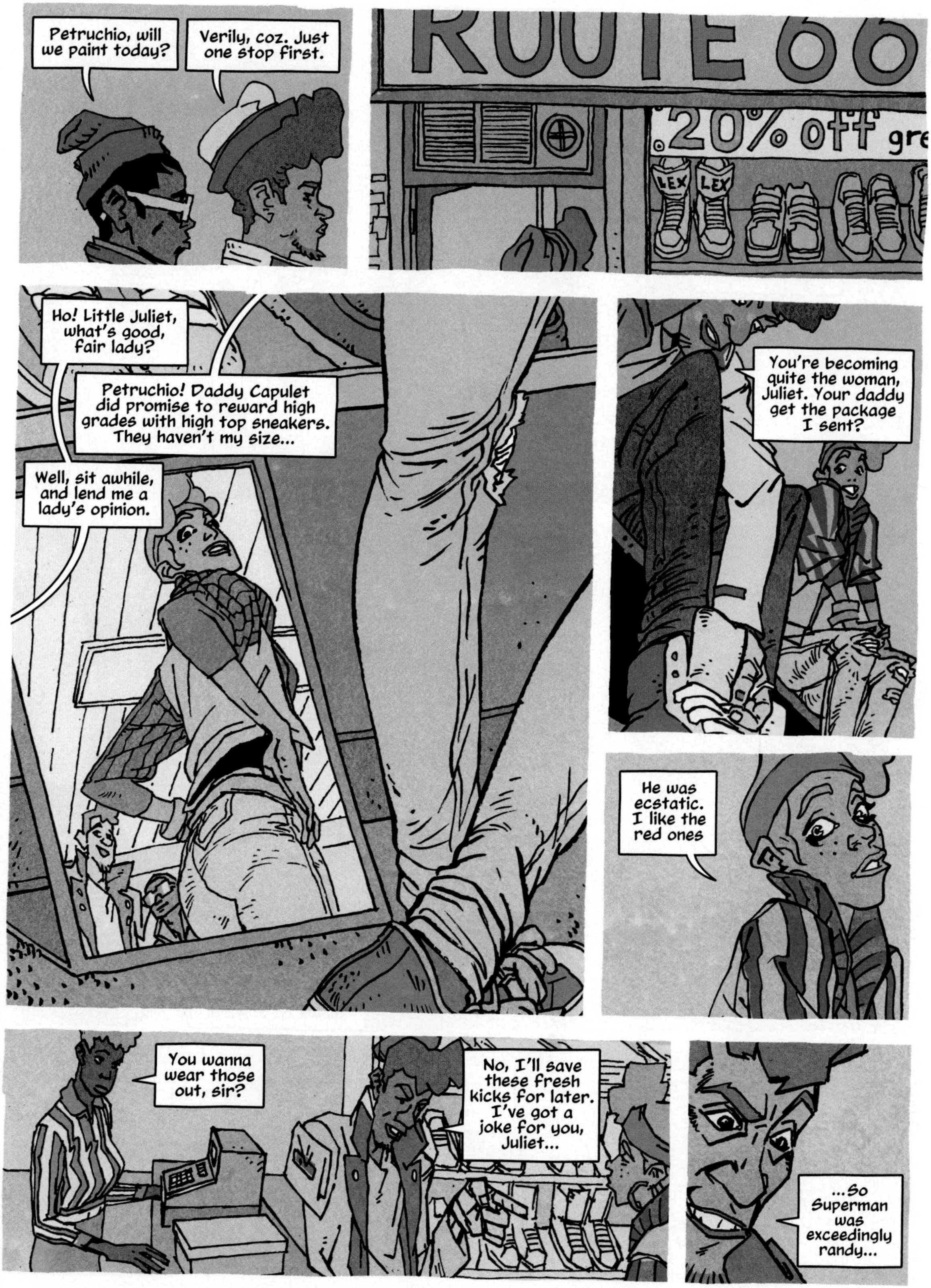
Petruchio, will we paint today?
Verily, coz. Just one stop first.
ROUTE 66
20% off gre
LEX LEX
Ho! Little Juliet, what's good, fair lady?
Petruchio! Daddy Capulet did promise to reward high grades with high top sneakers. They haven't my size...
Well, sit awhile, and lend me a lady's opinion.
You're becoming quite the woman, Juliet. Your daddy get the package I sent?
He was ecstatic. I like the red ones
You wanna wear those out, sir?
No, I'll save these fresh kicks for later. I've got a joke for you, Juliet...
...So Superman was exceedingly randy...

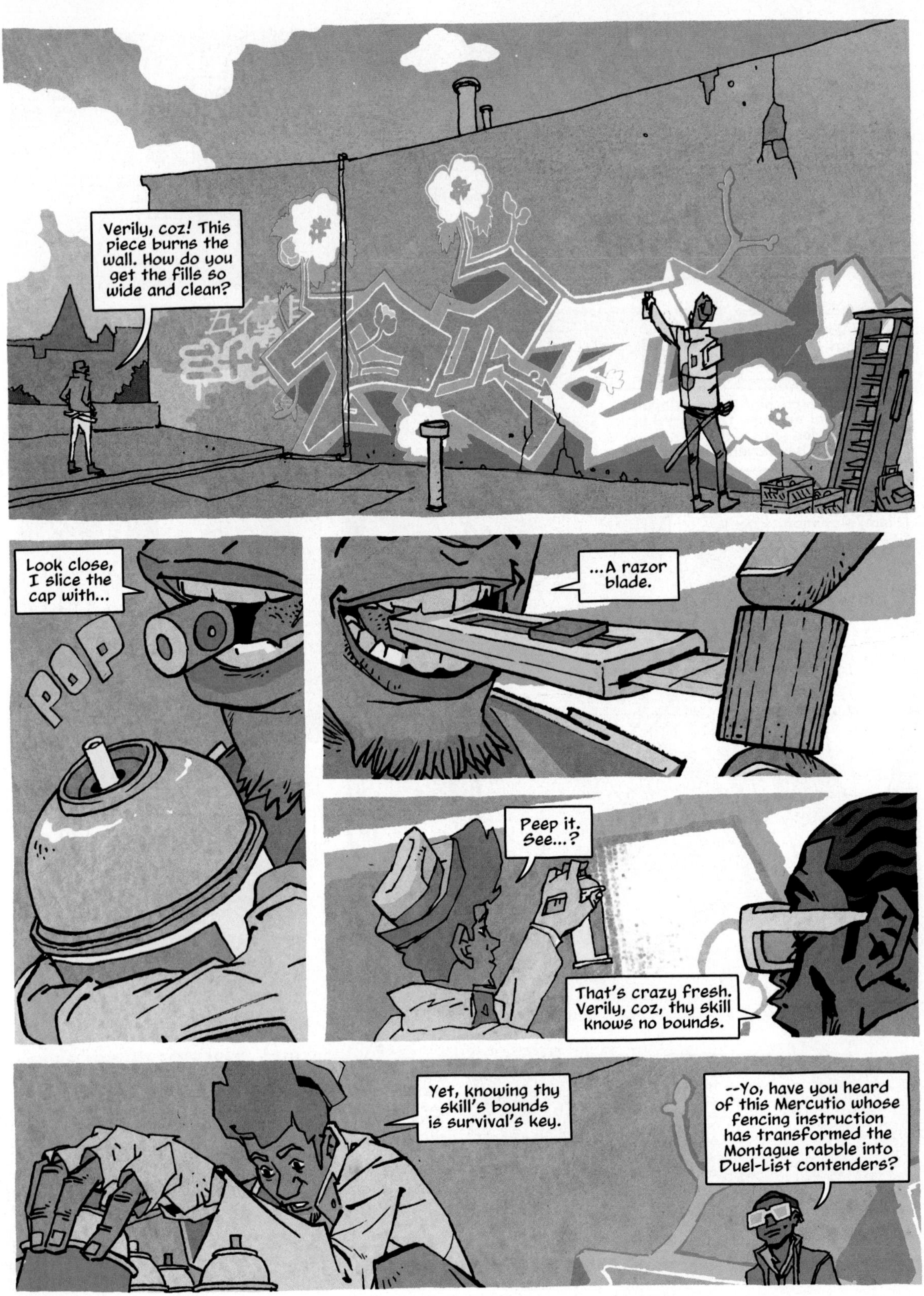
Verily, coz! This piece burns the wall. How do you get the fills so wide and clean?
Look close, I slice the cap with...
POP
...A razor blade.
Peep it. See...?
That's crazy fresh. Verily, coz, thy skill knows no bounds.
Yet, knowing thy skill's bounds is survival's key.
--Yo, have you heard of this Mercutio whose fencing instruction has transformed the Montague rabble into Duel-List contenders?

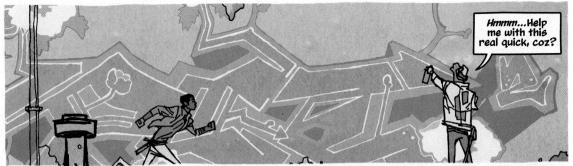

Hmmm...Help me with this real quick, coz?

Maaan, fuck a duel-list. I'm the King of Style...And I've got styles already that art more complex that nobody knowst about...

I mean super duty tough work.

See, a man caught in words can live forever.

Dope!

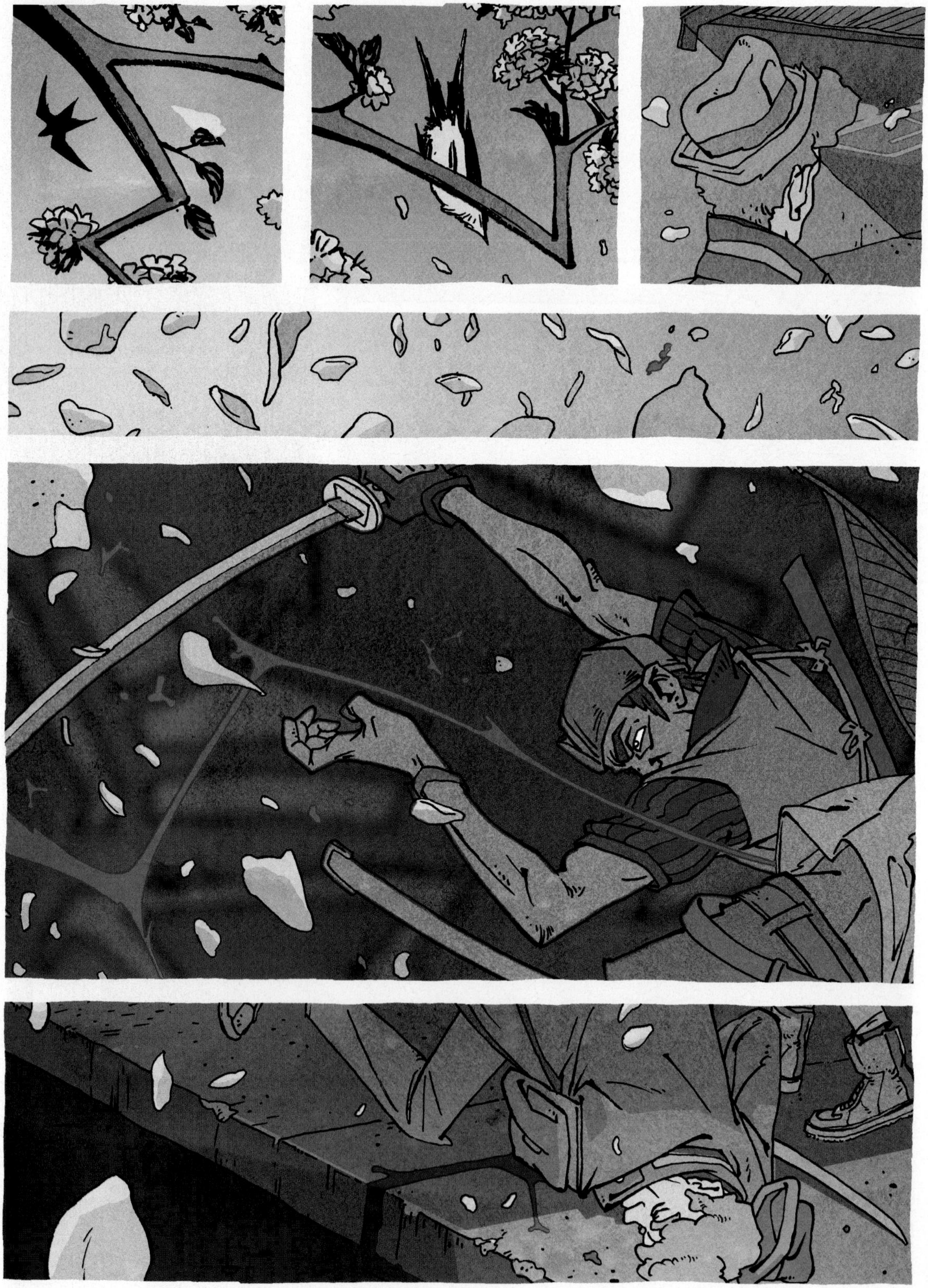

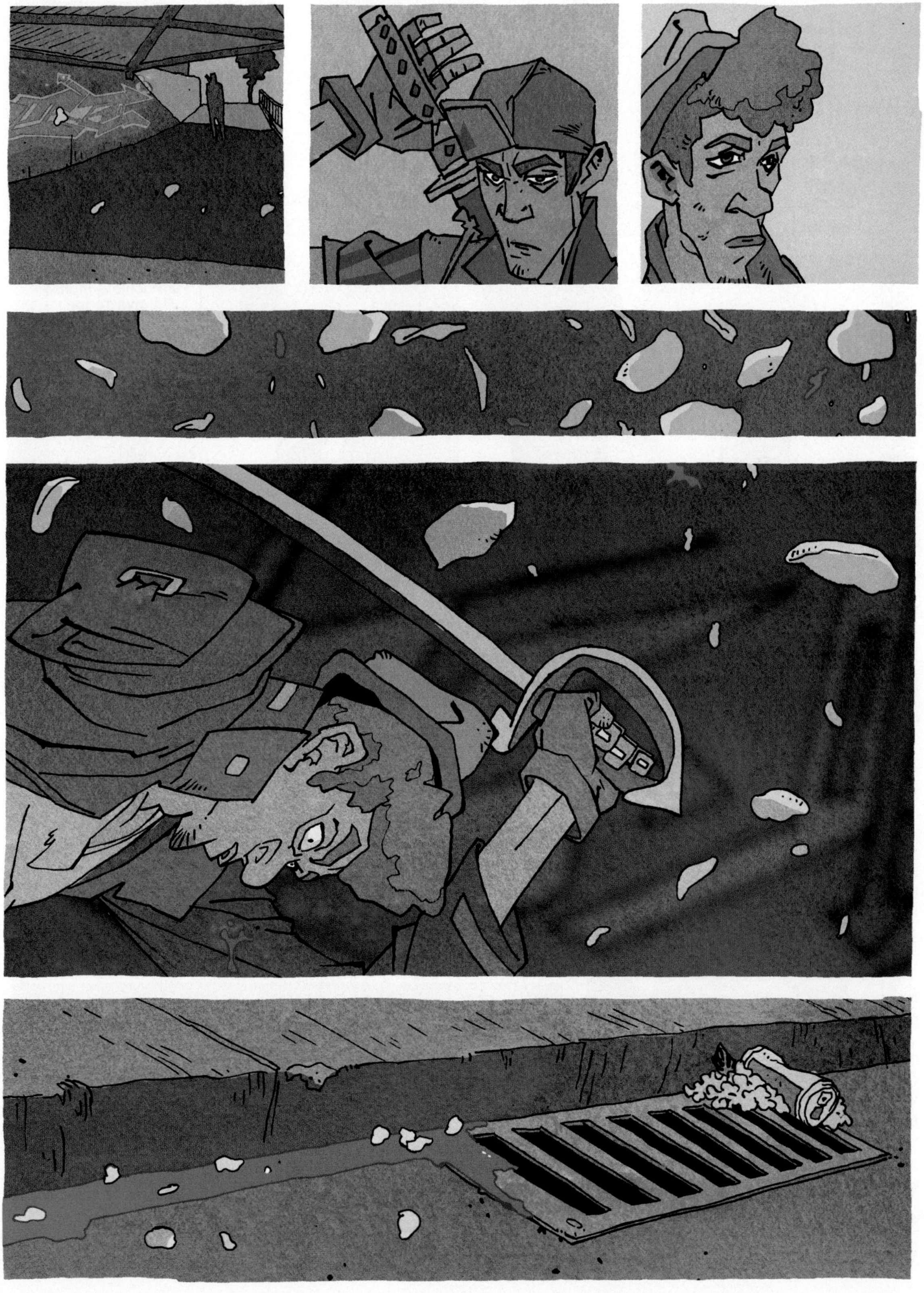

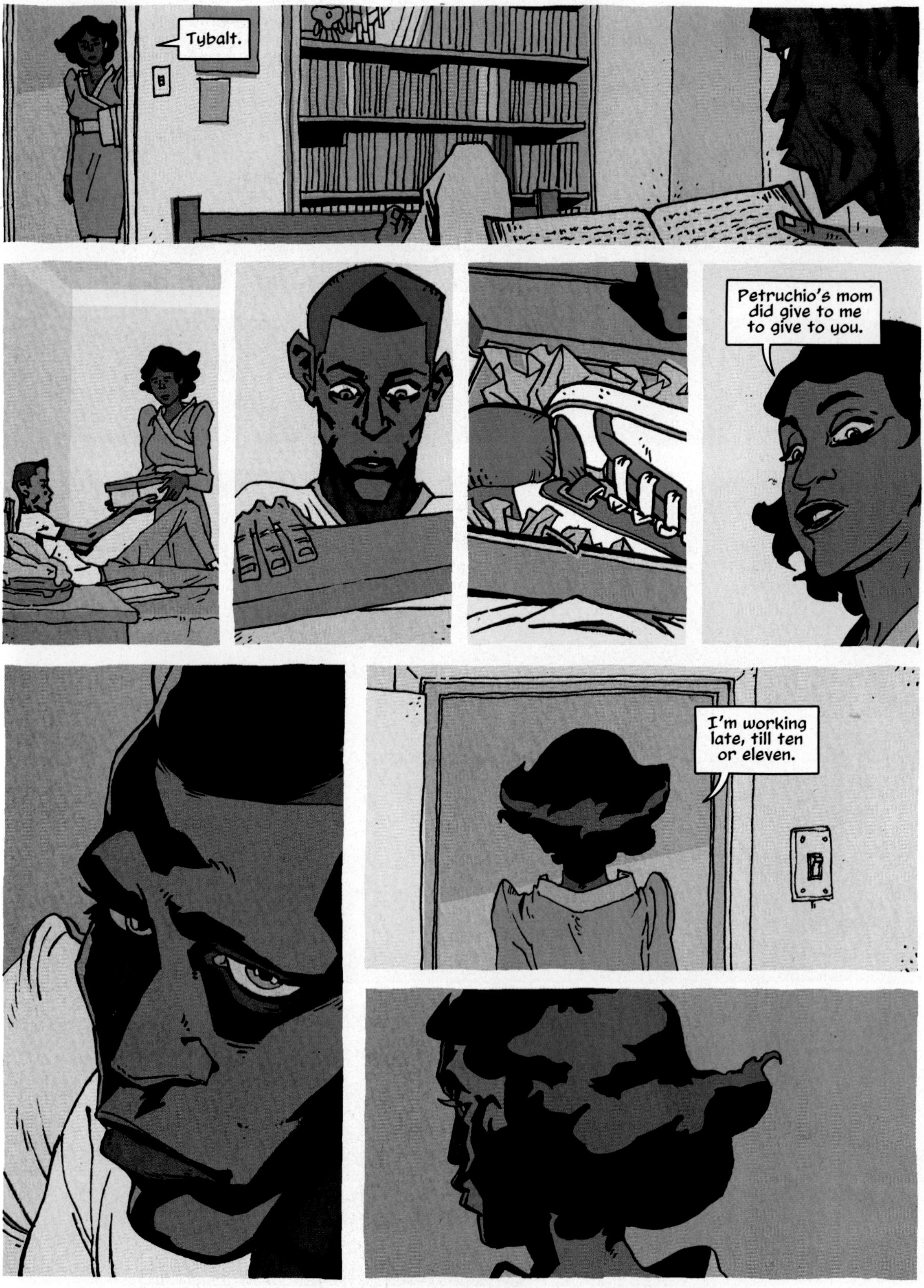
Tybalt.
Petruchio's mom did give to me to give to you.
I'm working late, till ten or eleven.

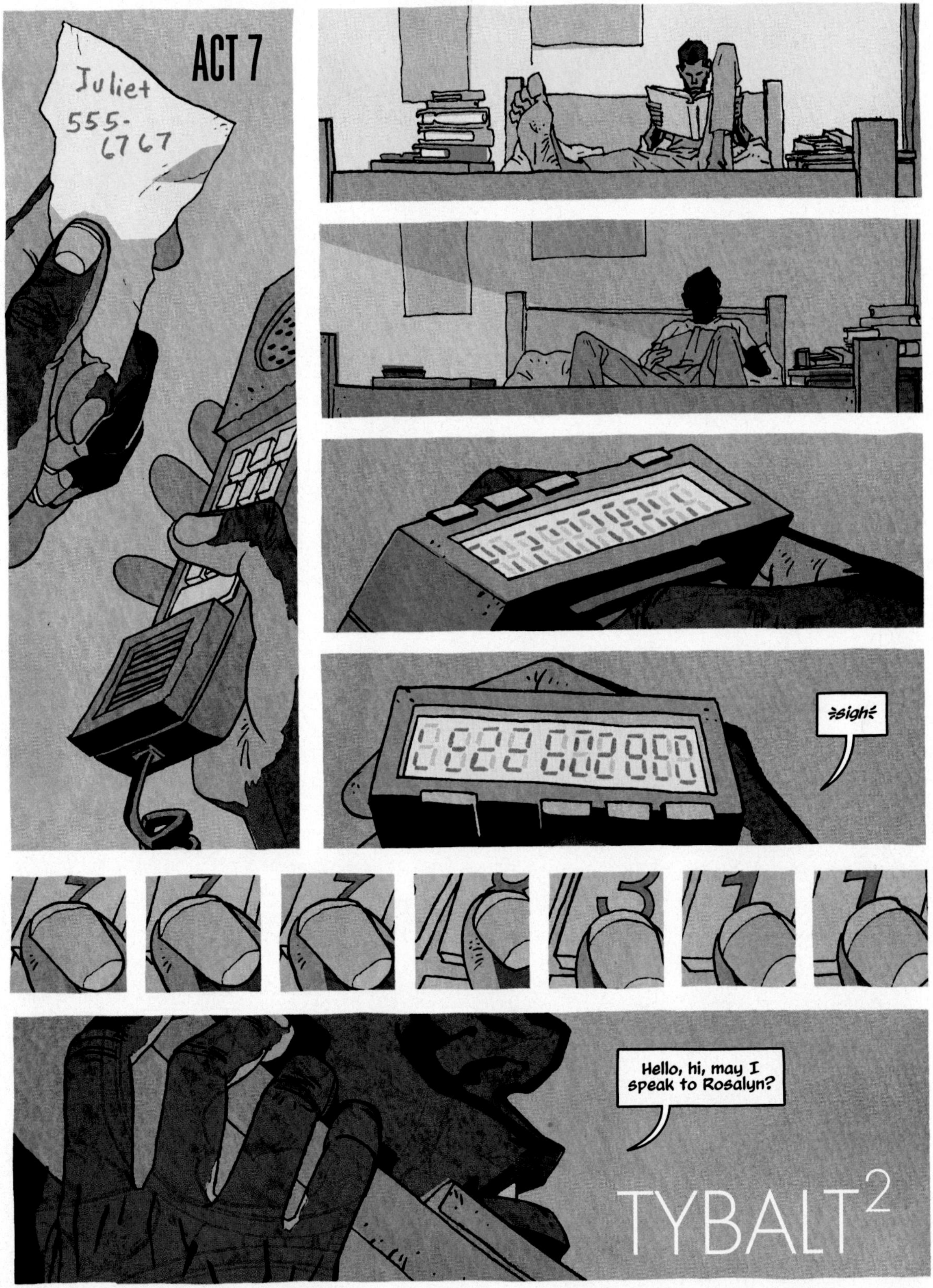
ACT 7
Juliet 555-6767
sigh
Hello, hi, may I speak to Rosalyn?
TYBALT2

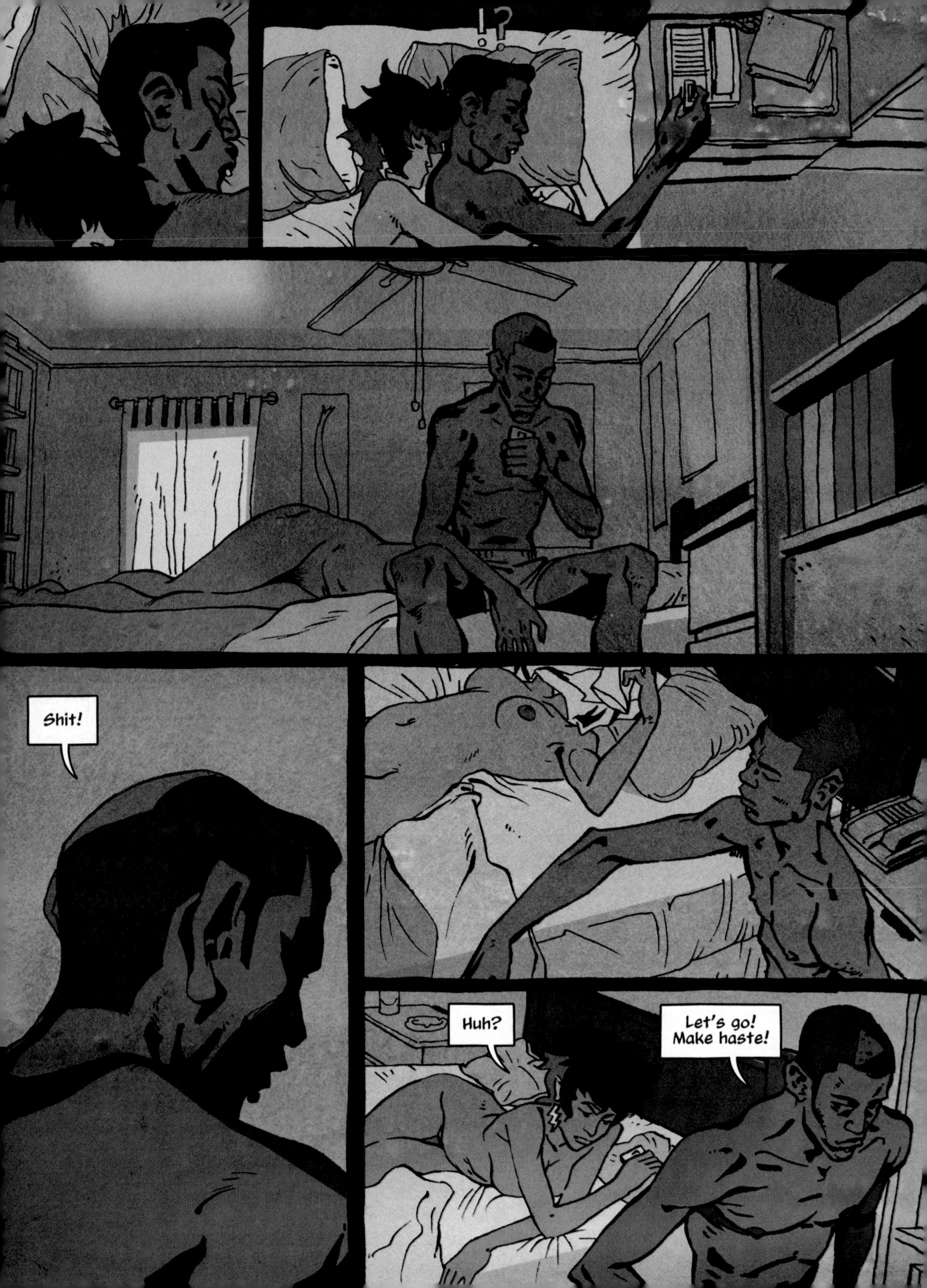
!?
Shit!
Huh?
Let's go!
Make haste!

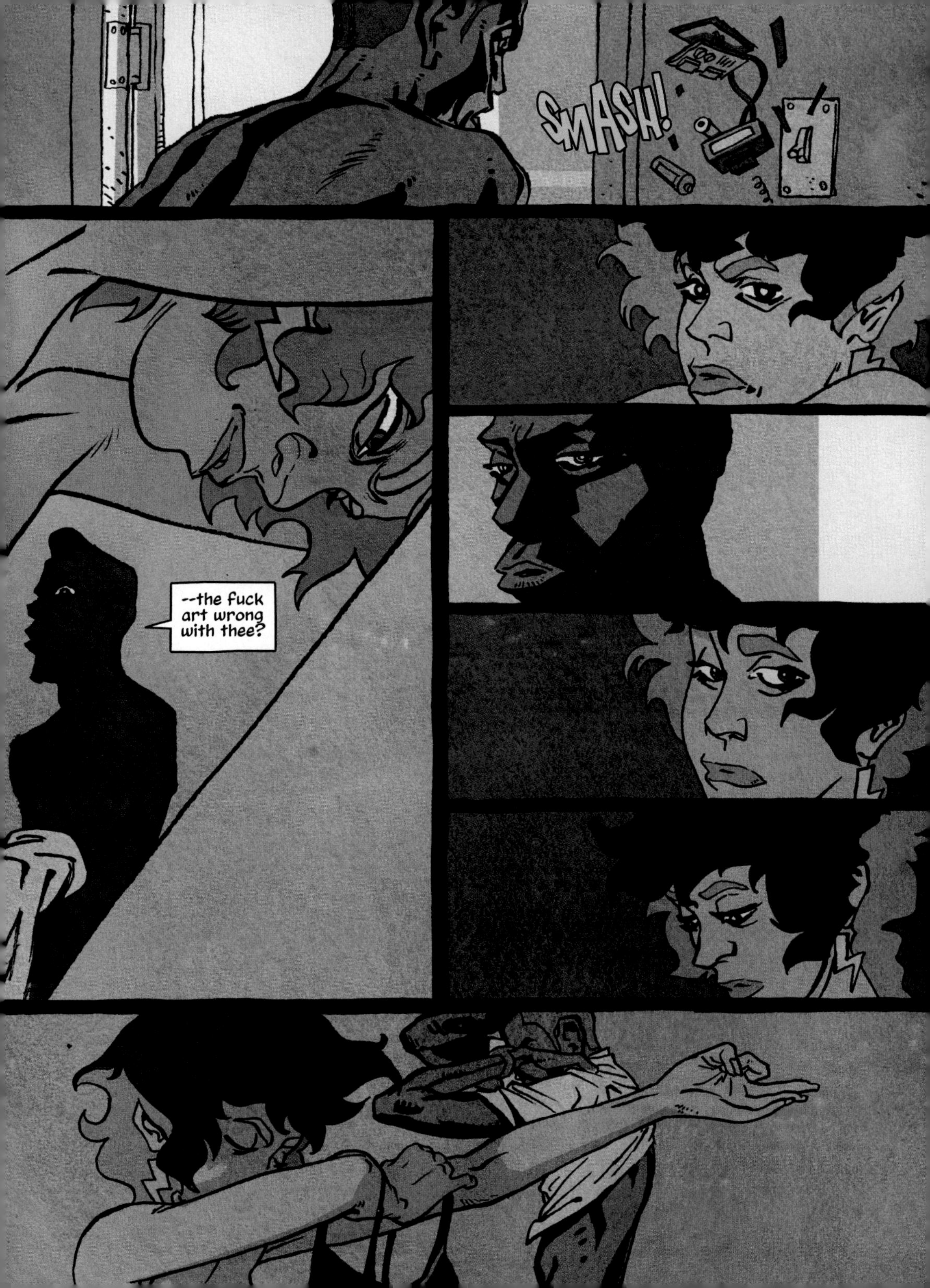
SMASH!
--the fuck art wrong with thee?

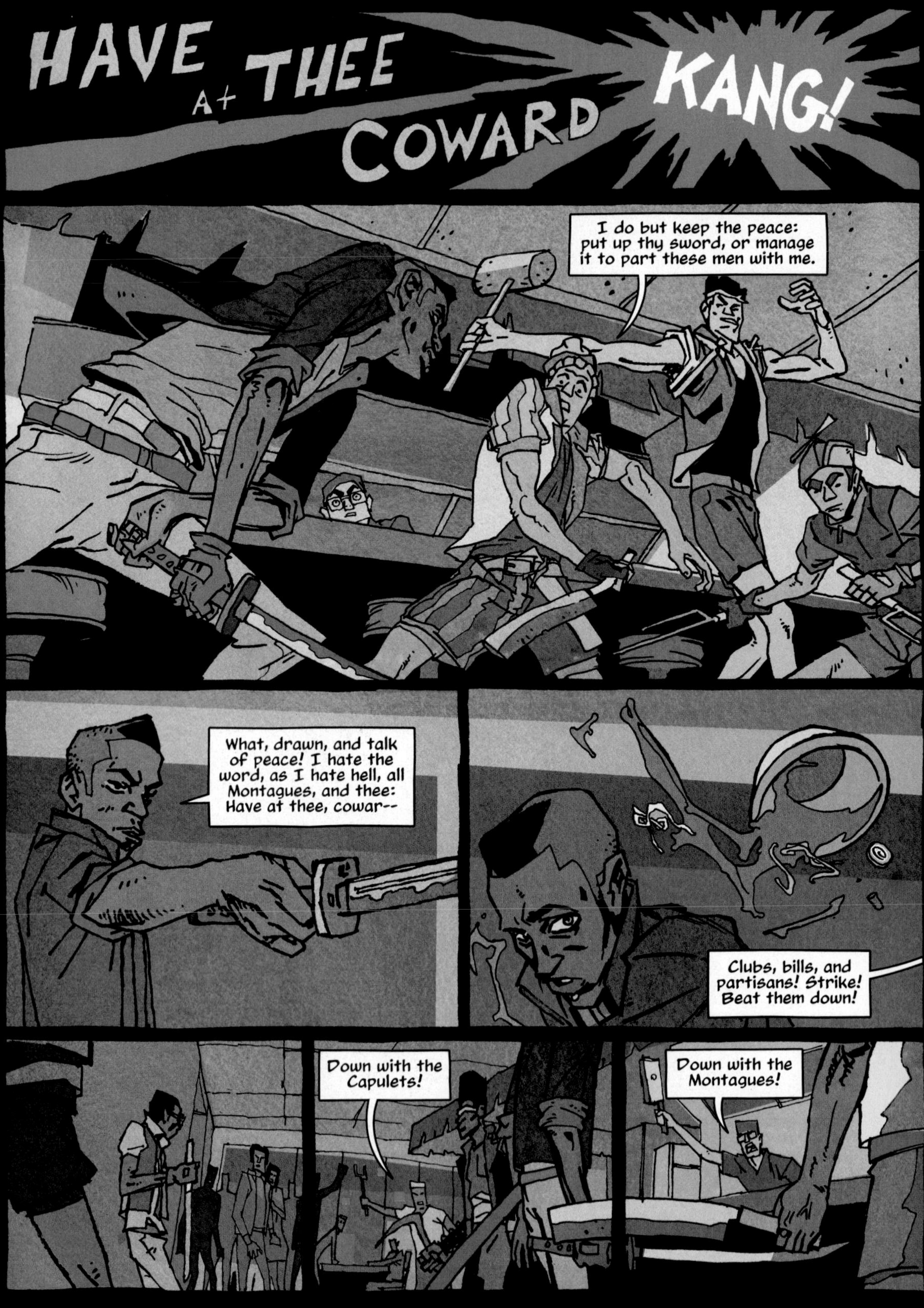
HAVE At THEE COWARD
KANG!
I do but keep the peace: put up thy sword, or manage it to part these men with me.
What, drawn, and talk of peace! I hate the word, as I hate hell, all Montagues, and thee: Have at thee, cowar--
Clubs, bills, and partisans! Strike! Beat them down!
Down with the Capulets!
Down with the Montagues!

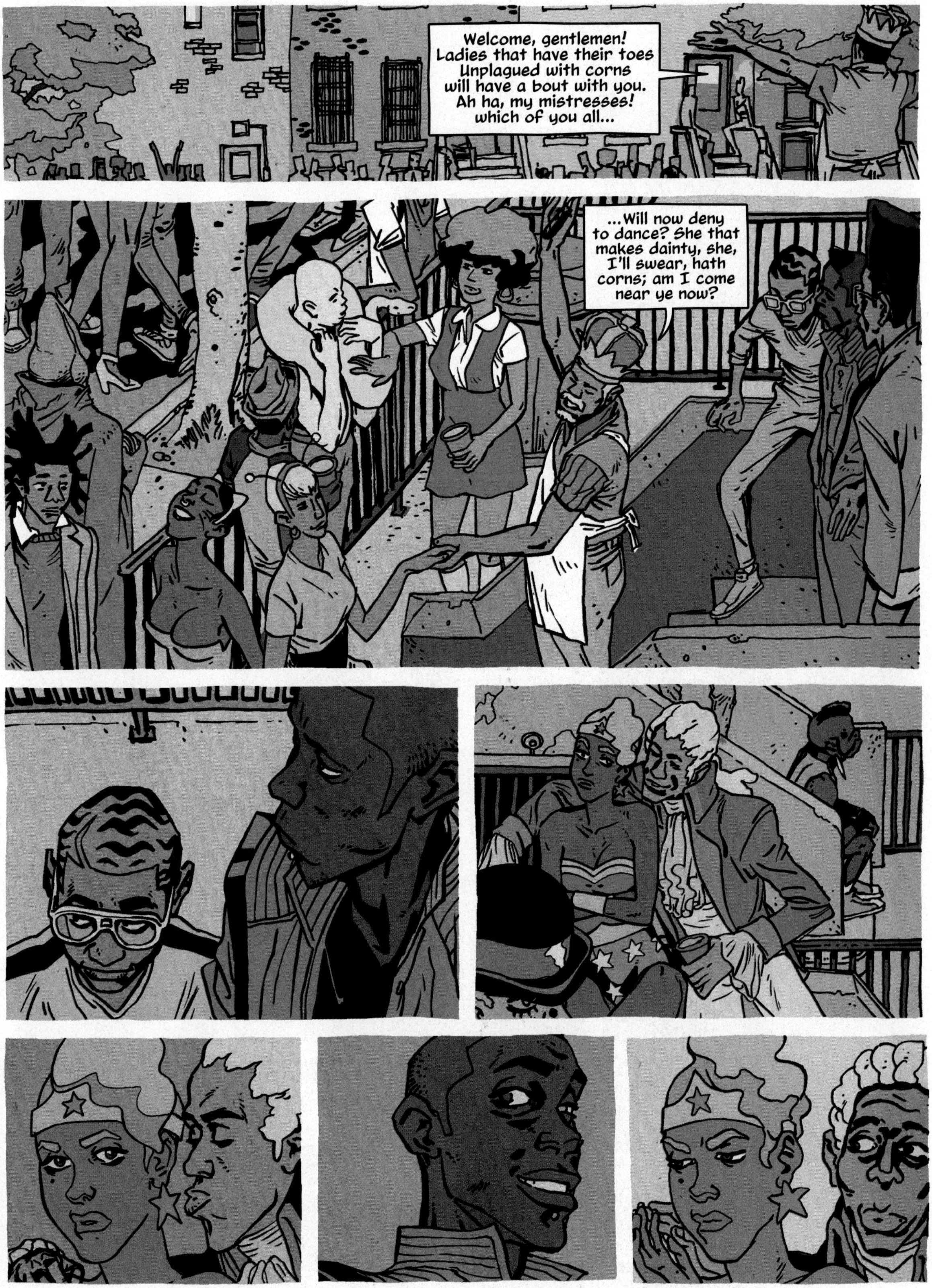
Welcome, gentlemen! Ladies that have their toes Unplagued with corns will have a bout with you. Ah ha, my mistresses! which of you all...
...Will now deny to dance? She that makes dainty, she, I'll swear, hath corns; am I come near ye now?

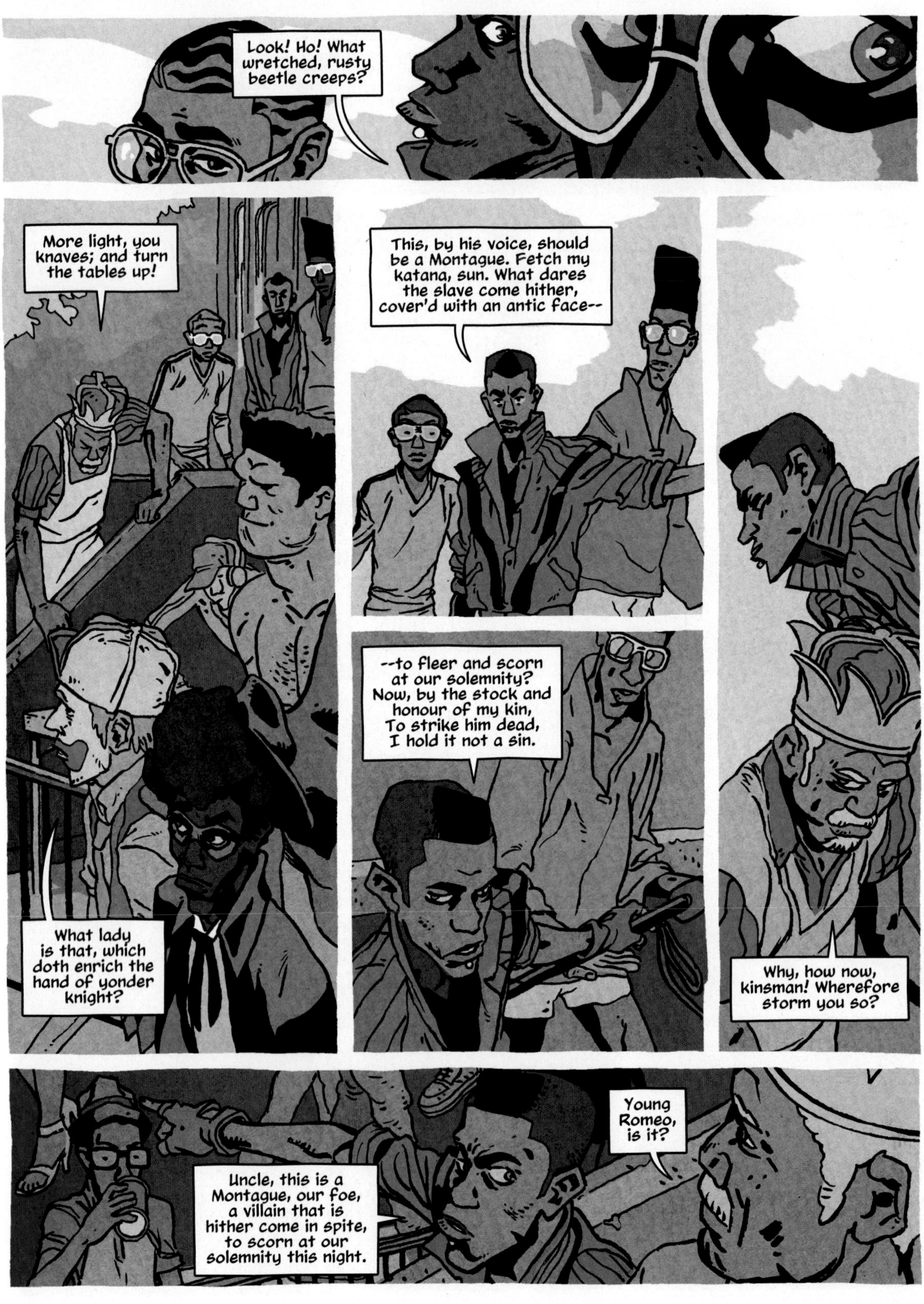
Look! Ho! What wretched, rusty beetle creeps?
More light, you knaves; and turn the tables up!
What lady is that, which doth enrich the hand of yonder knight?
This, by his voice, should be a Montague. Fetch my katana, sun. What dares the slave come hither, cover'd with an antic face--
--to fleer and scorn at our solemnity? Now, by the stock and honour of my kin, To strike him dead, I hold it not a sin.
Why, how now, kinsman! Wherefore storm you so?
Uncle, this is a Montague, our foe, a villain that is hither come in spite, to scorn at our solemnity this night.
Young Romeo, is it?

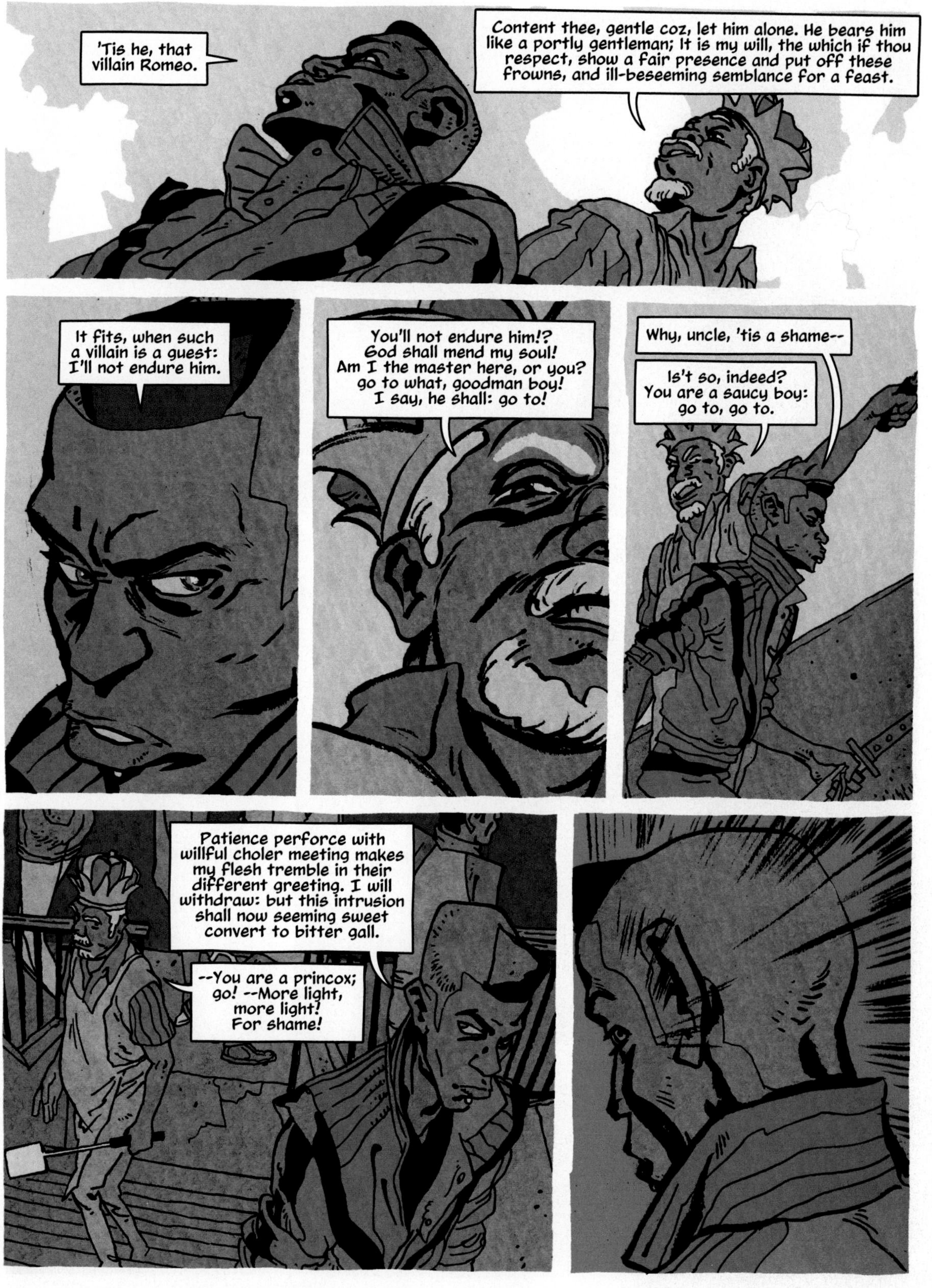
'Tis he, that villain Romeo.
Content thee, gentle coz, let him alone. He bears him like a portly gentleman; It is my will, the which if thou respect, show a fair presence and put off these frowns, and ill-beseeming semblance for a feast.
It fits, when such a villain is a guest: I'll not endure him.
You'll not endure him!? God shall mend my soul! Am I the master here, or you? go to what, goodman boy! I say, he shall: go to!
Why, uncle, 'tis a shame--
Is't so, indeed? You are a saucy boy: go to, go to.
Patience perforce with willful choler meeting makes my flesh tremble in their different greeting. I will withdraw: but this intrusion shall now seeming sweet convert to bitter gall.
--You are a princox; go! --More light, more light! For shame!

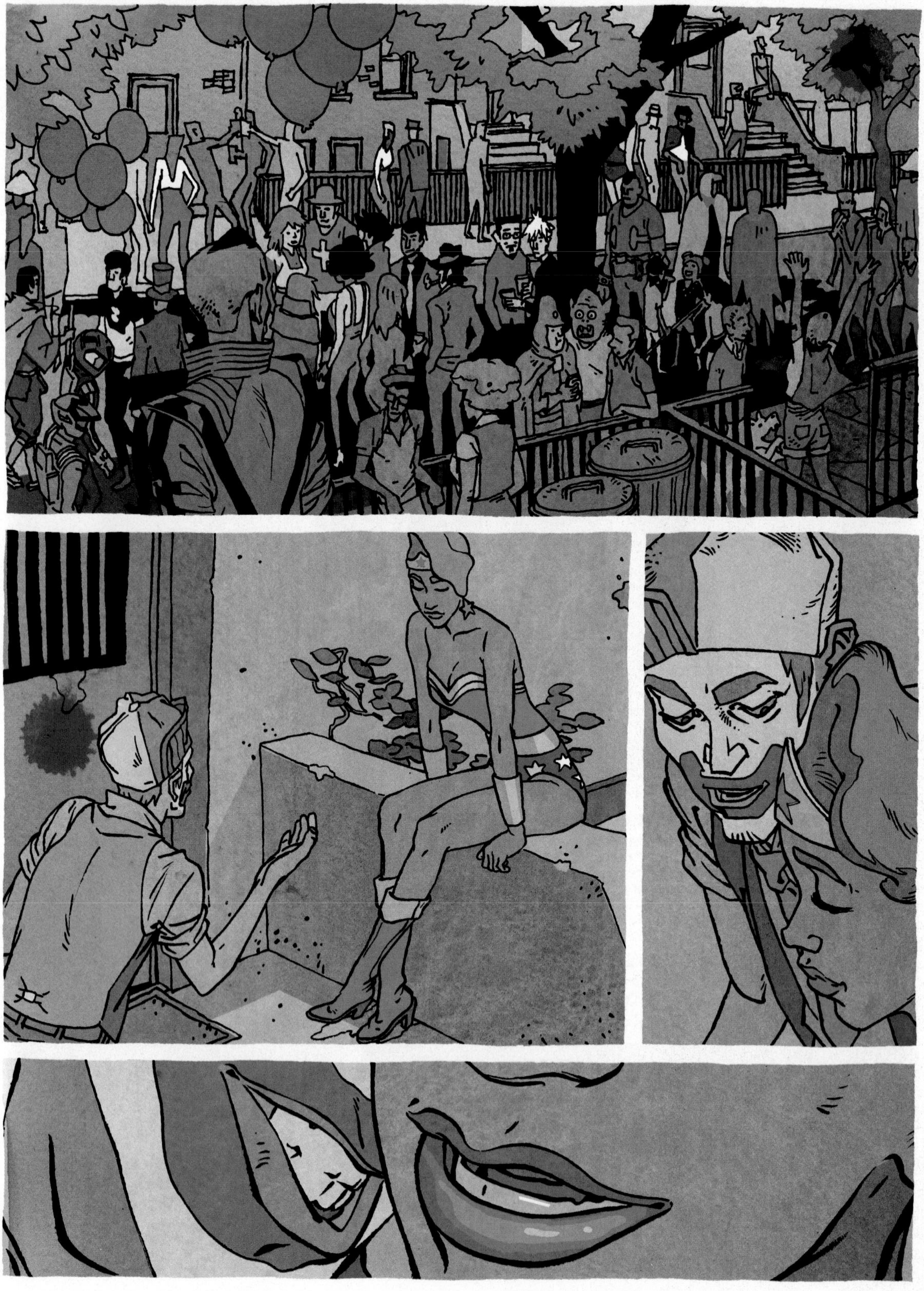

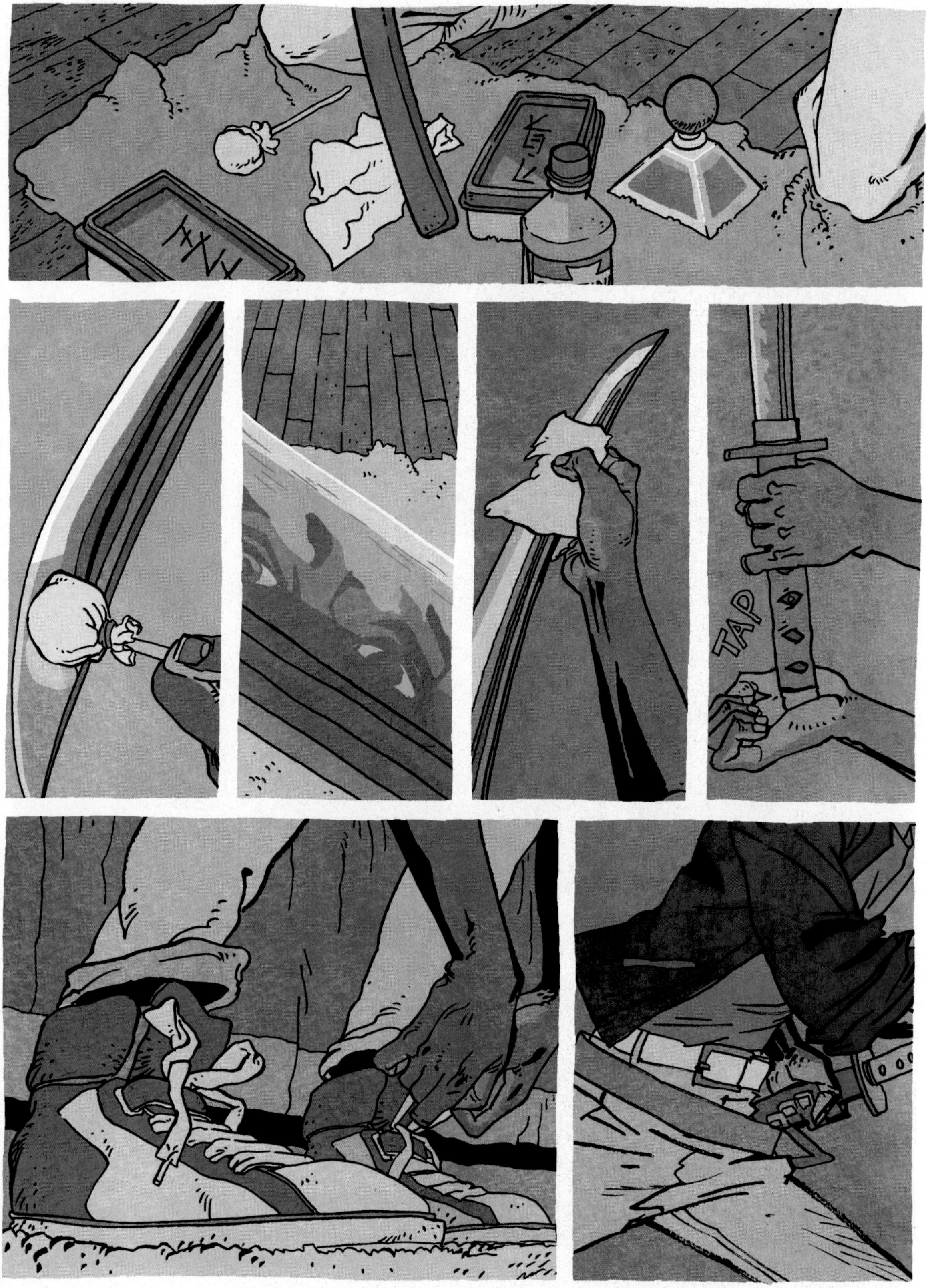
TAP

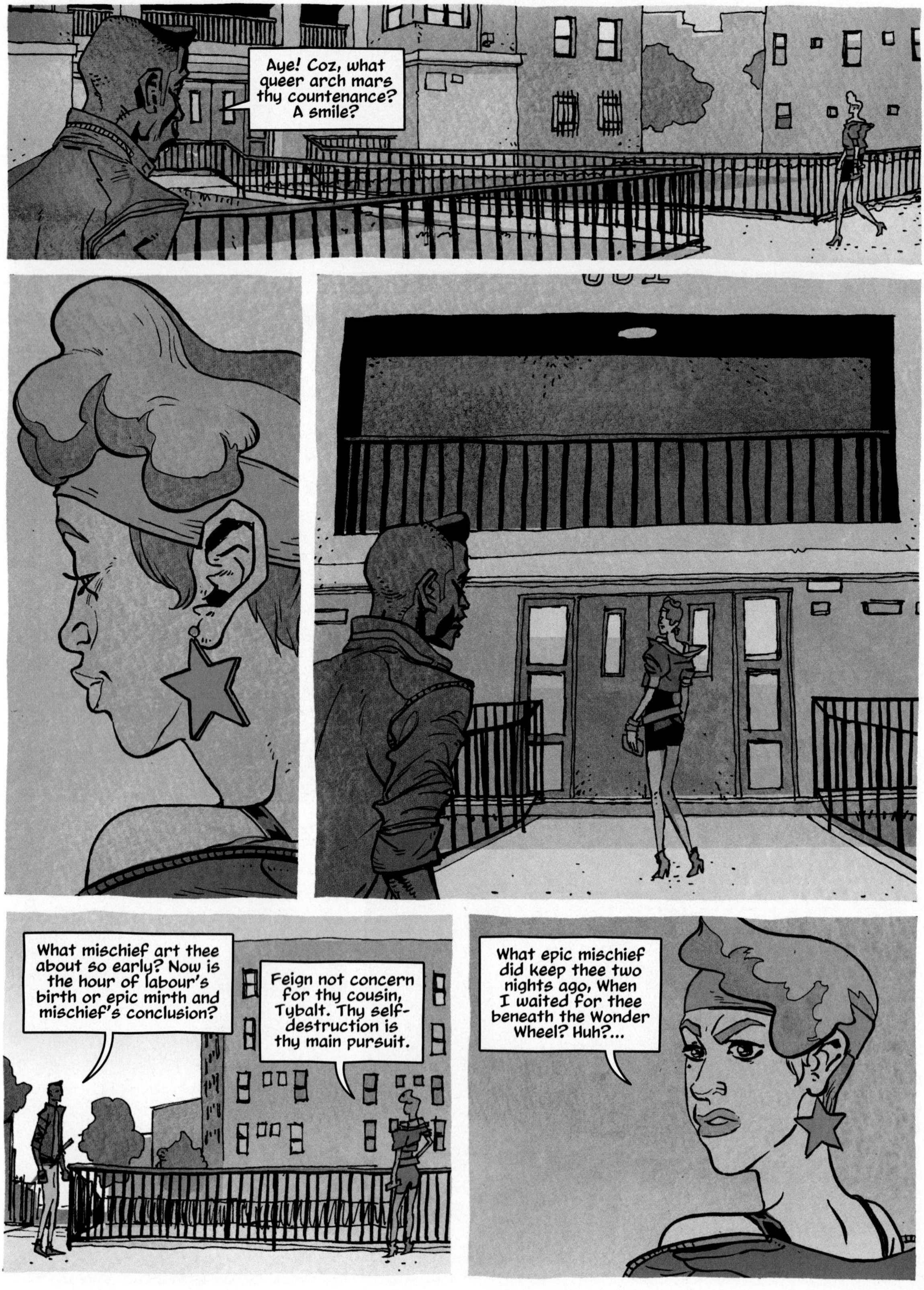

Aye! Coz, what queer arch mars thy countenance? A smile?
What mischief art thee about so early? Now is the hour of labour's birth or epic mirth and mischief's conclusion?
Feign not concern for thy cousin, Tybalt. Thy self-destruction is thy main pursuit.
What epic mischief did keep thee two nights ago, When I waited for thee beneath the Wonder Wheel? Huh?...

Romeo!

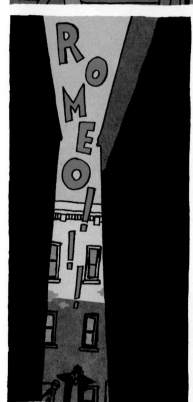

FLOYD'S
DELI & GROCERY

Gentlemen, good den: a word with one of you.

And but one word with one of us? Couple it with something--

--Make it a word and a blow.

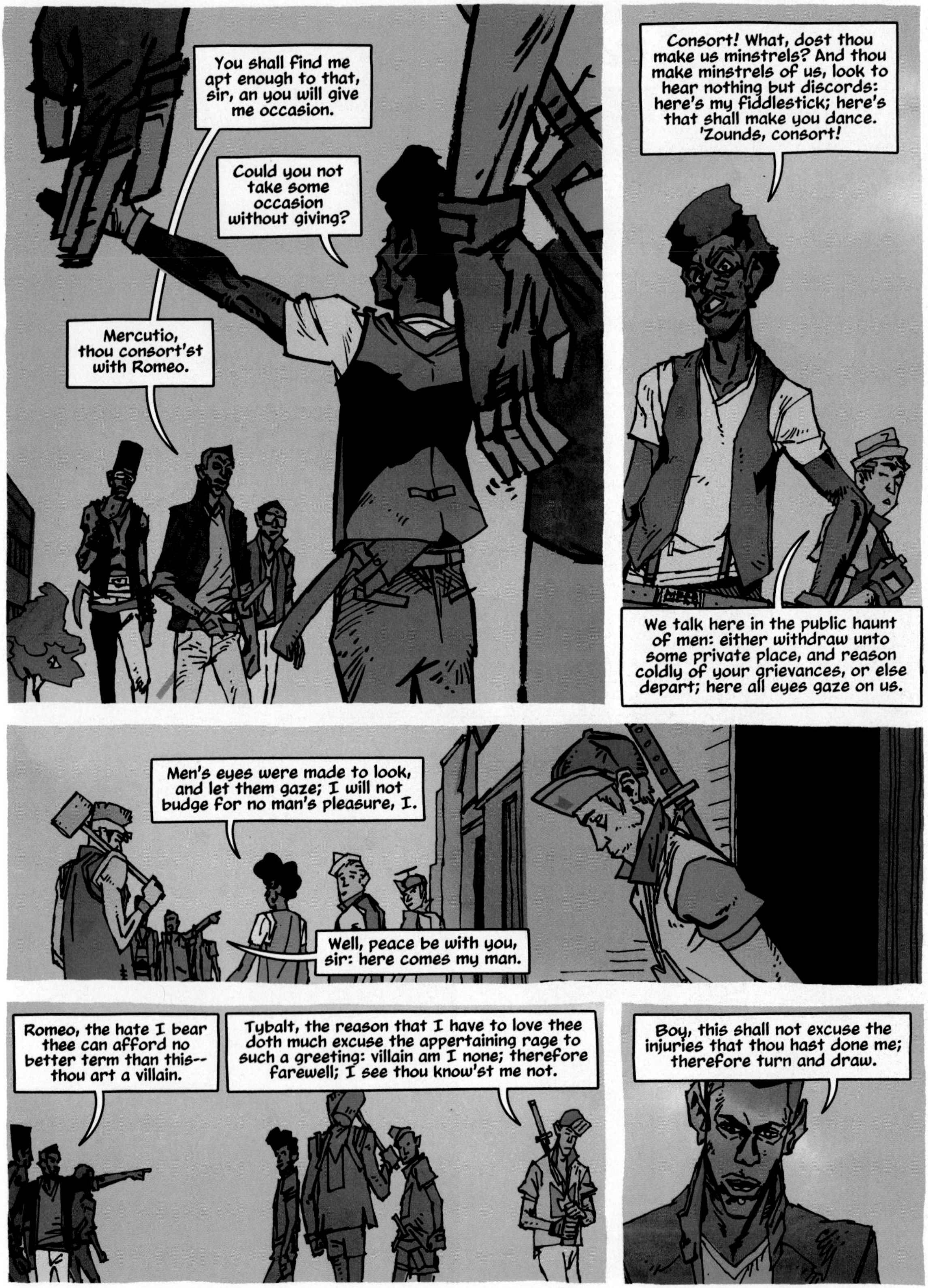
You shall find me apt enough to that, sir, an you will give me occasion.
Could you not take some occasion without giving?
Mercutio, thou consort'st with Romeo.
Consort! What, dost thou make us minstrels? And thou make minstrels of us, look to hear nothing but discords: here's my fiddlestick; here's that shall make you dance. 'Zounds, consort!
We talk here in the public haunt of men: either withdraw unto some private place, and reason coldly of your grievances, or else depart; here all eyes gaze on us.
Men's eyes were made to look, and let them gaze; I will not budge for no man's pleasure, I.
Well, peace be with you, sir: here comes my man.
Romeo, the hate I bear thee can afford no better term than this-- thou art a villain.
Tybalt, the reason that I have to love thee doth much excuse the appertaining rage to such a greeting: villain am I none; therefore farewell; I see thou know'st me not.
Boy, this shall not excuse the injuries that thou hast done me; therefore turn and draw.

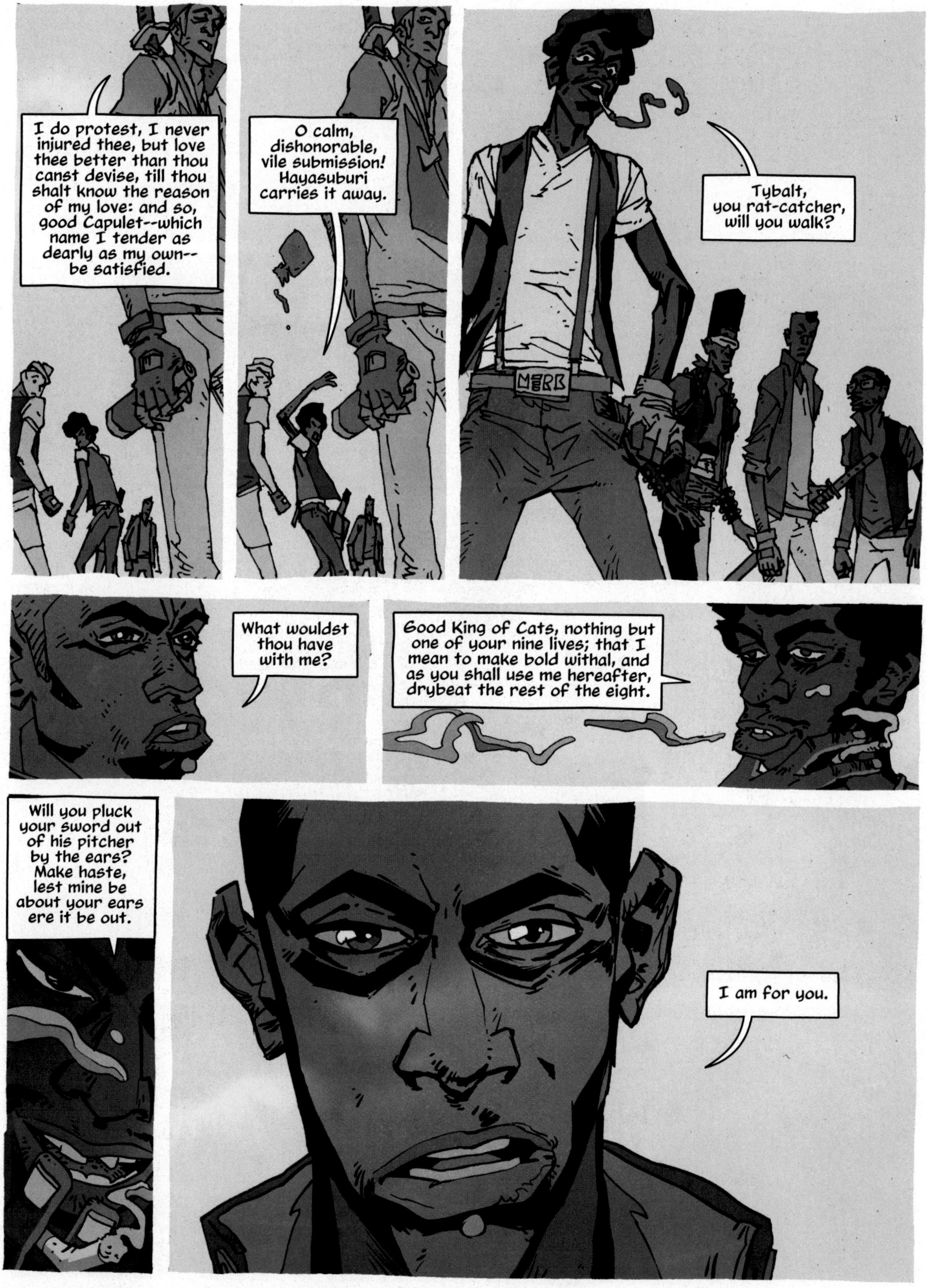
I do protest, I never injured thee, but love thee better than thou canst devise, till thou shalt know the reason of my love: and so, good Capulet--which name I tender as dearly as my own--be satisfied.
O calm, dishonorable, vile submission! Hayasuburi carries it away.
Tybalt, you rat-catcher, will you walk?
MERB
What wouldst thou have with me?
Good King of Cats, nothing but one of your nine lives; that I mean to make bold withal, and as you shall use me hereafter, drybeat the rest of the eight.
Will you pluck your sword out of his pitcher by the ears? Make haste, lest mine be about your ears ere it be out.
I am for you.

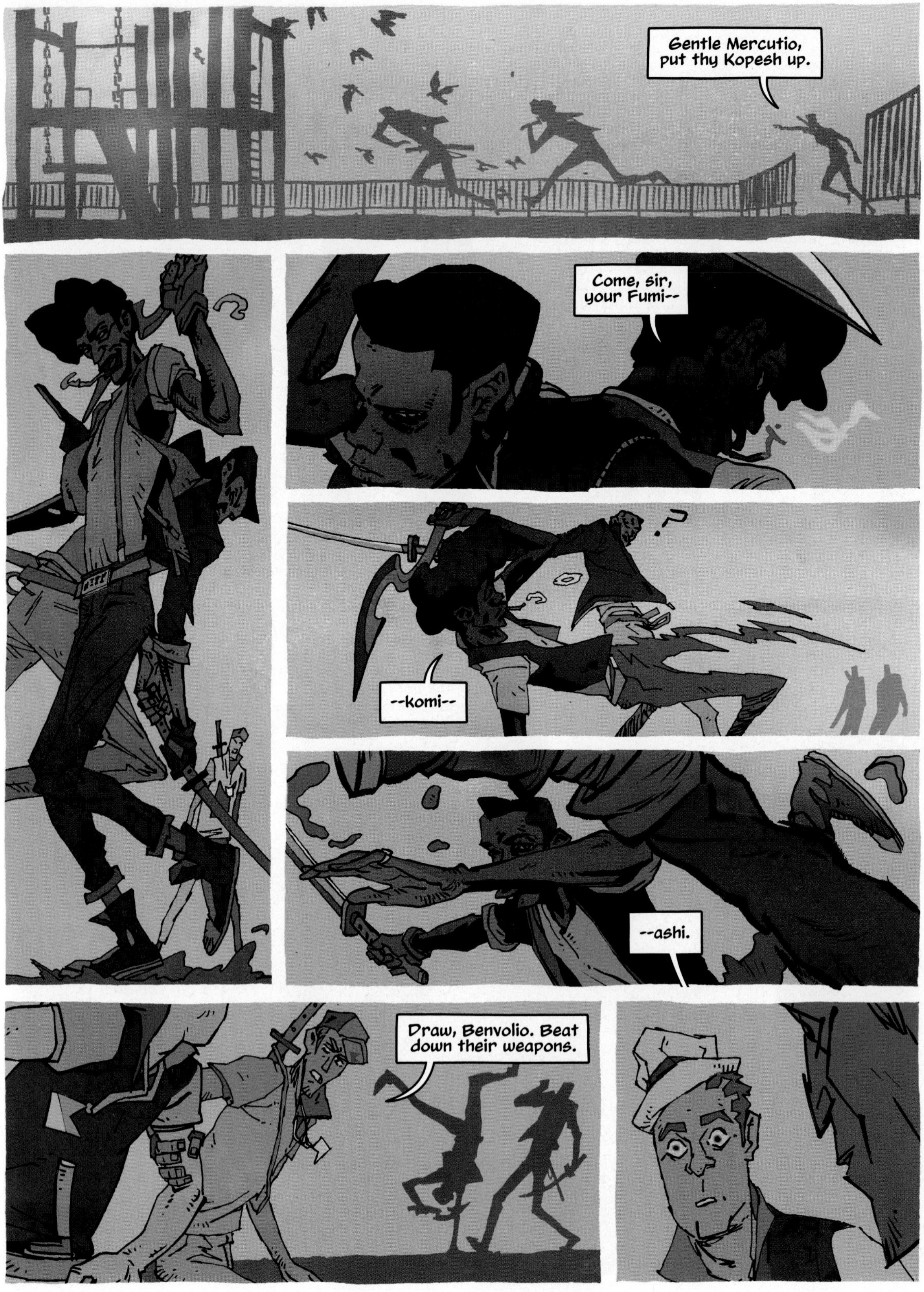
Gentle Mercutio, put thy Kopesh up.
Come, sir, your Fumi--
--komi--
--ashi.
Draw, Benvolio. Beat down their weapons.

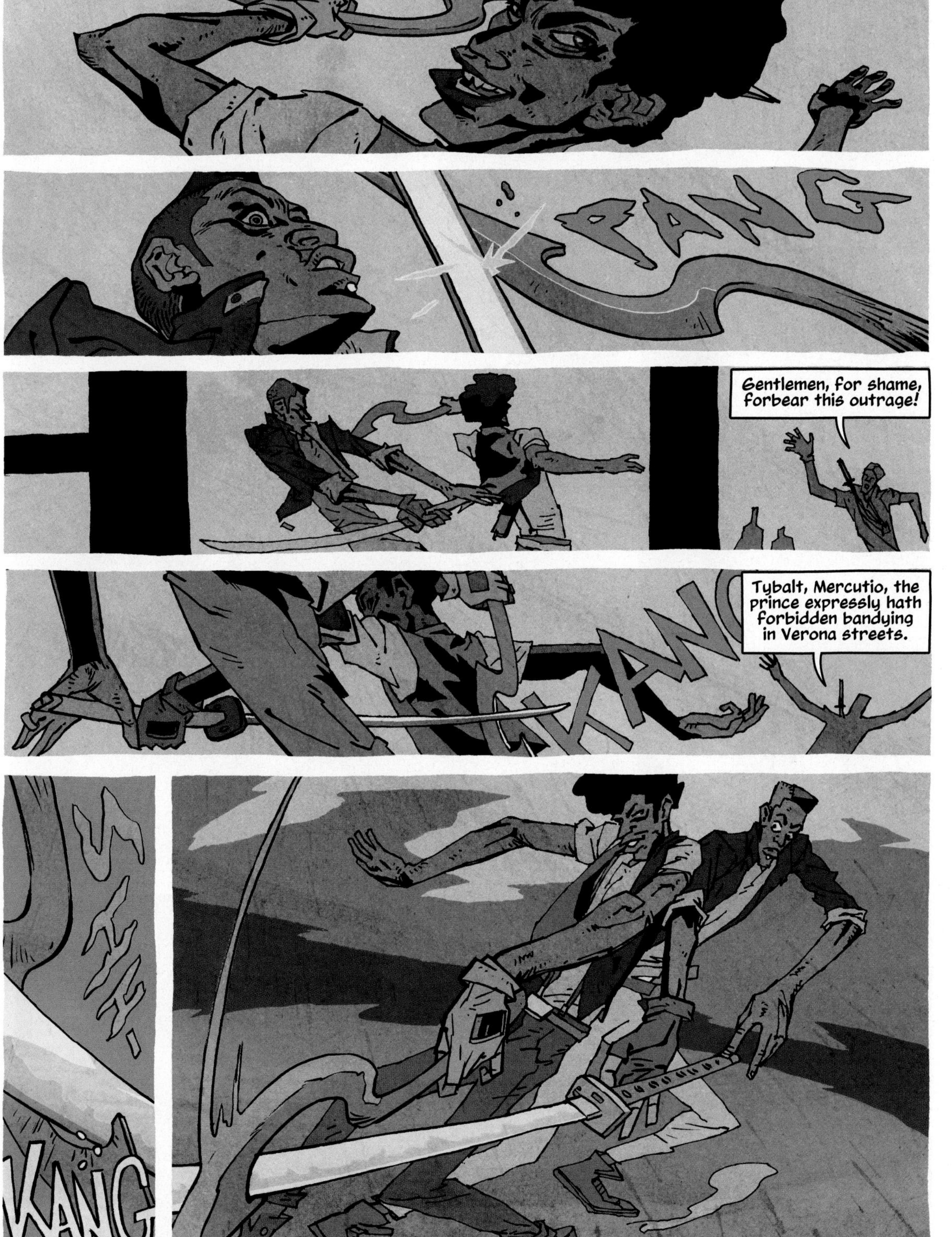

PANG
Gentlemen, for shame, forbear this outrage!
KANG
Tybalt, Mercutio, the prince expressly hath forbidden bandying in Verona streets.
KANG

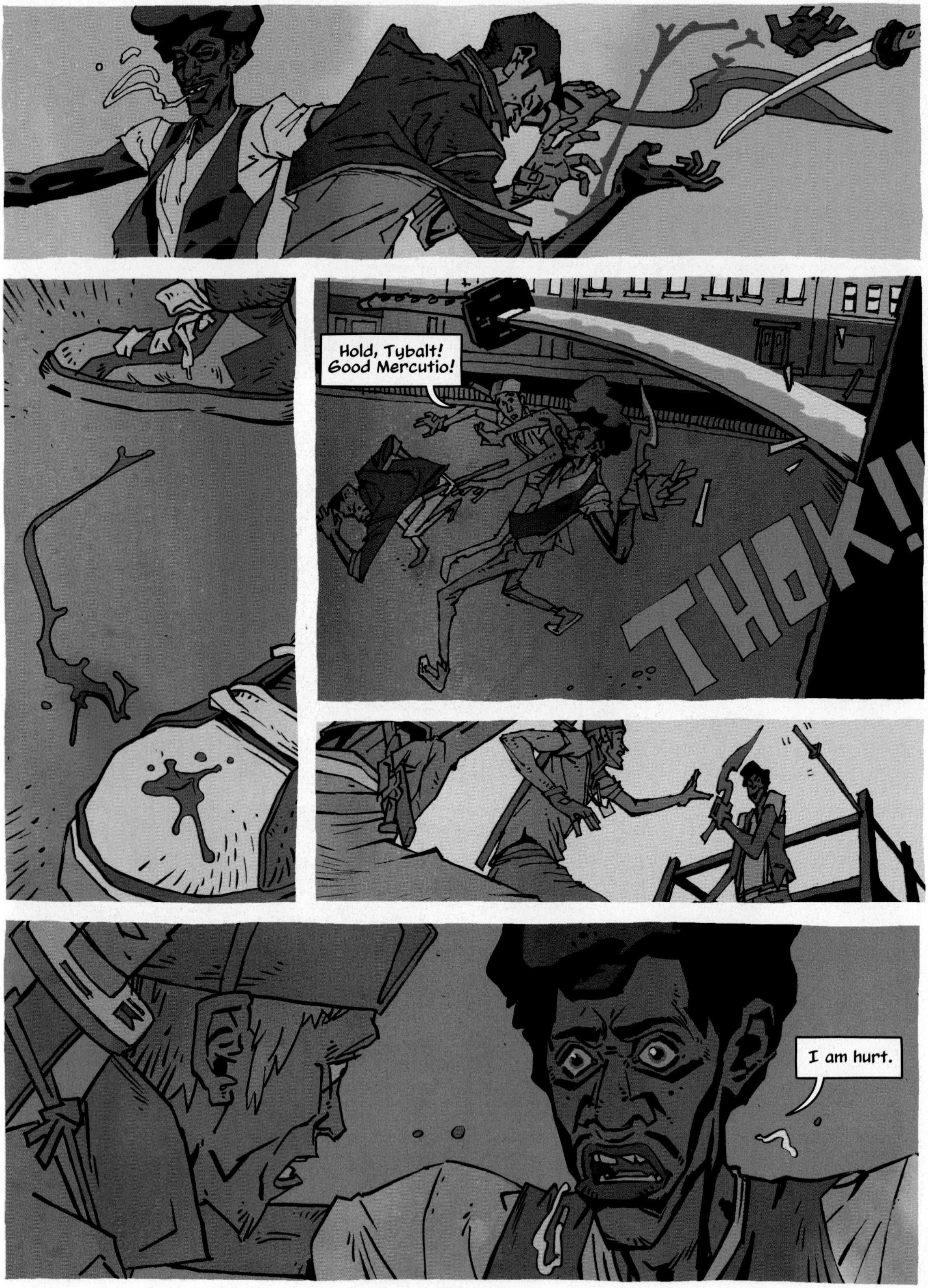
Hold, Tybalt!
Good Mercutio!
THOK!!
I am hurt.

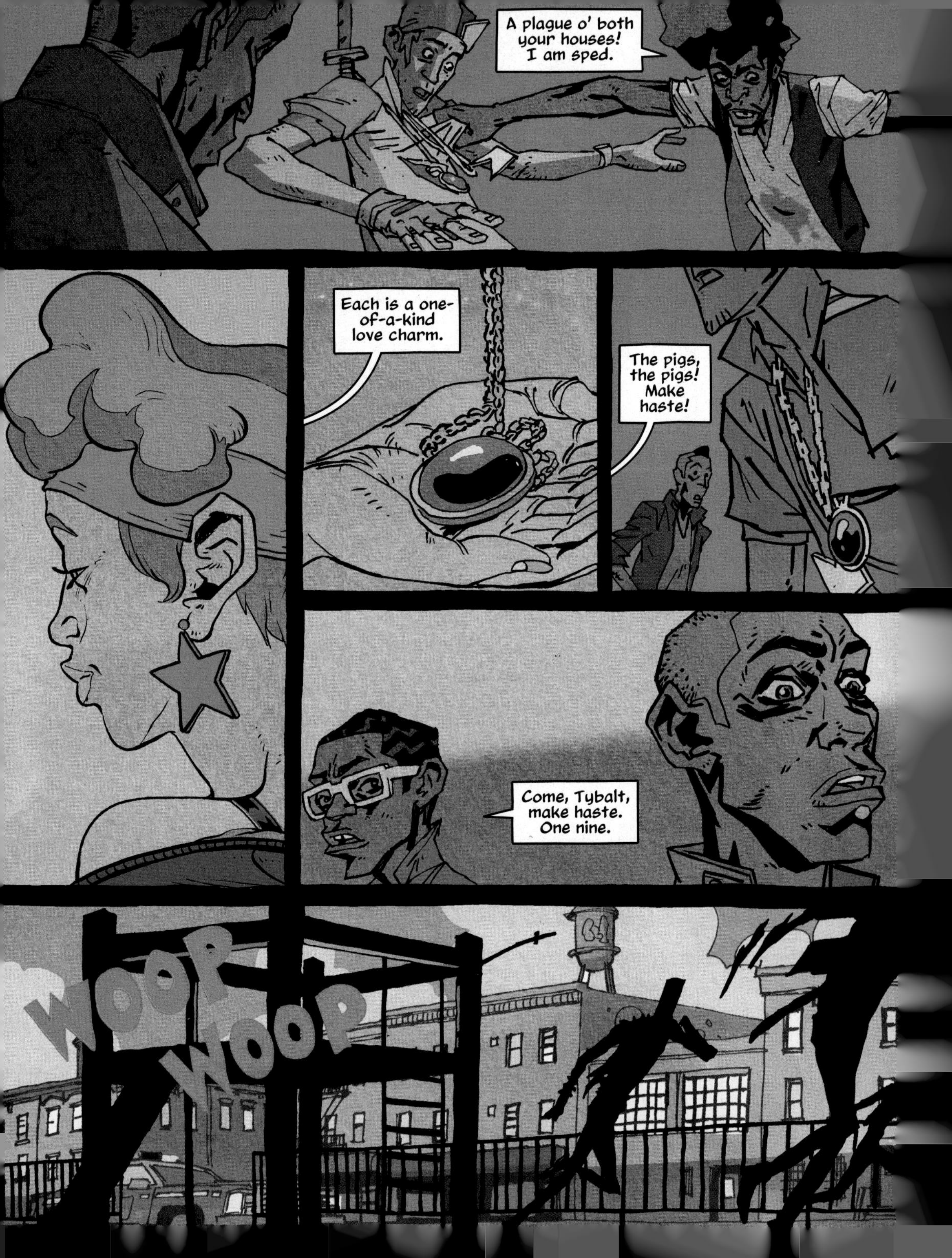
A plague o' both your houses! I am sped.
Each is a one-of-a-kind love charm.
The pigs, the pigs! Make haste!
Come, Tybalt, make haste. One nine.
WOOP WOOP

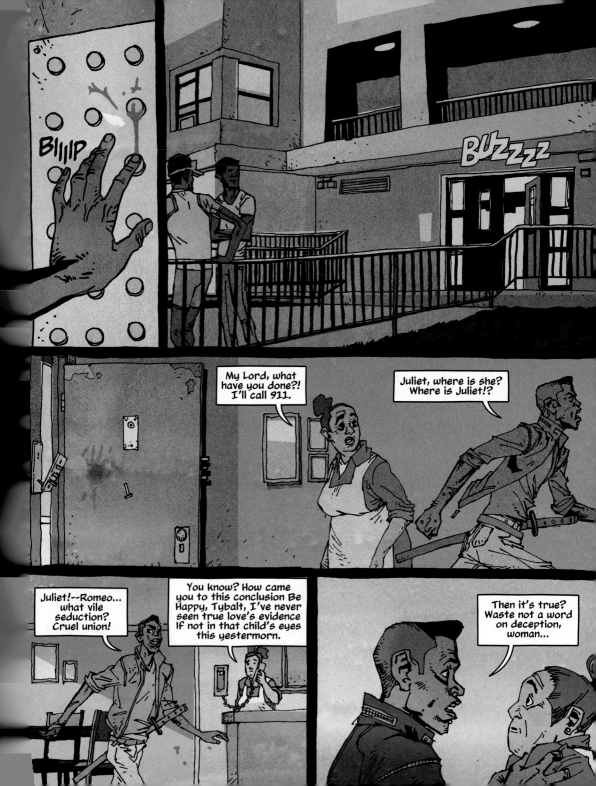

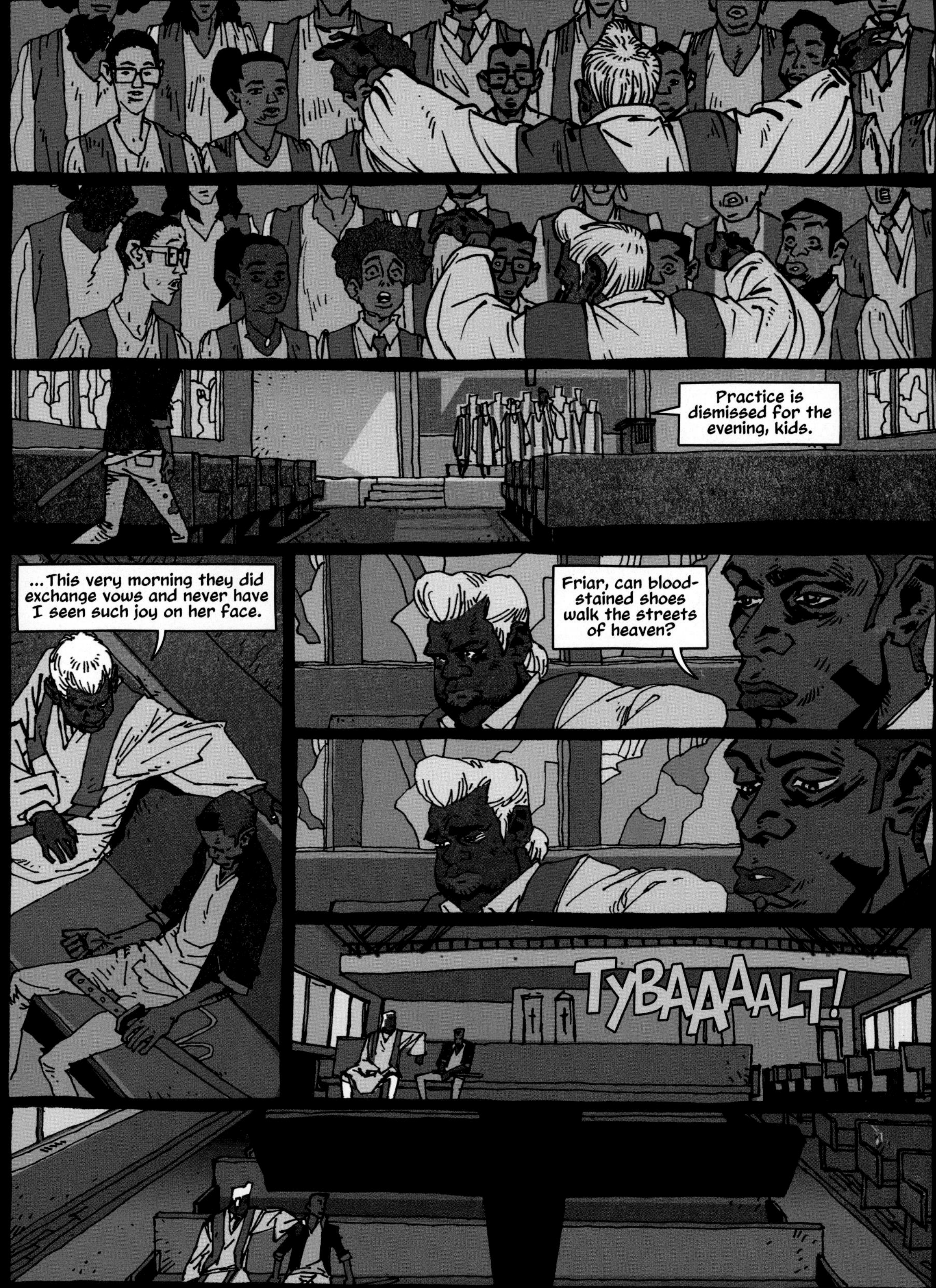
Practice is dismissed for the evening, kids.
...This very morning they did exchange vows and never have I seen such joy on her face.
Friar, can blood-stained shoes walk the streets of heaven?
TYBAAAALT!

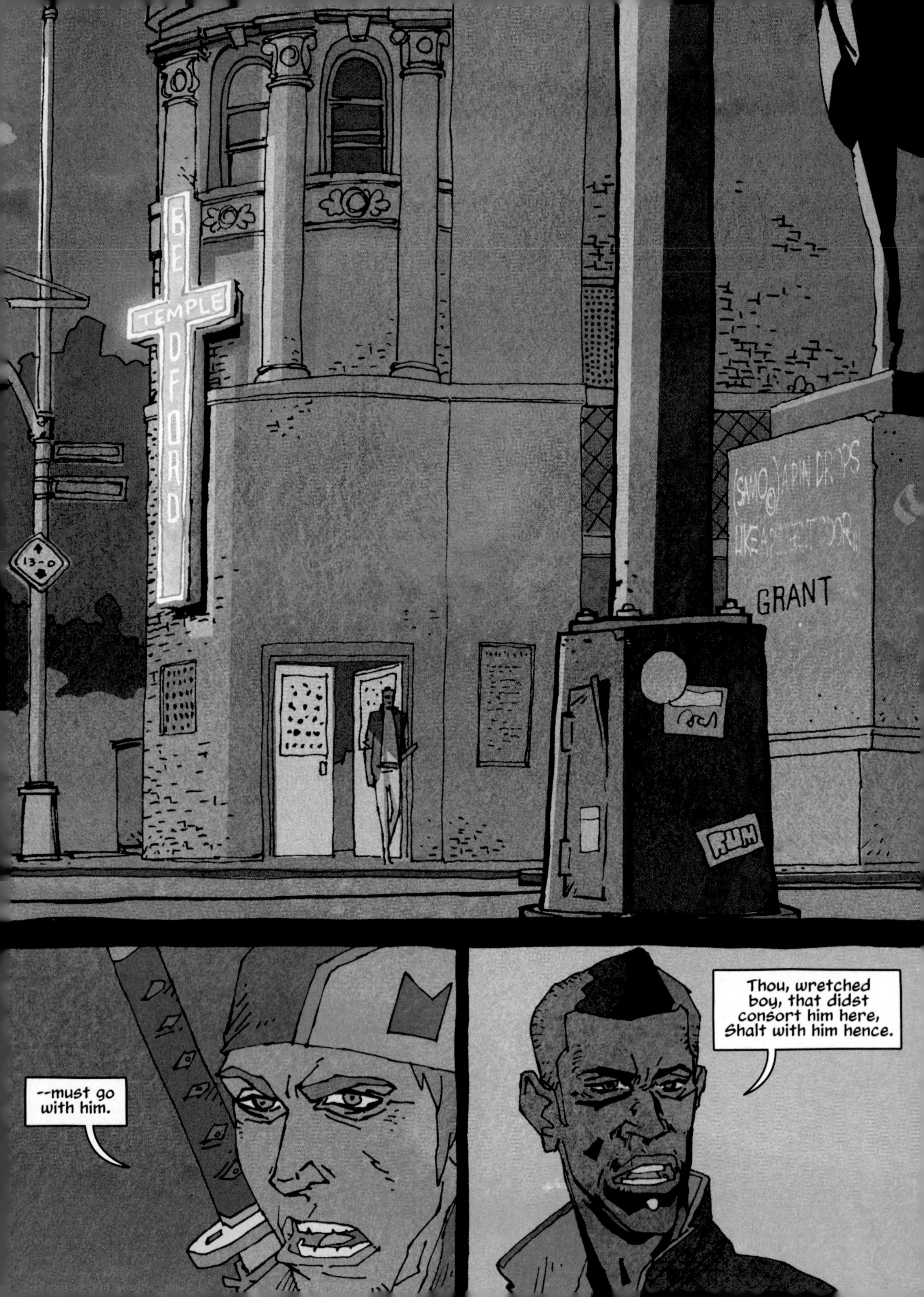
TEMPLE
BEDFORD
GRANT
--must go with him.
Thou, wretched boy, that didst consort him here, Shalt with him hence.

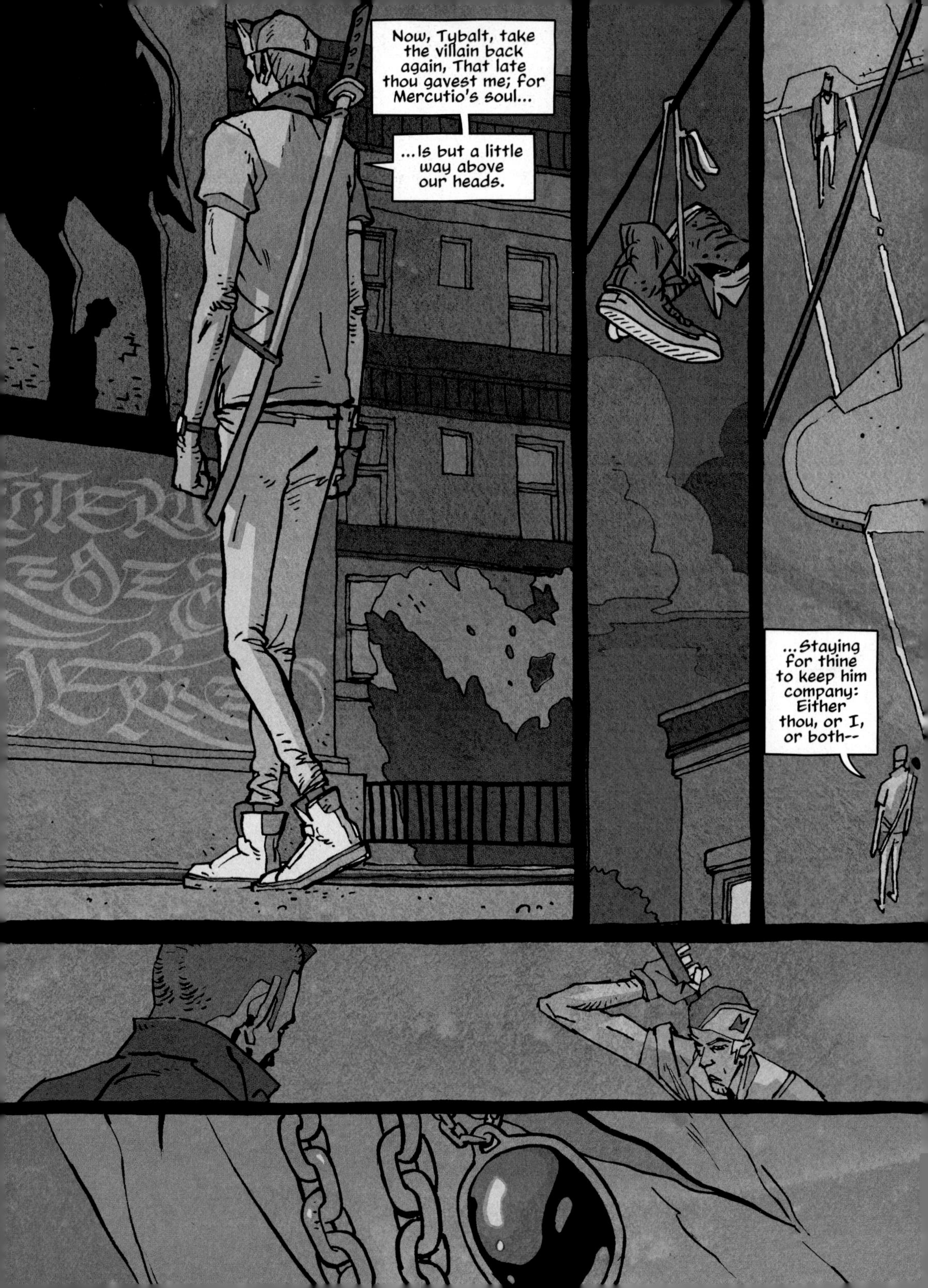
Now, Tybalt, take the villain back again, That late thou gavest me; for Mercutio's soul...
...Is but a little way above our heads.
...Staying for thine to keep him company: Either thou, or I, or both--

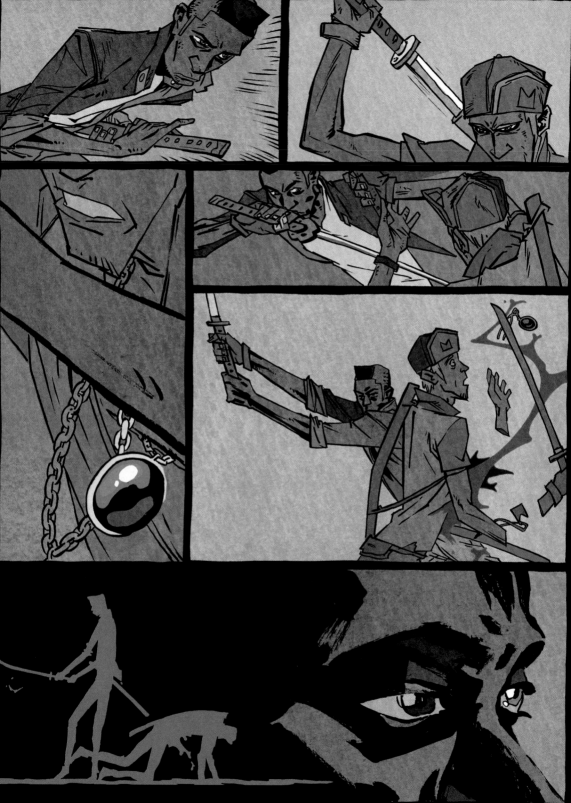

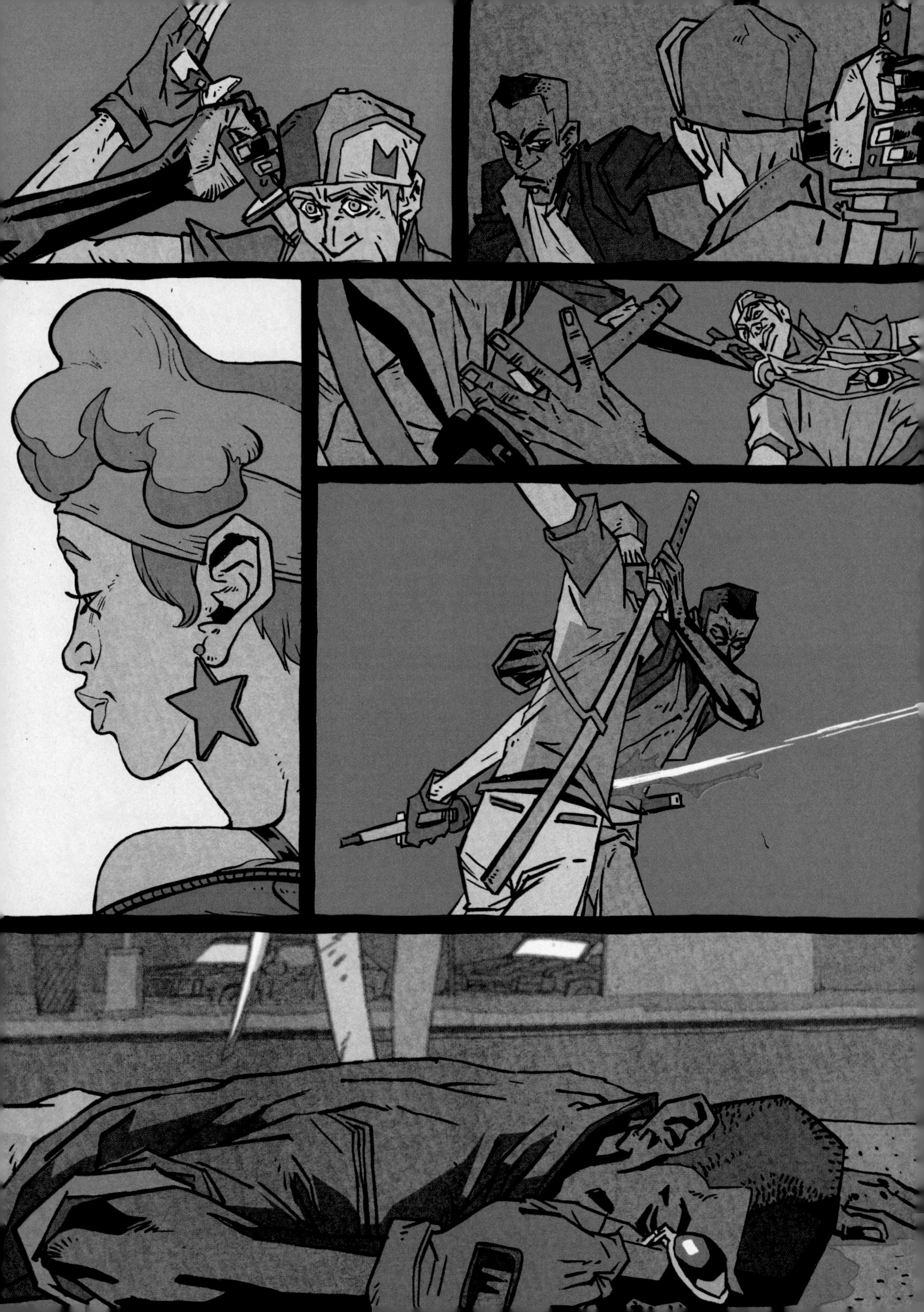

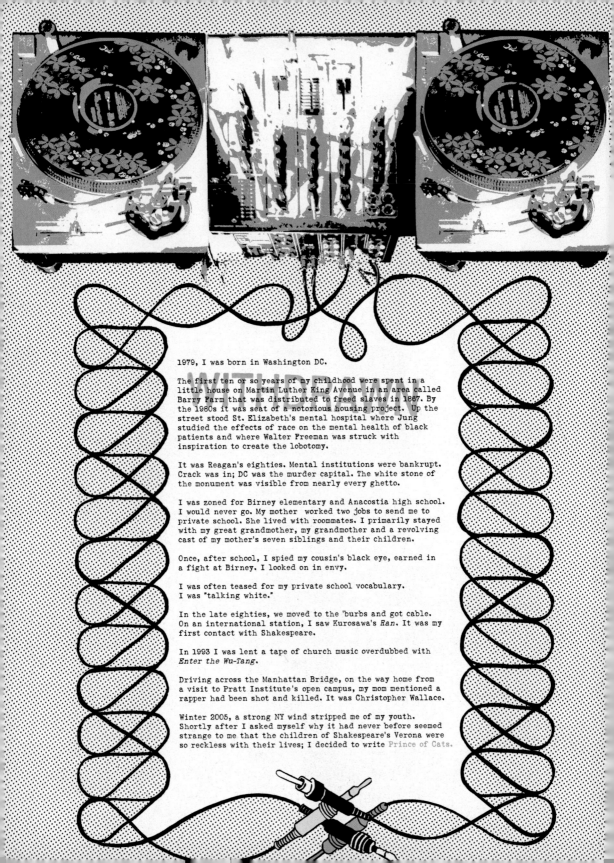

1979, I was born in Washington DC.

The first ten or so years of my childhood were spent in a
little house on Martin Luther King Avenue in an area called
Barry Farm that was distributed to freed slaves in 1867. By
the 1980s it was seat of a notorious housing project. Up the
street stood St. Elizabeth's mental hospital where Jung
studied the effects of race on the mental health of black
patients and where Walter Freeman was struck with
inspiration to create the lobotomy.

It was Reagan's eighties. Mental institutions were bankrupt.
Crack was in; DC was the murder capital. The white stone of
the monument was visible from nearly every ghetto.

I was zoned for Birney elementary and Anacostia high school.
I would never go. My mother worked two jobs to send me to
private school. She lived with roommates. I primarily stayed
with my great grandmother, my grandmother and a revolving
cast of my mother's seven siblings and their children.

Once, after school, I spied my cousin's black eye, earned in
a fight at Birney. I looked on in envy.

I was often teased for my private school vocabulary.
I was "talking white."

In the late eighties, we moved to the 'burbs and got cable.
On an international station, I saw Kurosawa's *Ran*. It was my
first contact with Shakespeare.

In 1993 I was lent a tape of church music overdubbed with
Enter the Wu-Tang.

Driving across the Manhattan Bridge, on the way home from
a visit to Pratt Institute's open campus, my mom mentioned a
rapper had been shot and killed. It was Christopher Wallace.

Winter 2005, a strong NY wind stripped me of my youth.
Shortly after I asked myself why it had never before seemed
strange to me that the children of Shakespeare's Verona were
so reckless with their lives; I decided to write Prince of Cats.

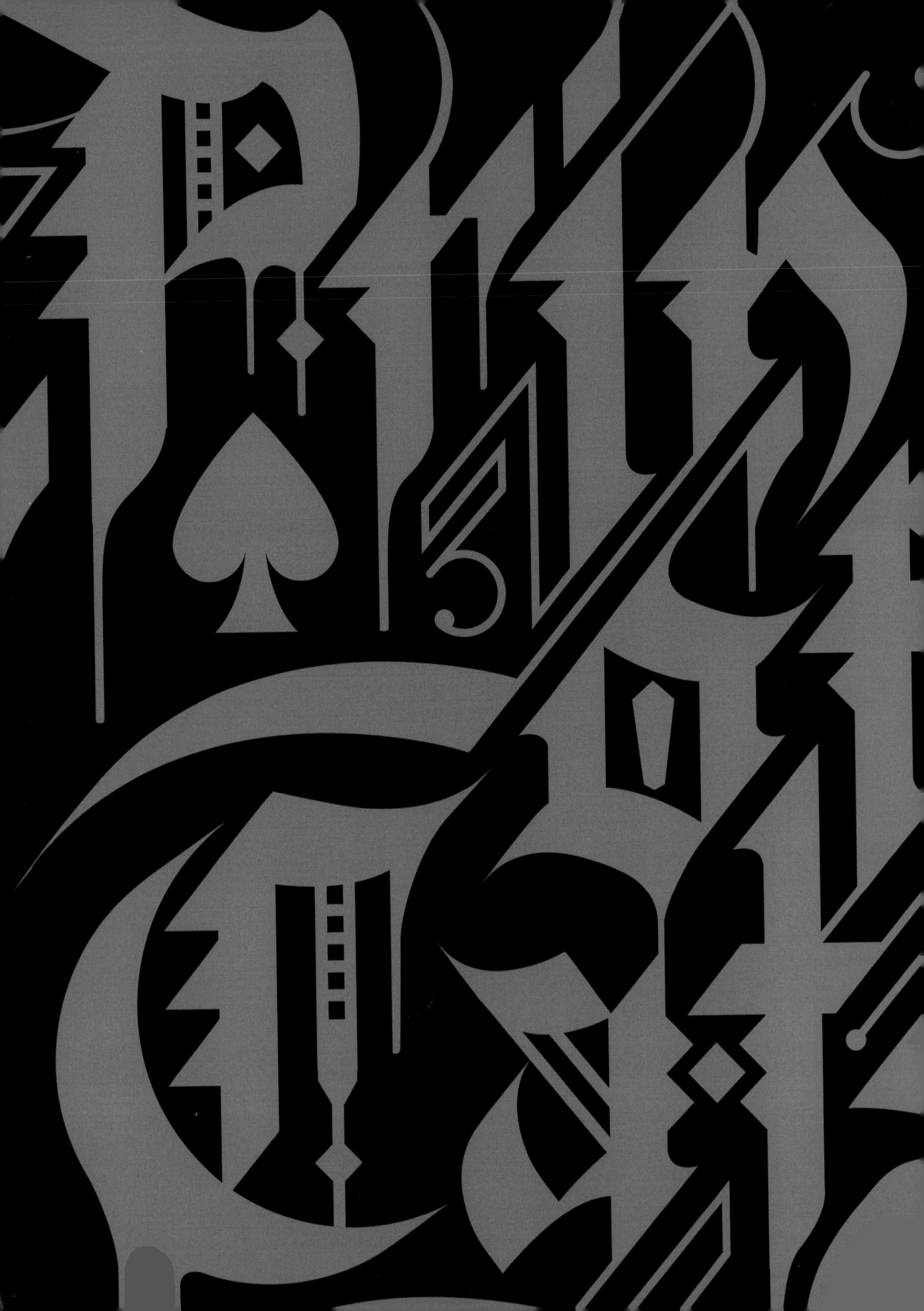

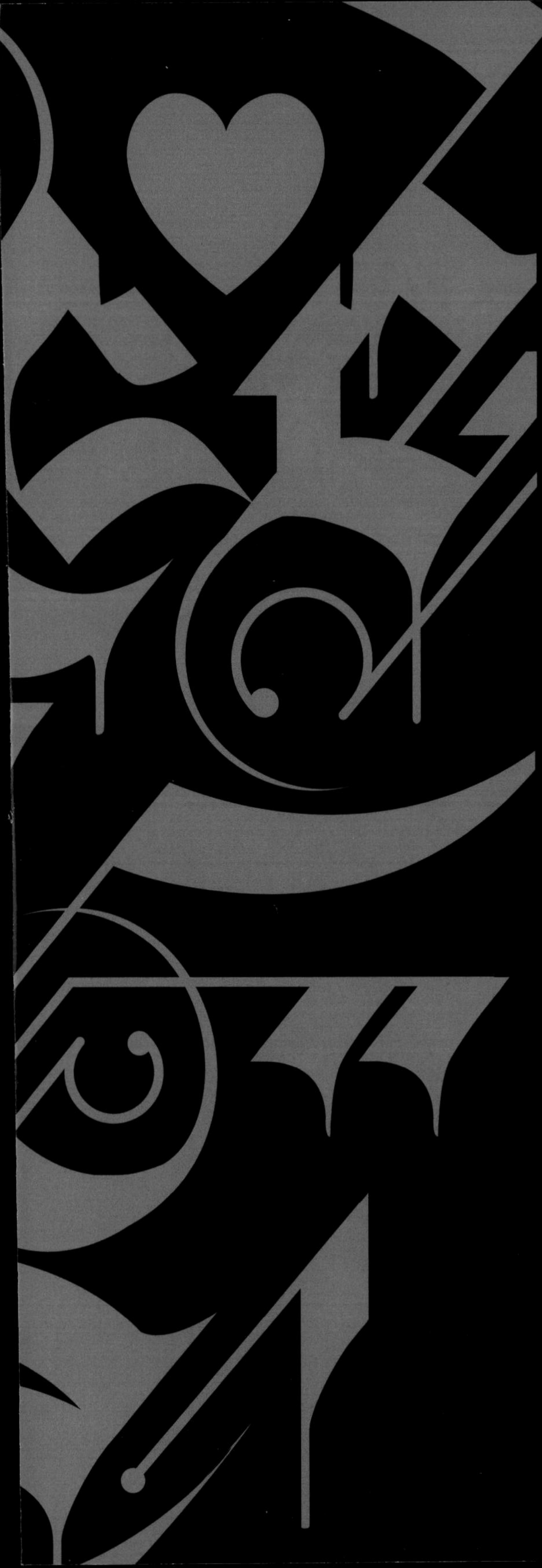

Ron Wimberly

Ronald Wimberly has worked as a writer/illustrator and comic book artist out of Brooklyn, New York, for ten years, and his work has been featured around the world. He is the artist behind SENTENCES: THE LIFE OF MF GRIMM, a graphic novel written by Percy Carey for Vertigo, and the authorized adaptation of Ray Bradbury's *Something Wicked This Way Comes*. He is currently working on *Black Dynamite* for Cartoon Network.

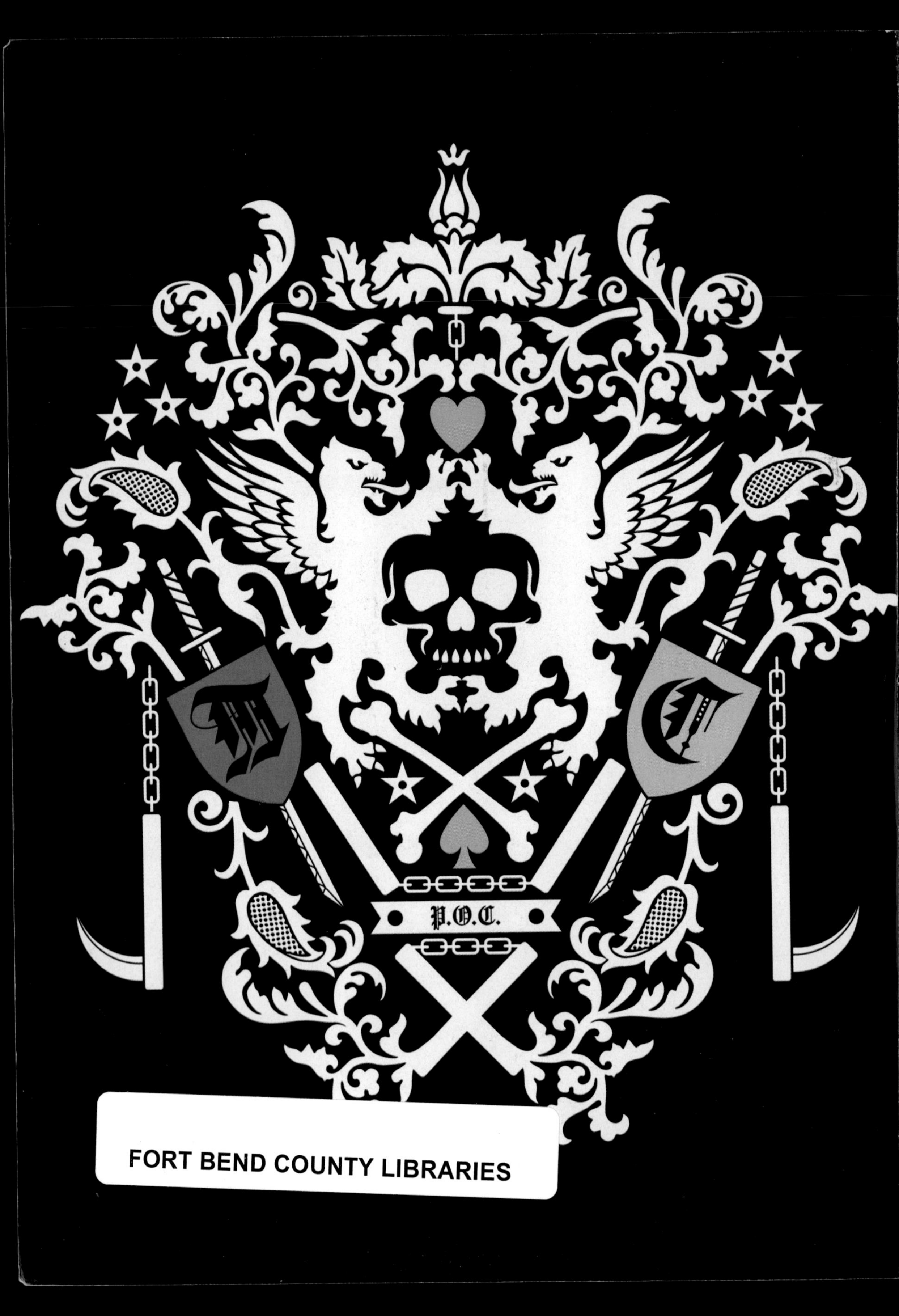
P.O.C.